HAPPINESS
AND VIRTUE
BEYOND EAST AND WEST
TOWARD A NEW GLOBAL RESPONSIBILITY

HAPPINESS AND VIRTUE

BEYOND EAST AND WEST
TOWARD A NEW GLOBAL RESPONSIBILITY

Edited by

KEVIN RYAN, BERNICE LERNER, KAREN E. BOHLIN
The Center for Character and Social Responsibility (CCSR)
at Boston University School of Education, USA

OSAMU NAKAYAMA, SHUJIRO MIZUNO, KAZUNOBU HORIUCHI
The Center for Moral Science and Education (CMSE)
at Reitaku University, Japan

TUTTLE Publishing
Tokyo | Rutland, Vermont | Singapore

The Tuttle Story: "Books to Span the East and West"

Most people are surprised to learn that the world's largest publisher of books on Asia had its beginnings in the tiny American state of Vermont. The company's founder, Charles E. Tuttle, belonged to a New England family steeped in publishing. And his first love was naturally books—especially old and rare editions.

Immediately after WW II, serving in Tokyo under General Douglas MacArthur, Tuttle was tasked with reviving the Japanese publishing industry, and founded the Charles E. Tuttle Publishing Company, which thrives today as one of the world's leading independent publishers.

Though a westerner, Charles was hugely instrumental in bringing a knowledge of Japan and Asia to a world hungry for information about the East. By the time of his death in 1993, Tuttle had published over 6,000 books on Asian culture, history and art—a legacy honored by the Japanese emperor with the "Order of the Sacred Treasure," the highest tribute Japan can bestow upon a non-Japanese.

With a backlist of 1,500 titles, Tuttle Publishing is more active today than at any time in its past—inspired by Charles' core mission to publish fine books to span the East and West and provide a greater understanding of each.

Published by Tuttle Publishing, an imprint of Periplus Editions (HK) Ltd.

www.tuttlepublishing.com

Copyright © 2011 Boston University and Reitaku University

Library of Congress Cataloging-in-Publication Data
Happiness and virtue beyond East and West : toward a new global responsibility / edited by Kevin Ryan ... [et al]. -- 1st ed.
    p. cm.
 Includes bibliographical references.
 ISBN 978-4-8053-1229-2 (hardcover)
1. Virtues. 2. Happiness. 3. Conduct of life.
4. Ethics. I. Ryan, Kevin, 1932-
   BJ1589.H37 2011
 179'.9--dc23
              2011044549

ISBN 978-4-8053-1229-2

Distributed by

North America, Latin America & Europe
Tuttle Publishing
364 Innovation Drive
North Clarendon, VT 05759-9436 U.S.A.
Tel: 1 (802) 773-8930; Fax: 1 (802) 773-6993
info@tuttlepublishing.com
www.tuttlepublishing.com

Japan
Tuttle Publishing
Yaekari Building, 3rd Floor, 5-4-12 Osaki
Shinagawa-ku, Tokyo 141 0032
Tel: (81) 3 5437-0171; Fax: (81) 3 5437-0755
sales@tuttle.co.jp   www.tuttle.co.jp

Asia Pacific
Berkeley Books Pte. Ltd.
61 Tai Seng Avenue #02-12, Singapore 534167
Tel: (65) 6280-1330; Fax: (65) 6280-6290
inquiries@periplus.com.sg
www.periplus.com

Printed in Singapore
First edition
15 14 13 12   5 4 3 2 1   1201MP

TUTTLE PUBLISHING® is a registered trademark of Tuttle Publishing, a division of Periplus Editions (HK) Ltd.

Contents

Preface

This book is the first fruit of an ambitious joint academic project involving the Center for Moral Science and Education (CMSE) at Reitaku University in Japan and the Center for Character and Social Responsibility (CCSR) at the School of Education, Boston University, in the United States. Its genesis was a visit to Reitaku in January 2009 by Dr. Karen Bohlin, a contributor to the present volume and a senior scholar at Boston University's Center for the Advancement of Ethics and Character (CAEC, the predecessor of the CCSR). The enlightening public lecture she gave on character education in the United States greatly inspired those listening, and a delegation from Reitaku decided to visit the CAEC in September 2009 to explore the possibility of academic and educational collaboration in the field of moral and ethical studies. Fruitful discussions with Dr. Bohlin and her Boston University colleagues, Dr. Kevin Ryan and Dr. Bernice Lerner, led to a full mutual understanding of the convergent academic and educational aims and activities of the two institutions, and a joint project was born. In 2010 both universities signed a Memorandum of Understanding for Research, Academic, and Educational Cooperation and Exchange, detailing their shared intentions to cooperate in the advancement of research, as well as in other academic and educational activities, and to foster links in these areas, especially in the form of intellectual exchanges involving faculty members, researchers, and students in undergraduate and postgraduate programs. At the very heart of this venture is a common desire to enhance mutual understanding, not just between two institutions, but also between the societies to which they belong.

For this reason, then, the present volume takes the form of a series of essays by authors from Japan and the United States who attempt to move beyond East and West to identify and explore the essence of the virtues prized in both regions, with the ultimate aim of allowing happiness to be realized in a globally and socially responsible manner. Each chapter examines, from both an Eastern and a Western perspective, one of nine virtues—courage, justice, benevolence, gratitude, wisdom, reflection, respect, responsibility, and temperance or self-mastery—and their practical importance in our lives. The book's final form owes much to the support and contributions of various individuals in both Japan and the United States. Its editors are particularly grateful to Jean Morrison, provost and chief academic officer of Boston University and Hardin L. K. Coleman, Ph.D., dean and professor of the Boston University School of Education. Special thanks are also due to Dr. Peter Luff, professor of Reitaku University, who read through all the essays by the Japanese authors, discussed their contents with them, and offered helpful advice and ideas where they were needed, especially in the conclusion; and to Elisabeth Carter, who edited the whole manuscript and wrote the introductions to the chapters.

♣　　♣　　♣

The English version of the book is intended mainly for Western readers, so a few words of explanation about the background of its Japanese contributors may be helpful. Since they are all associated with Reitaku University, a brief account should be given of its founder, Chikuro Hiroike (1866–1938), an eminent scholar and educator whose spirit and writings continue to play a central role in the concerns of the university. Hiroike firmly believed that education should provide students not only with knowledge but also with a high level of integrity and moral character. His personal commitment to knowledge and scholarship ran very deep. By his late twenties, he had established himself as a respected historian and so became a key figure in the national project to compile the *Encyclopedia of Ancient Things Japanese*. This was the largest work of its type ever published in Japan, and Hiroike himself was responsible for compiling a quarter of the entire work. In addition to this, he was the first scholar in the world to systematize the history of oriental law, receiving a doctoral degree in law in 1912 for this pioneering work. But his concern for the well-being of others led him far beyond the academic sphere, and he became increasingly preoccupied with addressing the central moral issues of the modern world. The solutions he offered in these matters were both original and fundamental in character. After more than ten years of thought and endeavor, he published his *Treatise on Moral Science: A First Attempt to Establish Moralogy as a New Science* in 1928. A three-volume English translation of the Japanese original did not become available until 2002 under the title, *Towards Supreme Morality: An Attempt to Establish the New Science of Moralogy*.

Reitaku University, with its foundations in Hiroike's moral philosophy and guiding spirit, has established two centers to support education and research on morality and ethics in today's world: the Reitaku University Business Ethics and Compliance Research Center (R-bec), and the CMSE mentioned earlier. The mission of R-bec, created in 2001, is to promote research into business ethics, compliance, and risk management, while CMSE collaborates with institutions like Boston University's CCSR that share its educational and scholarly concerns in the field of morality. The Reitaku approach to teaching at the university level is not especially common in Japan, where people tend to think that moral and ethical education is the province of education in the home and in elementary and junior high schools. Modern Japanese society is, however, faced with a mountain of issues, including environmental destruction, a general loss of morality, and a collapse of educational systems that render such a restricted approach untenable.

Responding to a clear need for a convincing answer to the question of how we should live in times of unprecedented transition,

Reitaku continues its search for a code of conduct that meets the needs both of individuals and of society as a whole. It has been said that the twenty-first century is the era of the "knowledge-based society," wherein new knowledge, information, and technology assume ever greater significance in the fields of politics, economy, and culture. Yet the mere enhancement of knowledge cannot deliver peace, security, and happiness to the people of the world. Knowledge cannot truly serve society unless it is accompanied by a high level of morality. At Reitaku, therefore, it is felt that moral and ethical education should go hand in hand with the work of scholarship in higher education, and that it is our task to rebuild morality in today's society while also reformulating areas of knowledge suitable for our new era. For this reason, the CMSE has published two textbooks on moral and ethical education at the university level, *A Moral Textbook for University Students: How Do You Live Your Life?* and *A Practical Moral Textbook for University Students: How Do You Think and How Do You Act?* These volumes represent, I believe, the first attempt to deal with morals and ethics in the sphere of higher education in Japan.

To better understand the distinctive character of the essays of the Japanese contributors in this volume, an awareness of the general approach to moral issues and virtues in Japan as a whole may also aide Western readers. The essence of that approach is not always easy to grasp. Japanese studies in the United States sometimes succumb to the heavy perfume of Eastern exoticism, while within Japan itself too much emphasis is placed, on occasion, on mere theories of Japanese uniqueness. The Reitaku contributors to this book try to avoid both extremes. They seek a middle path between overemphasizing the differences between Japanese and American views of virtue and dissolving all moral and ethical practices and their corresponding discourses into a flat postmodernist understanding of culture. They try to give proper weight, but no more, to what is genuinely distinctive about the Japanese concept of virtue.

One good example of an important background influence on their thinking is bushido, accurately defined as the spirit of the

samurai and the soul of the Japanese by the great Japanese interna-
tionalist Nitobe Inazo in his study *Bushido, The Soul of Japan* (1900).
Bushido can be described as a moral and ethical philosophy of life,
one that governed every action of the warrior caste of feudal Japan
for many centuries. To arrive at the heart of the Japanese approach
to virtue or morality, then, an understanding of the basics of this
philosophy and of how it permeates life in Japan is indispensable.
Inazo, for example, explains very clearly the significance of bushido for moral education in his country in the following passage:

> About ten years ago, while spending a few days under the hos-
> pitable roof of the distinguished Belgian jurist, the lamented M.
> de Laveleye, our conversation turned during one of our rambles
> to the subject of religion. "Do you mean to say," asked the ven-
> erable professor, "that you have no religious instruction in your
> schools?" On my replying in the negative, he suddenly halted in
> astonishment, and in a voice which I shall not easily forget, he
> repeated, "No religion! How do you impart moral education?"
> The question stunned me at the time. I could give no ready an-
> swer, for the moral precepts I learned in my childhood days were
> not given in schools; and not until I began to analyze the differ-
> ent elements that formed my notions of right and wrong, did
> I find that it was bushido that breathed them into my nostrils.

Another very important background influence on the thinking
of the Japanese contributors to this volume is their country's mythology. In the chapter about reflection, for example, reference is
made to the famous myth of Amaterasu, the Japanese Sun Goddess. This legend is a very old one, appearing in the very first works
of Japanese history, the *Kojiki* (*Records of Ancient Matters*, written in
712 A.D.) and the *Nihon Shoki* (*Chronicle of Japanese History*, written in 720 A.D.). Prior to the modern era, when Japan was not under the influence of Western rationalism, mythological events were
regarded as historical ones like any other. Even today, the people of

Japan begin their journey in search of their origins and identity in the unique and timeless mythology of the *Kojiki* and the *Nihon Shoki*. In our scientific age, people may view mythology from widely varying perspectives. Some may regard it as the imaginative story-telling of primitive people, while others may characterize it as pure fantasy or an early form of science fiction. Yet in traditional Japanese culture and spiritual life, and especially in the roots in Japanese Shintoism, its significance goes far beyond mere fantasy. It represents something very precious, a treasure of realities, or rather, the symbolic representation of Japanese spiritual or moral reality.

So some familiarity with bushido and the central features of Japanese mythology may serve as a bridge that Western readers may cross to arrive at a deeper understanding of the Japanese view of virtue. But there are many other such bridges, and not all of them are ancient. Indeed, new ones are being constructed all the time, as the following episode demonstrates so tellingly.

❧   ❧   ❧

On March 11, 2011, Japan was struck by a massive earthquake, followed by an even more devastating tsunami, resulting in the deaths of at least 15,000 people, with more than 9,400 others listed as missing. Communities and facilities along more than 300 miles of the eastern coastline of the country's main island were inundated, including the airport at Sendai, the region's largest city. The world watched transfixed as television pictures showed an unrelenting tide of water and mud sweeping far inland, demolishing dwellings like paper, picking up and tossing around countless vehicles, toppling trees, and engulfing all else in its path.

The tide of devastation eventually retreated, and in its wake it was clear to everyone that Sendai Airport, which would be crucial to any relief effort, was no longer usable. Nature, munificent in its gifts to the people of Japan, had made its power to reclaim those gifts very clear. Yet in an amazingly short period of time, the airport was transformed from a scene of destruction and abandonment into an image of hope and recovery. Shakespeare's words, "Sweet are the uses of adversity," ring as true as ever here, for the affected region certainly witnessed the birth of a new and priceless spirit of virtue in the days and weeks after the disaster. This appeared partly in the form of the perseverance and character of the Japanese people, as those who were most directly affected. But it was also manifested in remarkable acts of generosity and support from their American friends. To take one prominent example among so many, the restoration of Sendai Airport to its pre-tsunami condition in such short order would never have been possible without the contribution of the U.S. Air Force, Marines, Army, Navy, and other government agencies working in cooperation with the Japanese government bodies and its Self-Defense Forces. Within an astonishingly short space of time, American special operations forces air personnel began temporarily handling all airfield operations to make the delivery of aid possible, aid that Japanese workers were then able to use to start recovery operations.

The outcome of these joint labors was that the final transfer of airport operations from U.S. military personnel to the Japanese airport authorities took place as early as April 5. The following day Sendai Airport resumed full operations in exactly the same condition as it had been before the events of March 11. This was rightly hailed in the Japanese press as a "miraculous" recovery, a transformation that exemplified the meaning of the well-known proverb, "A friend in need is a friend indeed." So it will easily be understood why I wish to take the opportunity of these pages to express my own sense of the very deep gratitude that all my fellow citizens feel to every member of the U.S. forces who participated in Operation Tomodachi, and to all the American people who supported our country in its time of great need.

The story of the reconstruction of Sendai Airport has many heart-warming aspects. One such incident involved U.S. Air Force Colonel Robert P. Toth, whose unit specializes in restoring aviation facilities in disaster areas and which from the outset played a crucial role in the restoration of the inundated airport. Colonel Toth writes of how, flying in to take his leave of the airport after nineteen days of continuous work, he noticed, on the beach forming the final half-mile of the approach to runway 27, the Japanese word *arigato* (thank you) spelled out using twenty- to thirty-foot-high trees that had been laid flat by the tsunami. The sight of this word, a very Japanese way of expressing the country's gratitude to the American people, greatly impressed Colonel Toth. Even more impressive to the Japanese was the modesty and nobility of his response to this gesture. He began by saying that, on behalf of all U.S. forces stationed in Japan and those who had participated in Operation Tomodachi, "It was our honor to help the people of Japan, our hosts, friends, and neighbors." He then went on to quote Saint Augustine's unforgettable words, "We deserve no praise when we do things we ought to do and they are right." For this reason, he told the people of Japan, "A thank you is not necessary." These words, allied to his deeds, moved his Japanese readers very deeply indeed.

This episode shows us very clearly how virtue, in this case gratitude and a sense of duty, knows no national boundaries. Exactly the same is true of happiness. Almost all the contents of the present volume were written before the disaster of March 11, 2011. But what happened in its aftermath only serves to reinforce the underlying conviction of the contributors to this book that the virtues are vitally important for the realization of happiness, not least (indeed, perhaps especially) in the midst of difficulties and hardship. We hope that what follows will stimulate our readers to think afresh, to ponder more deeply the nature of our common global responsibility, and so help to bring about a new age of international cooperation and good will.

Osamu Nakayama

Introduction

BY THOMAS LICKONA

In his preface to this book, Osamu Nakayama graciously describes the gratitude his countrymen felt for the help Japan received from the United States after it was struck by the terrible earthquake and tsunami on March 11, 2011. At the time of the disaster, our College's Center for the 4th and 5th Rs (Respect and Responsibility) was hosting the year-long visit of a professor of moral education from Japan's National University, and his family. As the tragedy unfolded, we shared their anxiety as he and his wife awaited news from family members, one of whom was directly affected.

In the days and weeks that followed, I read reports in *The New York Times* of how the Japanese people were enduring their misfortune with stoic dignity; how workers at the damaged nuclear reactors had heroically risked exposure to dangerous levels of radiation in an effort to avert further catastrophe; how devastated villages, manifesting the Japanese talent for order and cooperation, had quickly organized themselves into teams and made remarkable progress in returning to normalcy; how shops and businesses had, with similar resiliency and group effort, repaired their buildings and sprung back into action; and how new college graduates, at first frustrated by the disaster's disruptive effects on their career plans and employment prospects, were in many instances drawn into helping with the recovery effort and found fulfillment in lending a hand to those whose lives had been much more profoundly disrupted.

Dr. Nakayama concludes his preface by saying that "what happened in [the aftermath of the disaster] only serves to reinforce the conviction of the contributors to this book that the virtues are vitally important for the realization of happiness, not least (indeed, perhaps especially) in the midst of difficulties and hardship." He expresses the hope that this book will stimulate readers "to ponder more deeply the nature of our common global responsibility."

The Challenges We Face

This book is not the first time Japan has reached out to colleagues in the West to consider the pursuit of virtue and the common social and moral problems that confront us. My first visit to Japan was in August 1987, when the Institute of Moralogy and Reitaku University sponsored the First East-West Conference on Moral Education. Speakers from many countries described the social-moral challenges their societies were facing. There was a shared concern about the breakdown of the family. There was a shared concern about the rise of the media-driven popular culture as a shaper of youth and societal values. There was a shared concern about increasing materialism and self-centeredness in the young and society at large. In the face of these troubling trends, there was also a shared conviction that education is the primary way society renews itself. In that belief, speakers from these many countries were looking to their educational institutions to lead the effort to improve their societies by building cultures of character.

The concerns that animated that 1987 conference are still very much with us. In his preface, Dr. Nakayama asserts that "modern Japanese society is ... faced with a mountain of issues," including "environmental destruction [and] a general loss of morality." Modern American society faces a comparable mountain of social and moral issues. In his concluding essay, Dr. Nakayama observes that there is a sense, common to East and West, that "the virtues are no longer prized today as they once were."

That observation called to mind a conversation I had during the 1987 conference with a thirty-year-old Reitaku University graduate student. We were discussing how virtues that appear to be com-

mon to all cultures are often enacted differently because of differences in cultural context. He cited respect for elders as a case
in point. He explained how, in his experience of Japanese ways,
respect for elders was such a strong and pervasive virtue that one
deferred to someone older even if the difference in age was slight.
He gave this example: "A good friend of mine is only six months
older than I am. But because he is older, when we enter a building
together, I always let him go before me. Or if we are with friends
having a discussion, I let him express his point of view before I
express mine."Although American culture affirms the virtue of respecting elders—we believe that teachers, parents, and grandparents are due such respect—there is clearly no American equivalent
of the nuanced Japanese attention to this virtue described by this
graduate student.

When I shared the story of the above conversation with a colleague during a 2010 visit to Japan, however, she said that Japan today faces new challenges to keeping its traditional respect for elders.
Families have changed. They have grown smaller as more mothers
have entered the workforce. According to my friend, more Japanese
children are coming to school with less respect for adult authority and less of the other-orientation that was typically fostered by
growing up with more siblings in bigger families. Discipline problems in classrooms are beginning to become more common.

American schools have long been struggling with problems stemming from changes in families. In 1960, only one in twenty U.S.
children was born to a single-parent family; last year that figure sur-
passed four in ten. Fatherlessness is now the leading predictor of
nearly every childhood and adolescent pathology, from insecurity
and depression to peer relationship difficulties and academic and behavior problems at school. Increasingly, American teachers have to
cope with the decline of things they used to take for granted: students' attention, respect for rules and authority, basic social skills,
and willingness to work. Indeed, the change schools see in children

is often cited as the main reason they have undertaken a more intentional schoolwide character education effort.

The Power of Culture

Even if our families and schools do a good job of teaching virtue—and even if all high school and college students were to read and take to heart a guide to virtuous living such as this book—our children will still have to function in a world that is, in many ways, increasingly hostile to moral values. We do well to remember that human behavior is a function of both *character* (the dispositions that make up our moral personality) and *culture* (the shared values, group expectations, traditions, and other factors that make up our social environment, which can call forth either the best or the worst of our character dispositions).

Put normally good persons in a bad moral environment, and they will often regress in their moral functioning. In a well-known study that simulated a prison environment, Stanford psychologist Philip Zimbardo randomly assigned undergraduates, all of whom tested normal on a personality inventory, to the roles of inmates or prison guards—and found that the "guards" were quickly transformed into sadistic tormentors. Even subtle situational cues can shape behavior. Experiments have shown that people are more likely to be rude if they just read words such as "assertive" and "interrupt," and are more likely to help others if there is the smell of fresh bread in the air.

In *The Altruistic Personality*, the most extensive study ever of those who helped to rescue Jews from the Holocaust, Samuel and Pearl Oliner report that three factors motivated people to rescue: (1) a belief in universal principles of justice (the motive for 11% of the 406 rescuers interviewed); (2) empathy for the victims (37%); and (3) a norm-centered orientation—that is, allegiance to the moral code of one's social group (52%). As an example of norm-centered orientation, the most common motive, a German woman said that she began helping Jews because her church was doing so. A Denmark man pointed to the moral code of Danish culture: "The basic morality in this little homogeneous country is to be nice to your neighbor and treat people well." In her essay on benevolence (Chapter 3 of this book), Bernice Lerner tells the stirring story of the French village of Le Chambon, whose Christian values impelled its members to save Jews—another example of the power of a positive moral culture to create a collective moral conscience.

Similarly, studies of organizational culture, such as Jim Collins's *Good to Great* and Charles Elbot's and David Fulton's *Building an Intentional School Culture*, have found that the companies, schools, non-profit enterprises, and other groups most successful in eliciting high-level behavior from their members have done so by creating a virtuous culture based on core values and norms ("This is our way—how we treat others, how we do our work"). This shared moral culture leads to a shared sense of moral identity ("This is who we are"), which is a powerful inducement to moral behavior even when others outside the particular group's culture are behaving much less morally.

Cross-cultural research confirms that culture matters. In a "lost wallet" study, passersby in some countries (such as Norway and Denmark) returned fully 100% of dropped wallets, with the fifty dollars in local currency intact, while in other countries the return rate was only a third or less.

There are two implications of the above studies: If we want readers of this volume and all present and future citizens to lead lives of virtue and take on higher levels of social and even global responsibility, then we do well to: (1) build a series of supportive "cultures of character" that bring out the best in their individual characters—beginning in families and extending to schools, communities, businesses, governments, and ultimately the whole society (clearly a tall order); (2) while we are working on the long-range project of transforming society by creating these concentric circles of character-supporting culture, simultaneously work to ensure that all young people, at some point in their development, have the experience of belonging to at least one formative moral culture that helps them develop an inner core of their character sturdy enough to stand up to the pressures of the less moral environments they will inevitably face. Ideally, we want to increase the number of principled people in any society who, in Kipling's famous phrase, will keep their heads even when all about them are losing theirs.

Japanese and American Approaches to Virtue: Where Does Culture Come In?

The idea that culture is important in shaping character and moral behavior offers a useful perspective from which to compare this book's Japanese and American essays on the virtues. In his thoughtful conclusion to the book, Dr. Nakayama states that the American authors rightly call our attention to the importance of the individual self as a moral agent, someone who makes and takes responsibility for moral choices, whatever the context. This is a basic moral capacity, Dr. Nakayama says, whose importance is beyond dispute. He also observes that the Japanese authors, compared to their American counterparts, more consistently call attention to the larger context in which the individual self functions. Reflecting their cultural heritage of Shintoist, Buddhist, and Taoist philosophies, the Japanese contributors more explicitly place the self "in its widest setting, in its relationship to all that the universe contains," including not only human relationships involving one's parents, ancestors, classmates, fellow workers, and even one's enemies, but also relationships with animals, plants, and everything in the inanimate world that enhances our lives.

This web of relationships can be viewed as a kind of all-encompassing culture—a "network of interdependence" of which Dr. Iwasa speaks in his chapter on benevolence. He points out that these interdependent relationships, if we are deeply aware of them, can bring out the best in us; they can give rise to "a benevolent mind" that serves "as the constant backdrop to all our thoughts and actions," a "permanent presence in our hearts and minds" making us grateful for all that we have received and motivating us to do good in return. Unlike other virtues whose manifestation may vary from situation to situation, benevolence in Dr. Iwasa's judgment is a "much more fundamental quality" that is central to our moral personality and functioning, and therefore should be the central goal of moral and character education.

As an American reader, I was also struck by two other ways the Japanese chapters reflect the importance of culture, membership, and interdependence. While both Japanese and American contributors tell the inspiring stories of individuals when they give examples of outstanding character, the Japanese authors more often describe the virtuous behavior of *groups*. We hear the story of Captain Kudo and his crew risking their own safety to save British sailors drifting in the Pacific after their ship had been sunk; the story of Japan's Oshima village rescuing drowning Turkish seamen and the reciprocal generosity of the Turkish government many years later in dispatching planes to take home Japanese citizens stranded in Tehran; the account of passengers on Japan's ill-fated Boeing 747 who penned notes to their loved ones in the face of impending death; and the story of the crew on the doomed Submarine Six who all dutifully stayed at their posts as they awaited their certain demise.

There is something especially moving about groups acting nobly. Americans did so during and after 9/11. They did so when upwards of 40,000 African-Americans, inspired by Rosa Park's refusal to go to the back of a segregated bus, boycotted Montgomery, Alabama's buses for more than a year, often walking long distances to their places of work. Americans come together in common cause when they gather by the thousands, as they often do, to march and speak up for those persons, born and preborn, whose human rights are unjustly denied. Japan's cultivation and celebration of altruistic group behavior remind us that it is important to tell such stories as we educate for character. They remind us of the power of deeply shared values. They remind us that the power of one is multiplied by the power of many. They remind us that we can and must become not only persons of character, but also a people of character.

❧　　❧　　❧

There is a second way the Japanese chapters treat the individual person within a larger context. Again and again, the Japanese authors invoke "the Japanese mind," "the Japanese way," the Japanese understanding of this or that virtue as revealed by a key cultural concept, an important mythical story, a revered moral or spiritual teacher, or a defining historical event. We are told that bushido, the spirit of the samurai, is "the soul of Japan" and crucial to understanding what is distinctive about the Japanese concept of virtue. We learn that the philosophy of "sharing losses equally among three parties" shapes the Japanese approach to justice. The writings of Chikuro Hiroike teach the concept of "moral causality," the notion that good actions have a chain of good consequences, often extending beyond our individual lives, just as bad actions always have bad consequences.

In the Japanese essay on gratitude, we learn that the concepts of *on* and *giri* underpin much social behavior in Japan because they teach people their responsibility to show gratitude to all their benefactors. In the essay on wisdom, we learn that for the Japanese, to become wise one must study the teachings of Confucius and Buddha. In the essay on reflection, we learn that *shikan* enables one to still one's thoughts, and that "[o]nly then can one observe the depths of one's being." In the essay on temperance, we learn that for Japanese, "the essence of self-control consists ... of maintaining a calm and poised mental attitude," not showing one's real emotions so as not to disturb the feelings of others and smiling even when criticized in order to gain time to restore one's inner composure. And so on.

What Is Distinctive about the American Approach to Virtue?

There is nothing comparable in the American essays. Why not? It may be more difficult to speak of "the American mind," "the American way," or what is distinctive about an American approach to virtue because we are not one culture but many. In a more homogeneous society such as Japan, it may be easier to speak of a "Japanese mind" about the duties involved in leading a moral life.

Moreover, the American authors, living as they do among people from many different lands, may be disposed to draw on stories and exemplars from many countries and cultures when they write about the virtues. Witness Kevin Ryan beginning his essay on respect with a famous children's story from Russia and Karen Bohlin, in her essay on gratitude, invoking the wisdom of the great German theologian Dietrich Bonheoffer: "[I]t is only with gratitude that life becomes rich." The American contributors may have consciously chosen to focus on the cross-cultural manifestations and universal importance of the book's nine virtues, rather than their distinctive manifestations in American culture.

Nevertheless, it seems to me that it may be worth speaking about what may in fact be distinctive about an American view of particular virtues. Americans' understanding of courage and justice, for example, is infused with admiration for heroes like George Washington and Abraham Lincoln, men who were great leaders because they had great character and a dedication to American ideals of freedom and equality. The American approach to justice is marked by a commitment to human rights and a strong spirit of egalitarianism that treats all people, regardless of social status, as moral equals.

Americans also have their defining historical events (such as the Revolutionary War, the Civil War, the Civil Rights Movement of the 1960s, and 9/11) and defining historical documents (such as the Declaration of Independence, the Constitution, the Gettysburg Address, and Martin Luther King's "Letter From Birmingham City Jail") that comprise our common cultural heritage, express the high value we place on freedom, democracy, and human rights, and shape our collective character. Many American youth are culturally illiterate about this rich heritage. We could and should do more to bring into sharper focus "the American mind" regarding the essence of good character and a good and just society as we educate our own students to become responsible American citizens—and as we engage in an East-West dialogue about what it means to be global citizens.

The World Our Children Live In

It is a tough time to be growing up. Our children face threats to their healthy character development that we didn't have to contend with. And when they become adults, they will likely still have to deal with a moral environment that often encourages them to lie, cheat, and steal to get what they want and to make self-interest their highest value.

I am currently reading *Light of the World*, a conversation between Pope Benedict XVI and the veteran journalist Peter Seewald. At one point, Seewald prefaces a question to the Pope with a stark description of the world we now live in:

> We see in our time a world in danger of sliding into the abyss. We see an unrestrained economic system ready to mutate into a predatory capitalism that devours values on a huge scale. We see that life in the fast lane robs us of our moral compass. We see the growth of a society that plunges ahead recklessly with no clear sense of direction, regarding today as right what yesterday was considered wrong. We have new addictions to things such as video games and pornography. We have the almost unmanageable stress produced by the mania for profit maximization that drives the business world. We have the precarious situation of children who suffer because of the loss of family relations. We have the dominance of the media, which have developed a culture bent on breaking our taboos, dumbing us down, and blunting our moral sense.

A sobering list. Let us focus for a moment on just one of these global problems: the "mania for profit maximization." In his 2009 encyclical on the global economy, soon after the world narrowly escaped economic meltdown, Pope Benedict addressed the causes of the economic and financial crisis. He argued that ethics must govern economics. Only concern for the common good and the dignity of the human person, he said, can restrain greed and guide economies toward the creation of a just, socially beneficial, and ecologically sound social order. In a similar spirit, Dr. Nakayama warns in his concluding chapter, "Economic globalization ... continues to produce the universalization of human greed, exploiting remorselessly our weakness in seeking to pursue our own interests...."

There is abundant evidence of the rapidly accelerating concentration of wealth in the hands of the already rich and powerful. The gap between rich nations and poor nations continues to widen. The same is true of economic disparities within nations. In the United States, in the late 1970s, the richest 1% of America's families took in about 9% of the nation's income; by 2007, the top 1% took in 23.5% of total income.

This past August (2011), England was shocked by widespread rioting and looting carried out by gangs of predominantly young unemployed males not for political protest but for criminal gain. In a recent commentary for *The New York Times*, British author Phillip Blond points out that in 1976, the lower half of the British population had 12% of the wealth but by 2003, their share had fallen to 1%. Blond is author of the book *Red Tory: How Left and Right Have Broken Britain and How We Can Fix It*. He blames cultural libertarians for undermining marriage and the family and promoting social welfare policies that have led to a tripling of the number of British children who live in single-parent households. He argues that the rioters are "morally denuded" and "shamefully emblematic of modern Britain," reflecting "the ruthless self-interest" that characterizes a self-serving economic elite.

When I was in Japan last November, I asked a university president what he considered the greatest challenge currently facing his country's young people. He paused for a long time before answering. Then he said, "I would say that the greatest challenge facing Japanese young people today is that they lack hope for the future."

Our conversation, mediated by a translator, veered in another direction and ended before I had a chance to clarify why the president thought Japanese young people were losing hope. But several months later, during the "Arab spring" that saw youth in Middle Eastern countries demonstrating in the streets for greater democracy and economic opportunity, I read a *New York Times* column by twenty-four-year-old Matthew Klein titled, "Educated, Unemployed, and Frustrated." It addressed the lack of hope that young people in many parts of the world are now experiencing. Klein wrote:

> My generation was taught that all we needed to succeed was an education and hard work. Tell that to my friend from high school who studied Chinese and international relations at a top-tier college. He had the misfortune of graduating in the class of 2009 and could find paid work only as a lifeguard and personal trainer. After more than a year, he moved back in with his parents.
>
> Millions of college graduates in rich nations could tell similar stories. In Italy, Portugal, and Spain, about one-fourth of college graduates under the age of twenty-five are unemployed. The cost of youth unemployment is not only financial but also emotional. The millions of young people who cannot get jobs are in danger of losing their faith in the future. They are indefinitely postponing the life they wanted and prepared for.

What are the implications of this situation for the young persons now coming of age, and for those of us who urge our youth to develop virtues such as those presented in this book? For our students and the young readers of this book, our message might be:

Don't lose hope—an important virtue in the face of all life's challenges. For now, do whatever work you can get. Keep pursuing your dream of more fulfilling work. Look for opportunities to do good in small ways in your daily interactions. These small acts of goodness will help to sustain you because you will be making a positive difference in the lives of others. Do what you can to support social policies that create better economic opportunities for all people. If you are fortunate enough to be in a position of influence or power, do whatever you can to promote economic justice for all. And if you ever get to run a company and it does well, use that good fortune to create more jobs, not to fatten your salary.

For our part as moral leaders, we can work to eliminate what Pope John Paul II called "structures of sin," such as a greed-driven capitalism that places maximization of profit and bonuses for the few above the common good and above giving people the work they need for their dignity, well-being, and simple survival. When we educate for character, we must be sure to include education for social and economic justice, something that character educators have sometimes been criticized for neglecting.

And when we educate for economic justice, we want to be sure to have students read books such as *The End of Poverty* by economist Jeffery Sachs. He reminds us that half of the world's six billion people are poor, and one-sixth of them suffer "extreme poverty," struggling to survive on less than one dollar a day, chronically hungry, lacking health care or safe drinking water, and unable to afford an education for their children. This, Sachs says, "is the poverty that kills," but it can be ended in twenty-five years by "a network of global cooperation" of the rich and powerful nations—if they have the will to do so.

Sex and Character
As Chapter 9 of this book recognizes, the virtue of temperance—the

disciplined control of our impulses, appetites, and passions—has long been considered a mark of good character. Sexual self-discipline, the aspect of temperance historically known as chastity, presents special challenges. In *The Courage to Be Chaste*, the spiritual writer Benedict Groeschel observes, "Sexual self-control is often the weakest link in an individual's self-control system."

One writer has observed that among all the challenges young people face, "Sex is the mountain." Their hormones are at full flood. They live in an increasingly sexualized popular culture that beckons them toward early and casual sexual involvement. If they can develop the self-discipline, respect, responsibility, and courage to resist sexual temptations and pressures, they will have conquered what is likely to be the greatest character challenge in their young and vulnerable lives. And they will have spared themselves and others the pain of mistakes they may regret for years to come.

For this reason, I think it would have been helpful to include a chapter in the book to show, with the kind of specificity and stories used so well to illustrate character in other spheres of behavior, how all nine of the virtues apply to the sexual domain. Many people, young and old, don't make the connections. Sex for many can be a kind of "moral free zone" where our lesser selves, uninhibited by moral judgment, dominate the better angels of our nature.

An honest discussion of sex must begin by recognizing that although sex is natural and good, not all sex is good. Sex can bring the joy of a new life into a family where parents are committed to love and raise the child, but it can also create a life that ends in abortion or comes into a world where there are not responsible parents. Sex can express and deepen committed and faithful love, but it can also be used to betray, demean, and exploit others. It is an unconscionable moral scandal that sexual exploitation is part of the dark underbelly of many societies, including those in the developed world. By one estimate, there are more than two million children worldwide involved in sex trafficking; the average age of entry into the sex trade is thirteen.

Wisdom about sexual restraint was swept aside by the sexual revolution, which hit the United States with full force in the late 1960s and is still making its way around the world, often fueled by the toxic sexualized media that America exports. The sexual revolution advanced a radical idea: that people should be free to have sex without the strictures of marriage, without commitment, and even without love. "Friends with (sexual) benefits" is now a growing pattern among college students and even high school students that has spread across cultural boundaries.

The new sexual freedom promised greater happiness, but it is now painfully clear that we suffer from a plague of problems stemming from the breakdown of sexual morality. These include increasingly precocious sexual activity on the part of the young; teen pregnancies; unwed births; abortions (worldwide, more than an estimated fifty million a year); an explosion of sexually transmitted diseases (fifteen million new cases every year in the U.S.); and a cluster of emotional and behavioral problems associated with uncommitted sex, such as higher rates of depression and suicide among sexually active teens.

Added to this is sexual harassment in schools and the workplace; pornography, which the author Sean Covey has called "the addiction of the twenty-first century"; the sexual abuse of children; single adults cohabitating with a series of sexual partners; the heightened risk of divorce associated with premarital cohabitation; rising levels of marital infidelity; and the weakening of marriage and the family caused by all of these problems.

Surveying this moral landscape, the essayist William Schickel observes, "Chastity, like honesty, is a civic as well as a personal virtue. When a society loses chastity, it begins to destroy itself."

How Is Virtue Developed? A Small Study

It is one thing to explain the nature of a virtue and its importance for personal and societal happiness. It is another thing to give useful tips that help us develop the virtues. When I asked about the goals of this book, one of the contributors said he hoped readers would "carry it everywhere and find hints for guidance for their everyday lives."

As I read the chapters, they set me to wondering: How, truly, is virtue developed in the lives of most people? How do good people I know—including contributors to this book and others who have spent much of their lives thinking, writing, and teaching about good character—go about trying to develop their own character?

To find out, I asked them. I emailed a dozen such colleagues and friends—half male, half female, including five contributors to this book and people of different cultures and faith traditions—and invited them to share responses to a number of questions:

1. How would you rate, on a scale of 1 (little or no importance) to 5 (very important) the following factors in terms of their impact on your own virtue/character development: family, school, religion, friends, mentors, role models, the community, and your personal, deliberate effort to become a better person?

2. What is one good habit—a virtuous pattern of acting—that you have deliberately tried to develop? What motivated you to do so? How, specifically, did you go about this? What obstacles, within and without, did you have to overcome? Did you ever regress, and if so, how did you deal with that? To what extent do you think you've succeeded?

3. What is one bad habit—a flaw, fault, or vice—that you have deliberately tried to reduce or eliminate? (followed by the other questions I had asked about the good habit)

4. In your own life, do you think that developing virtues, overcoming faults, and becoming a person of character have been: (a) mostly a matter of consciously striving to be a better person (e.g., working on developing good habits and curbing bad

ones); *or* (b) mostly a matter of less deliberate, less self-conscious, and less self-directed processes, such as having a good parent or teacher and experiences you didn't expect or control?

5. As you reflect on people you know, what do you think seems generally to be true of them—(a) or (b) in the question above?

6. What other thoughts would you care to share that might shed light on the development of virtue?

The results of this modest study show that, at least for this small sample (eleven persons responded), there are both similarities and differences in how people report they have developed virtue. Most, but not all, rated family as a very important influence (5). Most, but not all, rated religion and mentors as important (5 or 4). (A Christian friend, in response to the question about what motivated him to try to develop virtues and correct faults, answered simply, "Christ.") Most rated school and the community they grew up in as relatively *un*important (typically 2), although one gave his college education a 4.

Nearly everyone gave their own deliberate effort to become a better person a high rating (5 or 4). A few people cited authors whose books had a big impact on their moral and spiritual development. One said he used a "list of behaviors related to my selfishness that I score myself on daily" as an aid to developing selflessness. A woman said she learned to stop worrying about the future welfare of her family members by "making up my mind to just appreciate the essence of these people that I love so much and to enjoy every moment together." Another friend said that observing her great aunt's "beautifully ordered life" inspired her to develop greater discipline in her own life. A male friend wrote that "disgust and fatigue at the debilitating effects" of (sexual) "impurity," new habits of prayer, and a desire to imitate John Paul II's heroic virtues helped him to develop "the habit of personal purity."

One of the most thoughtful responses came from one of the Japanese authors, whose approach to developing personal virtue seemed to me distinctively Japanese. Note, for example, that he cites his cultural heritage and sense of indebtedness to others as central influences in his effort to lead a good life:

> My motivation [to develop virtues] came from my cultural heritage—to repay past indebtedness to various benefactors. I try always to think of others and not just chase my own interests. When I fail, I look for guidance by re-reading Hiroike's books on moral science. I have often made mistakes in judging other people and getting angry without knowing the complicated circumstances surrounding their actions. One of my teachers had to resign his post due to his past mistakes. Without knowing the ethical dilemma he was put in, I felt disappointment and mistrust, and even despised him. A Catholic friend, who happened to be a priest, taught me, "Man cannot judge people."

He then elaborated on what he saw as the important role played by ethical mentors:

> I have been lucky enough to meet the right people when I needed help. I have realized that less saintly or less holy persons such as myself need the help and protection of peers who are looking in the same direction—toward character enhancement. My advice to others is humbly to seek help, and then you will get answers to your questions and see the models you should follow.

Last, he reminded us that the struggle for character continues throughout life—and may get even harder in the twilight of our lives:

> I am far from being successful and am still working hard to overcome my faults. As I grow older, new tasks emerge. In these

modern times, when many people live longer, virtue development can become very difficult in the later stage of one's life. The true nature of your character will come out no matter how successfully you have developed your character through previous conscious efforts. We may find that we have strong self-preserving instincts and selfish desires.

This person's beliefs about the challenges we will face in our later years is confirmed by recent research on adult moral development. Our character is not static. Some adults become wiser, more patient, and more giving as they grow older; others, sadly, become more selfish.

An American contributor to this volume called attention to the importance of helping our young fall in love with the good. She wrote:

> I believe that the real engine that sustains the development of virtue is love, the desire to be a better spouse, a better parent, a better friend, a better student, a better athlete, a better professional. The desire to take care of someone in need, the desire to be more like the people we admire, the desire to become more worthy of their love. I don't think the literature and research on character development adequately addresses the importance of awakening and deepening this desire.
>
> Virtue preached isn't always attractive, but virtue lived is always attractive. Character education needs to make virtue desirable—not simply a means to good grades or a job—but rather as those habits that lead us to greater happiness, love, and freedom.

Another American respondent, not a contributor to this book but a developmental psychologist and researcher who has published widely on the subject of moral growth and character education, wrote:

I think the early years of parenting and education have a huge impact, and we are less captains of our own ships at that developmental point. Later we become more reflective and self-aware and better able to steer our own development, but change is harder then.

A friend from Singapore offered another perspective on early influences such as family. She said she was one of seven children in a home where her parents often fought violently, as did most couples in her poor neighborhood. Her mother left the family when she was eight. Her eldest brother beat her up. When she married, her husband drank heavily, gambled, and beat the children (she finally left him at age thirty-seven). But, she says, she experienced kindness from a third-grade teacher, her first boss, her own children, and her sister's husband, who embodied kindness in all that he did. "Many people would laugh at how 'silly' he was to be kind to everyone, but he became my teacher of kindness and selflessness. From his many kind acts, I have a lasting mental picture of what kindness looks like and feels like." Kindness is now her central value, and she has dedicated her life to trying to foster it in children and others. She wrote:

> Moral development is belief development. Change the belief, and emotion and behavior will change along with it. Good families don't always bring up good children who can endure adversity bravely and stay good. Surprisingly, many heroes come from broken families. Sometimes, you need darkness to recognize the light.

Finally, my American researcher friend offered this helpful caution against over-simplifying:

> The nature of humanity is too complex for the human mind to fully comprehend. It is a multifaceted and dynamic enterprise.

We certainly understand some of it, but when we try to simplify it to a few influences, we deeply distort it. This applies to virtue as well as to all other aspects of human development and functioning.

Humbly acknowledging the complexity of our challenging task, our quest for a deeper understanding of virtue goes on, aided in no small measure by the lifelong work of this book's authors and the wisdom they have shared in this volume. All of us, East and West, can feel gratitude for that.

I would like to thank my wife Judith—who, like me, was grateful for all we learned as we read portions of this book aloud together—for her prayers and helpful comments during my writing of this introduction.

CHAPTER 1

Courage

"To see what is right yet not do it is a sign of cowardice."
—Chinese

രാ രാ രാ

Courage is that which allows us to act in spite of our fears, to win over inner doubt and negativity, to do the right thing, no matter the risk. It is most appropriate to commence a discussion of virtues and happiness by focusing on courage, which we all must find within if we are to undertake a path of inner transformation toward living a fulfilling life.

Reitaku University President Osamu Nakayama states in the first essay, "Happiness bubbles up within us when we create value of some kind, but this is much easier said than done.... Essential is to launch ourselves into action." He illustrates two kinds of courage with a pair of true stories from different eras. In one, the captain of a Japanese destroyer vessel chooses to do the right thing and rescue British sailors after their ships had been sunk during a World War II battle. The story of Captain Kudo further illustrates the spirit of bushido, a code of chivalry from the samurai days. In the other, two college students with serious physical disabilities challenge their own limitations in the face of tremendous obstacles, one inspiring the other. Each of these individuals exhibits courage, which, as Dr. Nakayama describes, is the fruit of one's own initiative, can be inspired by others, and involves some significant risk of loss.

Kevin Ryan opens his essay by drawing from the book *The Things They Carried* by Vietnam War veteran Tim O'Brien to illustrate the lifelong struggle with courage an individual may face and how choices made along the way matter later. "Life tests us every day in small and large ways," writes Dr. Ryan, and "... our courage is continually on call." Courage allows us to face and transcend our "crippling fears," whether they involve being laughed at or excluded or killed, so that we might do the right thing, so that we can take action and become happy. Literature and other sources of story supply a rich garden of moral lessons, from which people from childhood to adulthood can learn.

Courage

BY OSAMU NAKAYAMA

It must have been about midday, for the sun was vertical and we were just south of the equator. About 200 yards away we thought we saw a Japanese destroyer. Was she a mirage? We all saw her, so perhaps she was real, but our first emotion was not joy or relief, for we expected to be machine-gunned. There was a great bustle aboard that ship, but the main armament was trained fore and aft and there was no sign of machine guns. The ship's sailors were lowering rope ladders all along the side of the ship. They were smiling small brown men in their floppy white sun hats and too-long khaki shorts. The ship came closer. We caught hold of the rope ladders and managed to clamber aboard. We were covered with oil and exhausted. The Japanese sailors surrounded us and regarded us with cheerful curiosity. They took cotton waste and spirit and cleaned the oil off us, firmly but gently. It was—extraordinary to relate—a friendly welcome.

I was given a green shirt, a pair of khaki shorts, and a pair of gym shoes. Then we were escorted to a large space amidships and politely invited to sit down in comfortable cane chairs. We were served hot milk, bully beef, and biscuits. After a while the captain of the destroyer came down from the bridge, saluted us, and addressed us in English: "You have fought bravely. Now you are the honored guests of the Imperial Japanese Navy. I respect the English navy, but your government is very foolish to make war on Japan."

That fine officer searched for survivors all day, stopping to pick up even single men, until his small ship was overflowing. An awning was spread over the fo'c's'le to protect us from the sun; lavatories were rigged outboard; cigarettes were handed out; and by a biblical type of miracle, our hosts managed to give all 300 of us food and drink …. The Japanese did not know, it seems, that there were no English submarines in the Java Sea. Yet they had continually stopped to rescue every survivor they could find.

Sam Falle, *My Lucky Life*

Sir Sam Falle, whose account of the above incident is taken from his autobiography, joined the British Royal Navy and served in the Far East during World War II. A little historical background will help us to grasp the full significance of what happened to him in the Java Sea between February 27 and March 3, 1942, soon after the outbreak of World War II in the Pacific. At that time, the Japanese Imperial Navy was engaged in combat with a combined force from the fleets of Great Britain, the United States, and Holland, during which it sank eleven out of a total of fifteen enemy warships in the theater. Among these were the British cruiser HMS *Exeter* and destroyer HMS *Encounter*, whose surviving crew members were forced to abandon ship and take to the water covered in fuel oil. Falle was among them. The next day, just as they were reaching the limits of their endurance, they were discovered by a Japanese destroyer, the *Ikazuchi*, which came across them by chance.

Falle shared the preconception, common among his countrymen at the time, that the Japanese were completely merciless, which explains his expectation of being machine-gunned on sight as he battled to stay afloat. As he says, though, the *Ikazuchi* did nothing of the sort. Quite the contrary, to his amazement and relief, it immediately set to work to save him and those of his fellow crew members still surviving in the water, flying the signal flag internationally recognized as notification of a rescue operation! By the end of the day, the *Ikazuchi* had pulled 422 individuals from the dangers of the open ocean. Then, as Falle goes on to recount, the captain of the ship, Lieutenant Commander Shunsaku Kudo (1901–1979), invited him and all the other rescued British sailors to repair to a large space amidships where they were met with "a friendly welcome" and the offer of water, food, clothes, and other conveniences.

The story of this encounter has much to teach us about the key components of the virtue of courage. Firstly, courage is the fruit of our own initiative; it does not appear at the behest of others. In the case of Captain Kudo, though his rank was certainly a precondition that made possible his courageous behavior, the spur to action was his conscience, not a command from his superior officers or even the advice of his colleagues. Indeed, one young officer aboard is on record as having expressed his dissatisfaction, complaining, "What on earth is our captain thinking about? We are here to make war!" But courage involves cleaving to what one knows to be right, even in the face of the objections of others.

Secondly, a courageous impulse can be inspired by the example of others. Though Sam Falle could not have been aware of it at the time, Captain Kudo was moved to act as he did by the object lesson afforded to him by the man he regarded as his role model, Vice Admiral Hikonojyo Kamimura (1849–1916). As Kudo gazed on the British sailors drifting helplessly amid the waves, the story of an incident nearly forty years before suddenly flashed into his mind. At the Battle off Ulsan (also known as the Battle of the Japanese Sea) on August 14, 1904, the second fleet of the Imperial Japanese Navy commanded by Vice Admiral Kamimura attacked the *Rurik*, a Russian armored cruiser, which eventually scuttled itself. Soon after, Kamimura, observing a large number of Russian sailors (627 in total, as it turned out) adrift on the sea, ordered three Japanese cruisers, the *Izumo, Naniwa,* and *Takachiho* to rescue as many of the enemy combatants as they could. This action was hailed as an example of the spirit of Japanese bushido (chivalry or ethical code) around the world.

The words of the song, "Admiral Kamimura," which his grandmother had sung for him as a child, echoed through Captain Kudo's mind as he gazed out over a similar scene in 1942. He heard again the third verse of the song's lyrics, which began: "The clouds above the Ulsan Sea clear away; when the Japanese fleet returns bravely after its triumphant pursuit and attack, the *Rurik* is sinking below the waves; though they are our bitterest enemies, they will die if we abandon them; You cry, 'Help them!'"

A third feature of such actions is that by their nature they expose courageous individuals to danger and the risk of serious loss, up to and including that of their own lives and those of others close to them. These possibilities must be fully admitted and squarely faced. In this way one readies oneself for any and all of the consequences of one's actions. The hallmark of courage is then revealed: a determined will to do what one believes to be right, come what may.

What kind of risks and potential losses did Captain Kudo choose to accept in acting as he did? Obviously, embarking on a rescue operation in an area that had recently witnessed major conflict was fraught with peril. Any encounter with an enemy submarine or warplane while his crew was distracted by the search for survivors might well have resulted in the loss of his own ship in short order. In his book, *Rescue Enemy Soldiers!*, Ryunosuke Megumi, whose professional expertise derives from his status as a former officer in the Japanese Self-Defense Force, details the dangers and unavoidable costs to which Captain Kudo decided to turn a blind eye. He believed, as Sam Falle notes, that there was a significant possibility that his ship would be attacked in the course of the rescue operation, and this was not a groundless supposition. A Japanese transport ship, the *Kamogawamaru*, had already been torpedoed in the same area, and combat reports show that between February 27 and March 1, the Imperial Japanese Navy sank seven enemy submarines in the vicinity.

There were also costs to be shouldered. Not least among these was the unanticipated expenditure of valuable fuel oil and water, the sacrifice of which might in time have endangered the *Ikazuchi*. Within months of the outbreak of conflict, oil had already become infinitely precious to the Japanese. The phrase commonly heard amongst them at the time, "One drop of oil is equal to one drop of blood," reflects how extremely limited were the country's supplies of that vital commodity. To consume it in the rescue of enemy combatants was not a decision to be taken lightly. The crisscrossing of a stretch of sea, with repeated stops, would eat into reserves that might well be crucial later in the voyage. But that was not the only extra drain on the oil supply. It was also needed to drive the machinery supplying the ship with pure water. This explains the tremendous efforts the crew of the *Ikazuchi* had made during the voyage to date to save pure water for washing and drinking. They had not spared themselves in the effort to economize on fuel, yet here they were being required to sacrifice their precious water and oil for their enemies. They were to provide the British sailors on board with a total of three tons of pure drinking water before they reached port, to which should be added the alcohol, gasoline, and water that was needed to clean off the oil in which they were covered.

Even if the rescued sailors were now prisoners rather than enemies, their presence aboard inevitably reduced the combat effectiveness of the *Ikazuchi* in a number of ways. Captain Kudo had a large awning hung above the front deck to shade those of the sailors who were wounded, and this made it impossible to use the main gun. But the ship was still in a war zone; nothing could be more dangerous than impairing its capacity to defend itself in this way. There was also the risk inherent simply in having such a large number of former enemy combatants aboard, twice as many, in fact, as the total crew of the ship itself. What would happen if they recovered their strength and tried to take over the vessel? When questioned about this risk, Captain Kudo replied half jokingly, "If they rise in revolt, it may prove fatal to us. They are tall and strong. However things turned out, we would be in an awful mess!"

All these risks and costs resulted from the remarkable zeal with which Captain Kudo conducted the rescue effort. He went far beyond what was normally considered prudent. On other similarly critical occasions during World War II, Japanese captains were forced to abandon efforts to save those who could not swim to their warships and climb on deck, even though they were their fellow countrymen. Captain Kudo, however, rescued all of the enemy sailors in view. In fact, some British sailors who were finally brought on deck had been too weak to hold on to a rope. So Japanese crew members held out bamboo poles to them and encouraged them to cling on, crying ""Don't give up!" in anguished voices. Even with this help, though, some of those in the water were too weak to hang on and sank beneath the surface. A Japanese sailor, unable to just stand by, jumped into the sea to rescue them despite regulations forbidding this. Captain Kudo did not prevent or punish those doing so; on the contrary, he ordered all the crew to join in. This alone explains how he was able to save twice as many enemy sailors as his total crew without abandoning a single severely wounded individual.

Captain Kudo's actions were clearly courageous, characteristic of bushido. His courage was identical in nature to that described by Nitobe Inazo (1862–1933) in his *Bushido, the Soul of Japan*:

> Nietzsche spoke for the samurai heart when he wrote, "You are to be proud of your enemy; then, the success of your enemy is your success also." Indeed valor and honor alike required that we should own as enemies in war only such as prove worthy of being friends in peace. When valor attains this height, it becomes akin to benevolence.

Captain Kudo displayed courage in action, accepting dangerous risks and discounting all potential costs. His wartime circumstances were far from ordinary, of course. But the essence of what was required of him has parallels with the courage that we may be asked to show when confronted with injury, illness, or other difficulties in our everyday, civilian lives.

A second true story will illustrate this point. Shingo Kunieda, a graduate of Reitaku University, is physically handicapped. But he has also become the number one singles wheelchair-tennis player in the world. Confined to a wheelchair since the age of nine by a tumor on his spinal cord, he overcame his disadvantage through a strong will and faith in life. He explains his attitude, encapsulated in his motto "everyone has infinite potential," in the following terms:

Not only in tennis but in every other thing we do, we will not be able to realize our true potential until we give it our best shot. However high our aims seem to be, we should tackle them with all our strength, never giving up at any point along the way. Wheelchair-tennis taught me that giving up is an act of choice, but I only learned this after I had given my all and been successful. On the way to my goal of becoming the number one wheelchair-tennis player, I practiced out of a desire to beat my rivals. But after I achieved my aim, I had no rival to overcome. Having lost that beacon, I went into a slump for several months. Fortunately, I was able to find a solution by myself; I realized that I had to continue to improve my own tennis. This opened up a limitless vista. I cannot imagine how strong I will be. As long as I try with all my strength, I think I will have limitless room for further progress.

In the process, I also came to ponder what I can do apart from playing my sport to a good standard. I found I needed to explain to others how wheelchair-tennis has brought happiness into my life. If I had not become involved in it, I would not have discovered many things that I can see clearly now. Meeting wonderful people through this sport has allowed me to find courage and to turn dreams into reality as my life in a wheelchair unfolds.

Kunieda's words reveal that courage can flow into us and allow us to achieve our dreams if we are ready to accept our destiny and

make the necessary effort, demonstrating patience amid tribula-
tions. That inflow of courage enables us to challenge ourselves and
to persevere.

❧   ❧   ❧

Of all the virtues, perhaps the one most necessary to the attainment
of happiness is courage. Happiness bubbles up within us when we
create value of some kind, but this is much easier said than done.
Creating value, spiritual or material, is seldom smooth sailing.

How is this to be done? The essential thing is to launch ourselves
into action. Like Shingo Kunieda in his wheelchair, we must be
indefatigable in challenging ourselves. To do this again and again,
against any and all odds, requires, more than anything else, courage.

And where is that to be found? The first place to seek it is within.
We must locate an aspiration to better ourselves. Without such an
ambition and the desire to accomplish something of worth, we will
never discover the springs of courage. They will remain buried if
we do nothing but run ourselves down, adopt a pessimistic outlook on our lives, and retreat into our own shells. Only action and
a change to a more positive way of thinking can release the inrush
of courage that follows from a belief that something will eventuate
if we act and from the acceptance that even failure can be a good
experience. Negative thinking is a guarantee that we will take no
action at all and therefore fail; the more negatively we think, the
more trapped we become in a vicious circle.

A second source of courage is a proper belief in ourselves. A
lack of legitimate self-confidence undoubtedly hinders the access
of courage. One of Kunieda's tenets is "I am the strongest!" The
question of which comes first, courage or confidence, is a chicken-
or-the-egg question, of course; they reinforce one another. We gain
courage through self-confidence, and we enhance our confidence
by acting courageously.

Certainly there are occasions when we cannot achieve the outcome we desire, no matter how hard we try. A third true story is relevant here. It again involves Kunieda. Another Reitaku student, Akitoshi Takehata, chose to come to the university on the strength of a keen interest in Kunieda's courageous way of life. Takehata, who was also a tennis player, had an osteogenic sarcoma in his left leg. Inspired by Kunieda's example, he wanted to fight against it. His ailment returned, however, and he had to leave the university for medical treatment after just one year. The doctor's verdict was that no therapy held any real prospect of success. Being told that he only had a five percent chance of surviving was a heavy blow, yet he did not throw in the towel. He was unable to accept an invitation to an alumni meeting in Kyushu, where he was born, being too ill and bedridden. But he did manage to send a video message. In it he said, "I have been very encouraged by my friends, including those from Reitaku University. I will never give up! If I give up, it would be ungracious to those who have supported me. In order to show my gratitude towards them, I will never give up." All the 240 people at the alumni meeting prayed for him, silently petitioning for his recovery. He made a slight improvement, but then in October, sad to say, he passed away. At the funeral ceremony, his father told those of us who were present, "My son's life of twenty-one years was so short, but he lived it to the full. He went to the university he really wanted to go to, and he met a lot of friends and teachers whom he really loved. Thank you so much."

In the course of our lives, we encounter numerous troubles and have to face seemingly insurmountable obstacles. In difficult times, anxiety amounting to despair may seize us. We may feel that whatever we do, success will elude us, that things are destined to go from bad to worse. Our future looms dark and unknowable. Such a chain of anxious thoughts is a horror and a torture. In such dire straits, we are tempted simply to seek to escape, but the further we try to run from our problems, the more serious they become and the more doggedly they pursue us. At such times we need to gather our courage and turn to face the harshness of reality. No matter how difficult our problems seem to be, we may then find, to our surprise, that meeting them head on diminishes them greatly. Timidity or cowardice magnifies all difficulties and makes them appear intractable. Courage is the antidote; it alone enables us to grow and achieve happiness, not just for ourselves, but for those around us too.

☘   ☘   ☘

Other lessons can help to imbed the virtue of courage deeply within us. The first is learning how to distinguish true courage from its mock variants. The hallmark of true courage is action, the doing of what is right. So the *Analects of Confucius* tell us that "to see what is right yet not do it is a sign of cowardice." The opposite, as described in the *Discourses of Mencius* (372–289 B.C.E.), is foolhardiness or the "humble man's courage." Reckless impetuosity without prudence or discretion should never be mistaken for courage.

Doing what is right can result in objections and mockery even from one's family, relatives, friends, and others who have previously been supportive. An access of true courage gives one the strength to endure criticism and scorn and persevere in doing what is right. Against the world if need be, we should follow the path we know to be correct.

Secondly, we must recognize that an act of courage is done of our own free will and can never be the result of compulsion. We must do what is right solely on our own initiative, and we must allow this freedom to others. Too many people in the world find enjoyment in picking holes in others and slandering them. Truly courageous people, though, not only take the initiative in doing good, they also publicly honour the good done by others.

A third step is to grasp the wisdom of the words of the *Analects* that say, "When you love courage but not learning, you will be rough and your influence harmful." "Learning" here refers not merely to academic or abstract knowledge. It means absorbing the words and deeds of courageous people, just as Captain Kudo learned bushido from Vice Admiral Kamimura and Takehata learned the courage of taking on a challenge from Kunieda.

Finally, we must understand that the key to nurturing courage within ourselves is benevolence. In the *Analects* there is this saying to ponder: "A man of virtue has always courage, but a man of courage does not always have virtue." This means that even when we are persecuted or become the victim of unlawful acts, we should respond with a blend of courage and benevolence. True courage is based on the lofty and impartial benevolence, which inspires us to love both foes and enemies without distinction. That is its wellspring. Having found it within ourselves, we can then experience how, from the unfathomable depths of the spirit of benevolence, surges the flood of self-certitude that will sweep us into courageous action.

Courage

BY KEVIN RYAN

Tim O'Brien, one of America's most gifted contemporary novelists, has written poignantly about his experiences as a soldier in the Vietnam War. In one book, *The Things They Carried*, he reflects back on his boyhood in a small Minnesota town. He tells of being in the fourth grade and being in love with Linda, a classmate. He describes the aching innocence of his feelings: "I just wanted to melt into her bones—that kind of love."

One day Linda showed up at school wearing a red cap with a white tassel. It was immediately the source of attention and curiosity. She wore it all day, even on the playground during recess. The class tough guy and show-off, Nick, repeatedly would sneak up on Linda and try to snatch it off her head. O'Brien describes how he stood on the sidelines witnessing Nick's cruel attempts to get the cap. While the other students watched, Linda kept a wary eye on Nick, protecting her cap and acting as if Nick's game didn't matter. A mixture of fear that his feelings for Linda would be revealed and fear of Nick kept O'Brien passively watching.

One afternoon during a spelling test, while the teacher was distracted, Nick snuck up behind Linda's desk and took his prize. What Nick and Tim and the rest of the class saw was Linda's glossy white skull with surgical stitches and a bandage. As her shocked classmates stared, Linda just looked forward. Finally, she turned and looked across the room to Tim. Although the look was brief and without words, O'Brien is convinced a whole conversation took place between them: "'Well?' she was saying, and I was saying, 'Sure, okay.'"

O'Brien carries memories of this moment into his adult life, reflecting on it while in the midst of his combat service in Vietnam. He regrets his role in the event with Linda and Nick on the playground. While Linda acted as if Nick's teasing grabs for her cap didn't matter, and he did nothing, O'Brien experienced an inner drama. He later wrote:

> For me, though, it did matter. It still does. I should've stepped in; fourth grade is no excuse. Besides it doesn't get easier with time, and twelve years later, when Vietnam presented much harder choices, some practice at being brave might've helped a little.

Later on in his narrative, O'Brien reveals that Linda, his pure first love, died of brain cancer that following summer. Nick, who after his terrible classroom stunt sympathetically had walked Linda home, remains insensitive. He hears of Linda's death from his mother at lunchtime and hurries back to school. With that certain callousness of youth, he rushes up to Tim and says, "Your girlfriend. She kicked the bucket."

Stories, by their very nature, deal with the moral life. Even seemingly minor stories, such as Tim O'Brien's childhood memory, are rich with moral matter. There is Linda, already burdened with illness and disfigurement, stoically enduring torment and then embarrassment. There is Nick, a bully, showing off to his schoolmates. He seems to recognize the pain he caused Linda, but later, with his callous announcement, returns to his pattern of bravado and insensitivity. And, finally, there is Tim and his quiet cowardice. It seems harsh to accuse a nine-year-old of cowardice, but as O'Brien himself acknowledges, his passivity was an act of moral cowardice.

While we may like to believe that children are the soul of innocence and incapable of moral cowardice, human history tells a different story. Young people, often very young, have performed stunning acts of virtue and strikingly dishonorable and immoral acts. The newspaper and television regularly present us with accounts of heroic acts on the part of children, such as that of a three-year-old seeking help from the fire department when her father collapsed. Sadly, too, we hear of sadistic school children who bully vulnerable others. To deny that the three figures in Tim O'Brien's story are not conscious moral actors is to deny their humanity.

While many stories simply describe moral and immoral actions, others probe further, presenting us with a more interior view of the actors. We discover that a cruel act is motivated by a long smoldering hatred or a hunger for another's wealth. We "live along" with these characters and experience some of their emotions as they perform their acts or endure their challenges. In O'Brien's story, we stand at the edge of the playground with Tim and watch the taunting. We feel his moral paralysis. Later, in the classroom, when Linda turns her bare and scarred head to Tim, we live his realization and his shame.

In this story, however, the author doesn't leave us simply reeling with the news of Linda's death and his dishonor. He takes us further. He tells us that a small act has consequences and that later on in Tim's life, his boyhood lapses come back to haunt him. "When Vietnam presented much harder choices, some practice at being brave might've helped a little." While it is unfair to take from this that the author demonstrated similar moral cowardice as a soldier, he evidently yearned for more personal courage.

More than this, however, his rueful wish that he had had "practice" at being brave reveals a fact of the moral life that is often obscured. There is a modern tendency to suggest that moral qualities, like kindness or persistence, are genetic endowments, such as height or intelligence. "Oh, she was born considerate of others." "He's always been that way…thinking of himself first." O'Brien's story reminds us that our virtues and our vices are not constant. One does not possess a virtue as one does his height or her gender. These elements of our characters are always in process.

Our human condition is such that we are always in the state of becoming. Musicians and athletes know that there is no resting on one's laurels. Without practice, skills and habits atrophy. There is an old joke about a man who, seeking directions to New York City's Carnegie Hall, asks a passerby, "How do you get to Carnegie Hall?" and receives the brusque answer, "Practice! Practice! Practice!" A musician wanting to know "How do I stay in Carnegie Hall?" should receive the same answer: "Practice! Practice! Practice!" Courage, like the other virtues, needs exercise. It needs performance. It needs practice.

The story reminds us, too, of the importance of attending to virtues, such as courage, from an early age. It seems to underscore the common wisdom that it is easier to acquire, and conversely to eliminate, a vice in what is aptly called the formative years, from ages three to sixteen or seventeen. While we know of no empirical evidence to this effect, anyone middle-aged or older knows how difficult it is to suppress a vice such as sarcasm and replace it with the virtue of generosity of spirit. Life tests us every day in small and large ways. Some trials are of our own making. Some are not. Some few are avoidable. Most are not. These challenges quickly call on our resources. We need to think about how we will respond to the rude request of a beggar or the news that a friend has betrayed us. We need to come to a judgment about what the right thing to do is. Often we need to struggle with our own emotions of fear or disappointment. And, we must act. At this point, we enter the arena of courage.

Courage is one of those large words, a word that encompasses so much of life and human behavior. Synonyms cascade: bravery, fearlessness, boldness, gallantry, audacity, valor, nerve. Perhaps courage has so many synonyms because it covers so much territory in a lived life. It begins with a child daring to take a step and cross the distance between a chair and its mother's outstretched arms. It ends with our final decision about how—if the opportunity presents itself—we will meet our own death. A potential feature of our daily lives, our courage is continually on call.

The poet Maya Angelou has written, "Without courage, you cannot practice any of the other virtues." Without courage, we cannot act responsibly. Without it, we cannot perform that action which we know is the correct thing to do. Courage is the very engine of the virtuous life. C.S. Lewis (1898–1963), scholar and writer on the spiritual life, captures its essential quality: "Courage is not simply one of the virtues, but the form of every virtue at the testing point."

We tend to associate the virtue of courage with action, often big and important action like Leonidas and his band of three hundred Spartan warriors crushing the ten thousand Persians at Thermopylae (480 B.C.E.). Or Sydney Carton's heroic self-sacrifice in taking the place of Charles Darnay in *A Tale of Two Cities* by Charles Dickens (1812–1870). But no less significant are small actions, such as taking an unpopular stand on an issue about which one has certain convictions; or for the shy, to step into a room full of strangers; or directly facing and dealing with fears such as airplane flight or heights. Dramatic action has a huge place in the virtue of courage, but so, too, does refusal to act, such as civil disobedience in the face of tyranny.

Our lives come at us in a stream of events: some manageable and some not manageable; some pleasant and some quite unpleasant. Many of our life-situations call not for action, but for standing still. They call for us to bravely withstand, to courageously endure. A young mother-to-be learns that the child she is carrying has Down syndrome. A promising dancer sustains a career-ending injury. A worker with no other options is trapped in an oppressive job. A student tries mightily to achieve an academic goal and fails. The list is endless. Eleanor Roosevelt (1884–1962) once said, "You have to accept whatever comes, and the only important thing is that we meet it with courage and with the best that you have to give." The courage of endurance in the face of disappointment has few of the satisfactions of actions, but it is the very stuff of courage.

Beyond these large disappointments and obstructions, there are the everyday calls for courage. The computer gets a virus. The car keys are lost. The much anticipated event turns sour. The favorite shirt is ruined in the wash. Theologian Michael Novak once claimed that modern men and women, adrift in a world of plenty, are the most mortified in human history. Be that as it may, how we meet these daily frustrations is an exercise in courage. Complaint, anger, self-pity, and searching for someone to blame are all retreats from the opportunity of courage.

🍀   🍀   🍀

There is a popular theory about the road to happiness based on the image of two travelers seeking this blessed state. One has his eyes continually on achieving his enshrined goal of happiness but is continually frustrated and upset because there are so many boulders that keep blocking him from his goal. The other traveler is seeking the same goal, happiness, but he expects life's boulders to roll into his path. When one does, he quietly and deliberately moves it out of the way and then attends with equanimity to the next boulder. This theory suggests that happiness is not achieved by laying out and working toward large goals, such as "being the best artist on the face of the earth" or "becoming a famous skater." Rather, we must look at our daily lives as a series of small and large challenges and calmly deal with them one after another. With the courage to confront and deal with our immediate "boulders" comes a calmness and peace.

Said another way, to achieve true happiness, we need to gain command of our lives. Not total control, because this is truly beyond us. *Command* means we are not paralyzed by our burdens and fears. We are neither passively fatalistic nor frantically trying to manage every detail of our lives. Philosopher and psychologist William James (1842–1910) said it best: "Act for the best, hope for the best, and take what comes."

Crippling fear is the great enemy of courage. It comes in many shapes and shades. We fear ridicule. We fear disgracing ourselves by having committed some heinous act. We fear not fitting in, being excluded. We fear not measuring up to the expectations of others, such as parents, spouses, teachers. We fear backing down from bullies or from life's challenges. Some of us are afraid of the dark and of sounds that go bump in the night. Some fear spiders. Others snakes. Some fear being too enclosed. Others fear being too exposed, too out-in-the-open. Many fear human intimacy. Some people are a bundle of fears, while others are cowed by one great fear, like the fear of failure. Tom Wolfe, the novelist, has written that our greatest fear is the loss of status. The list is endless.

Courage contributes to the possibility of happiness in that it is our shield and armor. It enables us to engage and, if not defeat our fears, hold them at bay. It helps us deal with stress, adversity, and the big and small pressures of our lives. The word itself has a military connotation in that this virtue, in particular, enables us to "fight the good fight."

The importance of courage to happiness suggests that its acquisition should be a central focus of our lives. Three ways of developing this virtue suggest themselves: confronting our fears; deepening our understanding; and practice.

Our fears lurk below the surface of our consciousness, like prowling predators. We know they are there, hearing their low snarls that sap our self-confidence and deny us peace. Typically, we find ways to ignore them, hoping that they will move away, only again to hear their growls at the most inopportune moments. On the other hand, bringing our fears to the surface and confronting them may be therapeutic. A phobia of spiders gives way to learning that only a tiny fraction of their species is poisonous, and all are more afraid of us than we of them. We are fearful of bringing up a delicate topic with a friend, only to discover that the issue evaporates when brought to light.

With this in mind we suggest that you stop here and confront your fears. What are three situations, personal failings, or challenges that you avoid? What is their real nature? What is their true cause? What would happen if you met them one by one, head on? What is the worst possible consequence? What good might come of your actions? How would your life be improved if you conquered such fears? This is not to suggest that exploring our fears is a magic elixir. There is much in life legitimately to fear. Aristotle (384–322 B.C.E.) tells us that "the person...who faces and who fears the right thing, from the right motive, in the right way, and who feels confidence under the corresponding conditions, is brave." Nevertheless, we urge you to take this step.

Second, we can grow in courage by expanding our knowledge of this virtue. Our knowledge about different subjects is like a computer database. We mentally call up a file on one particular subject, and the file has a few, disconnected entries. We call up a file on another topic, however, and we may find screen after screen of ideas, images, and reflections. Of all the virtues taken up in this volume, courage is one of the most accessible to our understanding, with lots of entries in our database.

One of the richest sources of our understanding of courage comes from literature, both fictional and biographical. Most of the great events at the center of a work of fiction are struggles between fear and courage. The young heroine in the perennial favorite *To Kill a Mockingbird* by Harper Lee, discovers her reserved father's bravery when he goes outside to confront a rabid dog that is terrorizing the neighborhood. But this is only a foretaste of her father's deep disposition to courage. She later observes how he agrees to defend a poor black farmer wrongly accused of raping a white woman. Military accounts of battles, such as Lieutenant General Harold G. Moore's *We Were Soldiers Then and Young*, are replete with acts of valor that transcend simple battlefield bravery as just so much adrenaline-driven, animalistic reaction to fear. Instead, we see the noble motivations working behind these courageous actions.

The theatre, and now films and television programs, have feasted on courage. Courage and its opposites, cowardice and recklessness, are not only quite common in our lives, but they can be made visual. While it can be challenging to discern wisdom or prudence on the stage or screen, fear and courage jump out at us. The great tragedies and histories of Shakespeare (1564–1616) rely on these emotion-laden themes, as do classic movies. At the heart of the archetypal western, *High Noon*, the hero, portrayed by Gary Cooper, puts aside his own safety and opportunity for happiness to confront a band of desperados planning mayhem for the town. The film's drama is the play of his valor against the craven behavior of the townspeople. In a more recent film, *Gladiator*, a conquering Roman general, played by Russell Crowe, is brought to his knees physically and psychologically, only to regain his courage and again save Rome from destruction. The fact that courage and its opposing vices are such a staple of books, film, and other media reflects not only the fact that these qualities are dramatic and easily represented, but also that they attract and inspire us.

Finally, there is the practicing of courage. It is useful, of course, to review how and where we can act more courageously. There are big situations in our lives calling for courage that require advance thought and planning. But we don't need to wait to practice courage. In the hundreds of small decisions we make each day, there are courageous choices waiting for us to seize them. For example, in our daily struggle between giving in to our selfish desires or reaching out to "the other," there is the call to practice courage.

We can think about areas of our lives where we are reckless or even foolhardy. Why is it risky? Who is in danger? What steps can I take to act with more measure and courage?

We can imagine ourselves fulfilling a daunting but important goal in life. What does it look and feel like? Now, plan backwards. To reach this goal, what steps do I need to take over the course of the next several weeks to make progress?

We can practice being brave for a moment. Choose something of which you are afraid. Speaking before a group? Dancing? Spiders? Take daily steps to confront those fears for brief periods. Gradually increase your exposure until the fear recedes.

In recent years, athletes have employed a technique called *imaging*, in which they develop a mental picture of a perfect golf swing or tennis serve. Before they hit a ball, they review and then attempt to execute the image. This imaging, combined with repeated execution, is the way to mastery. Imagining courage, or visualizing ourselves responding to our challenges with courage, is a way for us to be courageous. But we must act!

CHAPTER 2

Justice

"Justice is truth in action." —*Benjamin Disraeli*

෨ ෨ ෨ ෨

In the following pair of essays, numerous stories are cited to examine justice from the standpoints of both what is and what is not just, fair, or morally right. With the children's story *Crow Boy*, Toshitaka Adachi approaches the topic of justice by examining both injustice and redemption of the unjust. He compares Western and Japanese understandings of justice and uses the story to illustrate important elements of this virtue: respect for the individual, kindness, fairness, equal opportunity, and the opportunity to reflect and forge a new relationship. Drawing from a historic tale of a famous magistrate, as well as a story from the life of Reitaku University founder Chikuro Hiroike, Adachi further elaborates on unique Japanese concepts to illustrate how justice allows all parties involved to win. To move beyond winners and losers, he asserts, one first must "see matters from perspectives other than one's own," followed by respectful dialogue. Within this approach we see the Eastern values of securing harmony among people in order to build a more just and peaceful world.

Sources of injustice may include adverse conditions such as war, illness, or other disastrous events, or may be as intimate as a friend's betrayal, as explained in the following essay by Bernice

Lerner, who also examines this virtue from the perspective of one's response to injustice. She shares the story of her own father, who escaped from Hungarian forced labor during the anti-Semitism of World War II only to face anti-immigrant labor forces in the United States. She then analyzes several contemporary, real-life examples using Plato's theory of the three-part soul to illustrate how one can lead a happy and just life. This essay indicates the importance of learning and practicing good responses to injustice from an early age, which may include moderation, sensitivity to others, cultivating an attitude of appreciation, and nonviolent resistance.

Justice

BY TOSHITAKA ADACHI

On the first day of the elementary school year in a small village somewhere in Japan, a boy was missing from class. He was eventually found hidden away in the dark space beneath the floorboards of a classroom. Nobody knew who he was, but because he was very small, he was nicknamed Chibi (Tiny Boy).

Chibi's life at school was full of difficulties for the first five years. He was afraid of his teachers and could not make a single friend. He was left completely on his own during lessons and at play time. However, he quickly found many ways to enjoy himself. In class, sometimes he gazed up at the ceiling, while at other times, the top of his wooden desk was so interesting that he could study it for hours. In the playground, if he closed his eyes and listened carefully, Chibi could hear many sounds, near and far, and this was fun too. He would also watch and handle insects that most of his classmates would not touch or even look at. Because of his behavior, not only his classmates but also older and even younger pupils called him stupid and slowpoke. Despite all this, however, Chibi trudged to school every single day, come rain or storm.

Then in sixth grade, the final year of elementary school in Japan, Chibi's life was changed by his new teacher, Mr. Isobe. A very friendly man with a nice smile, Mr. Isobe was new to the school. He often took his pupils to play on the hilltop behind the school. There he was happy to find that Chibi knew all the places where wild fruit and vegetables grew, and he was also surprised to learn how much Chibi knew about all the flowers in the class garden. He liked Chibi's drawings and pinned them on the wall for others to admire. Chibi's calligraphy, which nobody but the boy himself could read, was tacked up on the wall too.

The most impressive of Chibi's hidden talents that Mr. Isobe discovered was put on public display at the annual school talent show. When Chibi first walked on stage, none of the children could understand why he was there, and they whispered to each other, "What can that stupid boy possibly do?"

Mr. Isobe announced that Chibi was going to mimic the cries of the crow. Chibi then gave perfect imitations of the sounds made by newly hatched crows, as well as by their male and female parents. He went on to demonstrate the cries they make early in the morning, when some sad accident happens to the village people, and the sounds they make when they are happy and playful. Listening to the boy's crow impressions, everybody's mind flew to the far mountain side where Chibi had his home. At the end of his show, Chibi made some special, deep sounds in his throat so that everybody could envision the far and lonely place where he lived with his family.

After this performance, Mr. Isobe explained how Chibi had learned those cries and calls: leaving his home for school at dawn and arriving home at sunset, he had heard them every day for six years. All the children in the audience began to cry, thinking of their unkindness to Chibi over the years and of how they had misjudged him.

At the graduation ceremony soon after the talent show, Chibi was the only one of his class to win an award for perfect attendance over the entire six years of his school life. After he left elementary school, nobody called him Chibi anymore. Everybody honored him as Crow Boy.

This story by the Japanese painter Taro Yashima (1908–1994) is based on his own life as a child in Japan before he went into exile in the United States and was published as *Crow Boy* here in 1955.

It won the Caldecott Medal, one of the most prestigious U.S. awards for picture books. About twenty years later, it appeared under the title *Karasutaro* in Japan, where it also won a special award for picture books.

Although the book was highly esteemed in both the United States and Japan, readers responded in rather different ways to the English and Japanese versions. A study was carried out in which bilingual children were asked to read both of them and then write their impressions of each. Many of the children responded positively to the English version; they wrote that it showed how hard Chibi worked to gain the trust of those around him, that it had a happy ending and was a story of how someone achieved success. The Japanese version, by contrast, left many of the children with a negative impression. They wrote that the essence of the story was the confession of guilt by Chibi's fellow students, that his experiences were of sorrow and loneliness, and that the tale emphasized the coldness with which human beings treat each other.

These differences are also apparent in the reactions of monolingual readers in the two countries. Many Americans praised Chibi's good character, his capacity for endurance, his generosity, and his kindness. Many Japanese, on the other hand, focused on the cruelty with which the other children treated Chibi, their nastiness or indifference towards him. These different perspectives are very interesting, but it is still possible to argue that both versions of the tale have a single message, one whose focus is justice, our subject here.

The Meaning of Justice

Before exploring what Chibi's story has to tell us about justice, we first need to define the word. Justice derives from the Latin word *jus*, meaning law, right, or judge. So in the United States, for example, the Justice Department is the federal office responsible for the administration and enforcement of the law. Modern people, therefore, regard justice as pertaining to the concept of law and law-related matters.

There are many legal institutions in the West that have chosen the figure of the Goddess of Justice, or Justitia, as their symbol, and the same is true in the East as, for example, with Japan's Supreme Court. The Goddess is depicted holding a set of scales in her left hand and a sword in her right. The scales imply that when judging any matter, she will take care to be fair and impartial, favoring neither side. Her sword symbolizes that she will use reason, not emotion, as her guide. She is also usually blindfolded, to show that she cannot be swayed by the status, power, reputation, and so on, of any of the parties to a dispute. In sum, she represents the ability to render an objective judgment. So the concept of justice is closely related to the law, and anyone connected with justice should be entirely objective in his or her deliberations.

The Japanese word for justice, however, has long been used not only in connection with jurisprudence but also with daily life. *Kojien*, a prestigious Japanese dictionary, offers four definitions: "right reasoning or logic, or the right way to secure a good life"; "the right meaning or interpretation of something"; "to realize and maintain order to secure the well-being of the whole of society"; and "individual virtue leading one to take the right action, for example, in distributing social goods." The dictionary says that the former two meanings appeared first in oriental classics, including the *Hsun-tzu* (an anthology of the words of the Chinese philosopher of the same name, ca. 312–230 B.C.E.) and other ancient Chinese books. They both relate to doing what is right and are therefore closely linked with morality or ethics. The other definitions are clearly Western in origin. They explain that justice is a state of the world in which the whole of society is happy and that the virtue of justice guides people to make this a reality. Like the first two, they also include a moral quality. The first two definitions of justice in *Kojien* do not define the *nature* of what is right. The third and fourth do, however, both from a Platonic perspective, where it is an act of duty done by an individual for the nation, and from an Aristotelian viewpoint, where it is the fair distribution of something on the basis of individual ability or capacity. Thus in Japan, justice has a variety of meanings, including fair and equal distribution, equality of opportunity, and increasing the good of the whole, among others.

Let us now look at *Crow Boy* from the perspective of justice and think especially about fairness. First, what can we say about how Chibi was treated by his classmates and the other children in the school?

Sadly, they were neither just nor fair to him. For example, they never bothered to find out his real name but used a nickname instead. Nicknames mostly fall into two groups, affectionate or insulting. *Chibi* was clearly the latter, a derogatory reference to his physical stature. Furthermore, he was sometimes called stupid or slowpoke when studying insects that other children ignored. Children sometimes tease someone who does strange things, and they tend to exclude those who act differently from the norm. Chibi was labeled as strange from the moment he was found hidden away under the floorboards. He had no friends and spent his time in school completely alone. There was no fairness in any of this.

How did the schoolteachers, who most probably knew of his problems, handle the situation? We cannot be entirely sure, since no teachers are mentioned in the story except for Mr. Isobe. However, as Chibi's unfair treatment continued for fully five years, we can surmise either that none of the teachers tried to remedy the situation, or that any attempts they did make were halfhearted and had very little effect.

The unfair treatment of Chibi changed dramatically as soon as Mr. Isobe appeared on the scene. He was quick to recognize Chibi's hidden talents, including his extraordinary knowledge of wildlife and his artistic gifts. He displayed Chibi's writing and drawings in the classroom to try to reveal these to the boy's classmates.

Before arriving at the school, it's likely that Mr. Isobe had been given some information about Chibi by the other teachers. As a result, he could have had a negative preconception of him as a problem child, which might have engendered a bias against the boy. This did not happen, however. Instead, Mr. Isobe observed him with an unprejudiced eye and so was able to discover Chibi's special abilities. He then tried to awaken others in the school to these. Mr. Isobe's approach as an educator reveals that he possessed the virtues of respecting children as individuals, caring for them without exception, and treating them all fairly.

Mr. Isobe's concern for Chibi, based as it was on justice, resulted in his encouraging the boy to enter the school talent show. When the audience, which included both the school children and their families, learned he was about to appear on stage, their reactions were uniformly disparaging. After his performance, though, they were all so moved that they came to recognize the boy whom they had previously treated with scorn as a valued member of the school and the local community.

Mr. Isobe probably saw the show as a very suitable, and probably the last, opportunity for the other school children to get to know the real Chibi and so remove the distorted labels that they had pinned on him. It was no easy matter to change the negative image of Chibi that his classmates had long held. But it was exactly these prejudices that had always deprived the other children of the chance to evaluate Chibi fairly, that never allowed him the same opportunities to shine that others had. Mr. Isobe believed that the talent show was a unique chance to set this matter right and to put the boy, for the first time, on an equal footing with all the other children.

After Chibi's performance, Mr. Isobe explained how the boy had obtained such a mastery of the many different sounds that crows make. At the time when the story was set, there were very few schools in remote rural locations and no public transportation there at all. As a result, children living far from the nearest school had no choice but to walk there and back. In Chibi's case, this meant leaving home at dawn and returning at sunset. Hard though this routine was, it did at least give him the chance to observe crows at different times of the day and in a great variety of situations, and this was the foundation for his remarkable performance in the show.

But it also reflected his complete loneliness. Although he went to school every day for six years, Chibi had no friends and was always alone. Only after the performance could the other children begin to imagine how they would feel if they had had to put up with such a situation for six whole years. This was how they were able to see that their treatment of Chibi had been so unjust. Given the chance to reflect deeply on their own behavior, they began sincerely to lament all they had done.

Mr. Isobe's explanation after the performance of how Chibi had acquired his skills had two aims. The first was to set Chibi's life at school in its correct context. Revealing the full truth about it gave others the information they needed to adjust their perspective. His second aim was to inspire the school children to reflect on themselves and their mistakes and thereby improve both their own behavior as individuals and the quality of their relationships with each other.

♣   ♣   ♣

This, then, is how we can relate Chibi's story to our theme of justice. Mr. Isobe's treatment of Chibi and his efforts to improve his life can certainly be described as just. They reveal him as a role model as well as exemplify the fairness with which teachers should treat students. We can also learn from his actions about some of the most important virtues we need to possess as human beings.

In terms of justice, these lessons can be summarized as follows. The first is to respect every individual as a human being, to approach everyone without bias and treat each with kindness. Following this rule will allow us to treat others fairly.

The second is to give everyone an equal opportunity. Denying someone the proper chance for self-realization shows a lack of respect for that person. Before Mr. Isobe arrived on the scene, Chibi's other teachers had probably not given him and his classmates such an opportunity. Providing that chance or removing the obstacles to self-realization, by contrast, allows others to evaluate the person properly as well, which is the hallmark of fairness.

The third lesson is that new relationships are made possible when people are given the chance of a fair view of one another, since this opens up different perspectives for them. In *Crow Boy*, for example, Mr. Isobe allowed the school community to get to know Chibi as he really was through his appearance at the talent show. After the teacher had explained Chibi's background, the school children deeply regretted what they had done to him, gave up their biased and scornful attitude, and began a new relationship with him.

The fourth lesson taught by the story, and one that is a precondition for the three already mentioned, is the vital need for an attitude of benevolence (see Chapter 3), or love towards people. Mr. Isobe surely wanted Chibi and all the other children to enjoy a fulfilling life at school. The virtue of benevolence explains why he behaved with justice, and it demonstrates how the concept of justice extends beyond judicial concerns to moral ones and how it connects the two. The Goddess of Justice wields the sword of reason when coming to a judgment, but this implies that an affectionate concern for people is excluded from the process. However, benevolence or love can play a very important role in giving a moral dimension to a just judgment. In *Crow Boy*, Mr. Isobe revealed his affectionate concern for both Chibi and the other school children, and his desire for justice was rooted in benevolence or love. We will explore this aspect of justice more fully in the next section.

♣   ♣   ♣

To help us grasp the real essence of justice, let us look at a story, well known in Japan, about a judgment made by a famous magistrate, Tadasuke Ooka (1677–1751). This story is a very clear illustration of the Japanese philosophy of *sanpo-ichiryou-zon* (sharing losses equally among three parties).

During the Edo period (1603–1868), there once was a maker of tatami mats named Sarobee, who lived in the old Reiganjima district of Tokyo. One December he found himself in need of some money for the preparations he had to make to welcome in the New Year. So he borrowed three *ryo* (an old Japanese unit of money) from a pawnshop. On his way home, however, he lost the coins.

They were later found by Chojyuro, a carpenter who lived in Kotenmacho, a different quarter of the old city. He figured out to whom they belonged because they were in a pouch that contained a memo with Sarobee's name at the top. Chojyuro took a leave from work and spent four days looking for the owner of the pouch. At last he found where Sarobee lived. When he tried to return the money, however, he was very surprised when Sarobee absolutely refused to receive it, claiming that it had ceased to belong to him once it had been lost. So, he said, the money now rightly belonged to Chojyuro. Chojyuro, in turn, refused to accept that it was his, at least in part because he had spent four days searching for the owner! A quarrel broke out between them and quickly escalated. Sarobee's landlord tried to arbitrate between them, but his efforts were completely in vain.

Sarobee and Chojyuro took their problem to the magistrate's office. There, Judge Ooka listened to both sides, and he was greatly impressed with the two men's honesty. After confirming that Sarobee indeed had no claim to the money after losing it, Ooka said, "The three *ryo* will be deposited immediately with the shogunal government, which will then return the money to you. Each of you will receive two *ryo*. That is my judgment in the matter." Sarobee and Chojyuro wondered how they could possibly get two *ryo* each, since that obviously made the total four *ryo*. They asked Ooka where the additional *ryo* came from. He answered as follows:

> I am happy to give one *ryo* myself on account of your honesty, to add to the three that were lost and found. So now, Chojyuro,

who found three *ryo*, will get two; Sarobee, who lost three, will get back two, and I will give one. In sum, all of us will lose one *ryo* each. This is called *sanpo-ichiryou-zon* (sharing losses equally between three parties).

The two men agreed to accept his decision. In terms of the true meaning of justice, this story has the following significant features. The first is that Ooka, acting as arbitrator, could not help but be impressed by the honesty or sincerity of both Sarobee and Chojyuro. His judgment was therefore influenced by his attitude towards those who had brought the matter to him. The second is that both Sarobee and Chojyuro were more than satisfied with his judgment; they took it deeply to heart, and it changed their relationship.

The behavior of Judge Ooka has some similarities with that of Mr. Isobe from the standpoint of justice, even though their occupations were different. Essentially, they each conceived of their responsibility as not just requiring them to make a judgment of right or wrong for the parties involved, but to make it in such a way that these parties could enjoy a better relationship and live more rewarding lives. In other words, they thought of justice not as something that produced winners or losers, but as that which allowed both parties to win. To achieve this, of course, requires the qualities of deep insight into, and warm feelings towards the people involved. Only such tenderness can produce behavior such as Mr. Ooka's taking one *ryo* from his own pocket and Mr. Isobe's spending so much time with Chibi and the other children to enable them to refashion their relationship.

Tadasuke Ooka's judgment, in which both parties and the judge himself all lost one *ryo*, exemplifies what has been termed "sharing losses equally among three parties." But though each of the three people suffered a monetary loss, they all gained some measure of satisfaction from the case. The two petitioners admired and accepted the wisdom of Ooka's judgment, and Ooka himself was happy to be able to offer his own money to create harmony between them. Therefore the judgment pleased all three parties.

This type of justice is termed *sanpo-yoshi* or *sanpo-zen* (the good of all three parties). Recently it has come to be adopted as the management philosophy of merchants in the Omi, Shiga, region of Japan, whose aim is to do business in ways that benefit the seller, the buyer, and society. Its influence can also be seen in the following episode in the life of Chikuro Hiroike, the founder of Reitaku University, which reflects what has been recognized as a moral norm in Japan.

In 1929, Dr. Hiroike and two of his followers were taking a train to Mitajiri, in Yamaguchi Prefecture, where he was to give a lecture. However, a tunnel collapse caused a serious delay, and since their schedule was tight, they could not afford to wait for the line to be cleared. One of Hiroike's followers arranged for a taxi driver at the nearest station to take the three of them to their destination for a fare of twenty yen.

Just as they were about to leave, an office worker and a student came up to ask if they could share the taxi. Both, for special reasons, were in a great hurry. Unfortunately, there was no other taxi at the station. Out of pity, one of Hiroike's followers agreed to their request. Just as they were all about to get into the taxi, Hiroike asked them to wait a moment and made the following suggestion:

> The three of us agreed to pay the driver twenty yen for our fare to Mitajiri. If you both share our taxi now, though, it will consume extra gasoline, the tires may wear out much faster, and each of us will have less space. So I propose that we three each pay five yen, and I will ask both of you to do the same.

Hiroike then said to the driver,

> As there are now five of us, I think you will need more gasoline for the journey, and the tires might wear out faster. So we will

pay you twenty-five yen, five yen more than our previous agreement. Is that all right with you?

The two people who had asked to share the taxi agreed to this suggestion with great pleasure, and the driver was happy as well. Everyone involved benefitted from the new arrangement. The office worker and the student were able to take the taxi they needed. The driver received five yen more than initially agreed upon. Hiroike's group was to pay five yen less than before. All three parties, the two additional passengers, the driver, and Hiroike's group, were happier as a result.

The main point of this story is not about saving money for particular individuals but about behaving in a way that results in good for everyone involved. In the arrangements for the sharing of the taxi, Hiroike made his suggestion taking into account the situation and interests of a direct party (the office worker and the student), an indirect party (the taxi driver), and his own group. This concern to look at a situation in its entirety and to consider the interests of everyone involved can be held up as a model of true justice. By attending to the good of all the parties, the resolution achieved might be seen as what Plato calls "a completely balanced situation."

The Contribution of Justice to Human Happiness

As we see, justice as a virtue varies in content and operates in different ways and on different levels. Some people might object that the type of justice which mandates doing something good for all parties involved is too idealistic, and they might be skeptical about how it could apply to everyday life. They could perhaps accept the incident of the taxi just described as a rare case where a type of ideal behavior based on the virtue of justice can work in reality; but they might argue that the concept of justice where one party wins and the other loses is the norm, which of course will not satisfy all parties, enhance their mutual understanding, nor improve their lives.

Nonetheless, mutual understanding and general satisfaction are crucial in our daily human relationships and in those between countries in the contemporary world. A failure to secure mutual understanding can only produce more serious conflicts, which is why it is dangerous to insist only on our own claims to justice. Such an approach will put the creation of a peaceful world out of reach forever. This is evident in current worldwide problems like terrorism and global warming.

☘   ☘   ☘

How can we move beyond the concept of justice as a matter of winners and losers? The first important step is to try to see matters from perspectives other than our own. We need to ask ourselves repeatedly how we would feel and what we would do in somebody else's position. By training ourselves to look at a situation in which we are involved from a variety of different perspectives, we can raise our awareness of what we need to do to treat others in a spirit of fairness. If we look at ourselves and our situation objectively, we can gain perspectives that have been hidden from us until now. This approach also allows us to survey the whole situation from higher ground and understand it more completely.

The second important step is to engage in dialogue with the other parties on as broad a basis as possible. Through dialogue, we will get the chance to reflect on our conduct, rid ourselves of bias, and test whether our understanding of others is correct. A proper dialogue demands that we have and show respect for others. Without this, we will never reach a successful resolution in any dispute.

By proceeding in this way, we may find that we can cultivate an attitude of real and deep concern for others within our hearts. That will then open up the road that leads to the concept of justice "bringing good to both parties" and "considering the good of three parties." The virtue of justice, understood in this way, can then make its vital contribution to the well-being of humankind.

Justice

BY BERNICE LERNER

At the time of this writing, I am mourning the recent loss of my father, a simple man who endured extreme circumstances. What do I mean by "a simple man"? In Hebrew, the word for simple is *tam*. *Tam* is related to the biblical word *tamim*, which means whole, intact. My father was whole, a person of integrity; a person for whom life was not easy, but for whom it was uncomplicated. He had only to figure out the right thing to do and do it. His moral compass would guide him in all situations. He was the same person in public as he was in the privacy of his home.

My father delighted in simple things. At the last, he loved the soft, warm comforter covering his frail body. When he was a boy, he loved sleeping on fresh-smelling hay—the family barn in summer was one of his favorite sensory memories. Unfortunately, not all of his memories were happy ones.

My father, Sidney Mermelstein, was the fifth of nine children born to Elias Mermelstein and Rachel *nee* Froimovitz. His identity was shaped by his tight-knit family and the community in which he was reared. His teachers would ask him why he was not smart like his brother Hershu, about two years his senior. But his interests lay not in school. He was, rather, intensely interested in the occupation of his father and his eldest brother, Jack: cattle dealing. He loved to guess what they paid for calves they brought home. By age ten, he was determined to be part of the action. Skipping school, he trailed stealthily behind his father and Jack until they reached a distant village. When he appeared before them, his soft father did not send him home.

My father excelled at business—and at saving. From his earliest years, hard-earned money was never squandered. By the same token, my father was a generous soul. People who knew him as a kid told me his happiness was to buy and give candy out to other kids.

My father was seventeen when Hungary annexed the part of Czechoslovakia (the Carpathian Mountain region) in which he lived. It was 1938. Anti-Semitism escalated. In the coming years, his three older brothers were conscripted into Hungarian forced labor, a system heavily influenced by Nazi racial policies. In the fall of 1942, my father, too, was inducted into slave labor. Marching from place to place, his battalion would build bunkers and perform other hard labor on behalf of Hungarian soldiers. Given little to eat, the men scavenged what they could. Once, when they happened upon a farm, my father carefully watched a hen to see when it would lay its egg. At the moment the egg appeared, he quickly drank its contents and disposed of the shell in a nearby river. Another time, he encountered woodsmen having their lunch. He traded his last possession—a wallet—for one of their bowls of soup. When his battalion was assigned to work in a forest, my father reveled in eating berries. Catching him in the act, an overseer cracked a stick down on his head—it took weeks for the resulting welt to subside.

Once, my father demonstrated for me a punishment that was meted out to many of his comrades—they were forced to kneel with a stick behind their knees. He described what happened to a man who had to step out of line to relieve himself—a bullet to his head caused his brain to spill out on the ground. When my father questioned the existence of God, when he spent the night lying in mud, he wished not to awaken the next day.

By October of 1944, many of the original two hundred in my father's battalion were gone. So were other boys who had joined them. (My father knew by newcomers' shiny shoes—a sign of a privileged life—that they would not survive.) Soon, the prospect of certain death hung over all. But the group shrank not only on account of wanton killing; every once in a while, one or two boys managed to escape. One fateful day, while the battalion parked by a road, it started to rain. My father crawled under a wagon for shelter. Exhausted, he fell asleep. When he roused, he realized he was alone; the group had moved on. Here was his chance. Emaciated, with rags on his feet and shovel in hand, he made his way through familiar territory. Three days later he was in his hometown of Chinyadevo, the first Jew to return. Five months earlier his parents, sisters, and younger brother had been taken to Auschwitz.

The war was still raging, and my father had to use his wiles to evade capture by the Russians. He learned that his brother Hershu was alive, then that his brothers Jack and Irving had survived, and months later, after the war's end, that his sisters, Helen and Esther, had miraculously made it through hell. He regained his strength and ability to feel. While most eligible survivors were pairing off, he chose to wait. He spent more than two years at a displaced persons camp in Germany, where he worked with and among many local Germans. Though there were opportunities to torment those who supported Hitler, my father chose not to exact revenge. It was not in his nature to harm any human being.

My father arrived in the United States in 1948 and within one year opened his own butcher shop. It was not long before a representative from the butchers union came around and invited him to join the organization. Knowing nothing about unions, he decided to attend a meeting. There he heard American butchers complain bitterly about the "greenhorns" (refugees) who were taking away their business. On the meeting agenda: What to do about this "problem."

It had never occurred to my father to bring to justice brutal Hungarian overseers or Nazis who murdered members of his family. Such individuals, cogs in an overwhelming system of evil, seemed an abstraction. But here, in a free country, at an open meeting, his blood boiled. My father stood and gave his first and only public speech, educating those present on the circumstances in Europe from whence the "greenhorn" butchers had come.

Primo Levi (1919–1987), Viktor Frankl (1905–1997), and other Holocaust survivors have written of the post-war pain of encountering callous others, individuals who not only did not care to hear about what occurred during the war but who were preoccupied with their own suffering or grievances. The insensitivity that gave rise to a warped sense of victimization on the part of some of the union's butchers pained my father and triggered his outburst. He surely did not stop to analyze their sentiments or his reaction. He simply could not contain himself in the face of justice violated.

That members of the butchers union hoped to prosper was understandable. Let us now consider why their agenda item, i.e., to stop competition from "greenhorn" butchers—men who had to learn a new language and new mores, who struggled to forge new lives after having endured devastating loss—exemplified injustice. Let us turn to Plato's *three-part soul*, a construct that enables us to discern whether certain habits of heart and mind, and actions stemming from these dispositions, are ethical and just.

Plato's theory says that our soul is comprised of three parts: *reason*, *spirit*, and *appetite*. When reason, i.e., practical wisdom, captains the team of three parts, the virtue of justice is displayed. The souls of those members of the butchers union who wished to undermine "problem greenhorns" were not properly ordered. Their *spirit* and/or *appetites* overshadowed their *reason*. They cared more about satisfying their personal ambitions and monetary needs than fair practice.

There are many ways in which we humans blindly pursue goals and miss the larger picture. Are we so intent on advancing in our career, in gaining recognition, that we neglect those dear to us? Do we spend hours surfing the Internet or watching television and thus fail to attend to our responsibilities? Do we indulge in second helpings of rich desserts when we know we will later feel unwell? Our spirit and our appetite are both vital, but when they are not properly moderated, we risk hurting ourselves and/or others. We need only pick up the newspaper (or read a book or view a film) to test the validity of Plato's theory.

Take the story of Mr. C, a brilliant, self-made businessman who owns dozens of upscale hotels around the world. One of his close friends observed that he is not entirely satisfied with his station in life—he wants to be wealthier still. Despite having more money than he could ever spend, Mr. C continually sets new, harder-to-reach goals. Though he is generous as a philanthropist, a lack of harmony in Mr. C's soul is evident in the way he treats certain others. Given to yelling, he tends, his workers say, toward unreasonable toughness. To work with him, explained one of his chief executives, one must don armor. Disposed to quarrels, legal battles, and animosity, he has alienated many. Moreover, ever looking to expand his empire, Mr. C is too busy to enjoy other aspects of life. Is Mr. C's *spirit*, or ambition, running amok within his soul, causing him to lash out at at least some who do not deserve such treatment, and likely causing injustice, in some respects, to himself?

Now let us take the example of Ms. D, an entrepreneur whose design of greeting cards, children's books, and music CDs for children have earned her accolades, awards, and monetary success. Though she has long been fascinated by business and appreciates having "a sense of self-sufficiency," Ms. D believes that people consistently overvalue material goods. She values, foremost, her artistic autonomy and her relationships. Ms. D works in a studio near the comfortable (far from lavish) farmhouse where she and her husband raised three children. She works long days because she loves what she does and the songwriter partner with whom she collaborates. She cares deeply about the quality of her creations and says that she does not need more money than she has. Though she attributes her stance to common sense and "not revolutionary philosophy," her views accord with those of Plato; she seems to embody a harmonized three-part soul.

We can judge as well-ordered and moderate individuals whose choices benefit themselves and others. And we can assume that a part of the soul (most often the spirit or appetite) is driven to excess in those who cause undue harm or distress to themselves and others. When a person's reason, spirit, and appetite are well integrated, he or she is able to lead a moral, just, and happy life. Given human frailties, there are, of course, internal obstacles to this state. There are also external challenges that threaten to upend our potential for happiness. Nowhere is this more evident than in the case of injustice done to us.

We may have little or no control over the laws to which we are subjected, which may be just (if they accord with natural law, and are fair) or unjust (wherein losses and gains are not in proportion to what people deserve). Beyond man-made laws there are adversities, conditions, and circumstances that can thwart happiness and that are features of the human condition. There is the ineffable injustice of being caught at the wrong place and time in history, such as a war or a natural disaster. There is the injustice of isolated terrible events, such as having to deal with a debilitating illness or the loss of a loved one. For those who are relatively blessed, there are less earth-shattering injustices, such as being covertly discriminated against, defrauded, or downsized out of a job; having to deal with unreasonable demands on one's time and energies; or having costs associated with accidents that one did not cause. There is no limit to the docket of injustices that could be brought before cosmic small claims courts. And few among us escape some such instance in any decade of our lives.

A friend, Ms. G, faces no small injustice in her role as wife and caregiver of a man who has fallen prey to the ravaging physical disabilities of primary progressive multiple sclerosis. That this disease of "seemingly intractable evils" has befallen her sweet, ethical, and humane husband might have enraged or embittered the active career woman and mother of two. And yet, she explains, "I have been blessed with the insight to perceive that this enemy's invasion of our lives has served only to render our marriage stronger, our love for each other deeper, our days together more precious." Ms. G's perspective has been shaped, too, by the loss of two close friends to cancer. She and her husband hold fast to an attitude of gratitude, defying the hold of an injustice that could easily possess them.

❧   ❧   ❧

Most of us learn early about injustice. An insensitive teacher dismisses a question; a friend betrays a confidence; a beloved pet—or worse, family member—dies. To the extent that young people gain practice at choosing well from a range of responses to such situations, they attain measures of a moral stance. Parents and teachers can fortify young people by putting before them historical or literary exemplars that inspire just thought and action, even—or especially—in the face of injustice.

It is important here to note that extreme cases can illuminate ordinary affairs. American author and naturalist Henry David Thoreau (1817–1862) wrote about non-violent resistance as a response to aggression during the Mexican-American War (1846–1848). The "Father of India," political and spiritual leader Mohandas Karamchand Gandhi (1869–1948) pioneered satyagraha, a philosophy of resistance to evil in his times (i.e., British colonial rule) through active, non-violent resistance. Having studied the experiences—and internalized the words—of those who came before him (including Thoreau and Gandhi), Martin Luther King, Jr. (1929–1968), a Baptist minister and American civil rights leader, wrote a letter to his fellow clergy while jailed in Birmingham, Alabama. Knowing that he was imprisoned for unjust reasons, for leading a peaceful demonstration for the rights of blacks, he explained:

> There are two types of laws: just and unjust …. One has not only a legal but a moral responsibility to obey just laws. Conversely, one has a moral responsibility to disobey unjust laws. A just law is a man-made code that squares with the moral law or the law of God. An unjust law is a code that is out of harmony

with the moral law. Any law that uplifts human personality is just. Any law that degrades human personality is unjust.

King, who famously observed, "The arc of the moral universe is long, but it bends toward justice," is among those who point the way to thoughtful, moral action in the face of injustice.

Though most of us are unlikely to hold such powerful positions, we are all capable of recognizing and respecting the dignity, rights, and needs of others, of tempering our selfish instincts and engaging in action that constructively addresses problems. Beginning at home, and branching out to our communities, we can do our part to bend the arc toward justice. We can help a neighbor who is unable to obtain groceries, speak up when we witness wrongdoings, and cooperate with colleagues in striving toward shared goals.

Justice promotes human welfare and liberates us from the tendency to dwell on our own hardships or pleasures, for we are challenged not only in the face of adversity, but also to the extent our world is rife with temptations. In the story of "Gyges's Ring," Plato relays how a shepherd who finds a magical ring uses its power to turn himself invisible. Because there are then no consequences to his behavior, he commits a series of egregious acts. The question at hand is: What do we do when no one is looking? Are we mindful of how we treat others? We need not plunder or sleep with the king's wife (as does Gyges), but few among us are not on occasion ruled by our desires, thus causing to ourselves and/or others undue harm. And this is why we may, on occasion, hope or pray for mercy, a light sentence—and not justice—from those by whom we are judged. To flourish in this life is to make such supplication as unnecessary as possible, to aim, in all of our activities, toward virtue. How can we attain a disposition toward justice, which is, truly, within everyone's reach?

Let us momentarily examine instances in which we ourselves are prey to injustice. How ought we to respond? With all parts of our soul ordered, we may opt to display outrage or acceptance. We may count blessings or reframe the difficulty at hand. We may choose to redouble our efforts toward some achievable goal. A combination of responses may also be called for. How do we choose wisely from the range of options and their infinite permutations? By paying attention to what we feel and striving to display these feelings in the most excellent way. How can we locate this way? By realizing that it exists somewhere between two extremes: one of defect and one of excess. A person of fine character will neither under-react nor overreact but will respond with decency to particular circumstances. He will know how he is temperamentally inclined to respond and, in trying to get it right, consciously lean toward the opposite tendency. He might ask what the most judicious person he knows would do in the same situation. And he will aim toward producing the least pernicious outcome.

When there is no time to reflect, we will respond to injustice in our usual way. This is why it is crucial for young people to develop good habits of heart and mind, i.e., to practice dealing constructively with the unfairness to which they are subjected. This may mean striving toward positive goals, directing attention to the disadvantaged or the needy, speaking out against discriminatory practices, or lobbying for a noble cause. Given their natural tendencies, given the situations in which they find themselves, young people will thus be equipped to deal with what life may bring.

Honing one's empathy for others is crucial to developing a sense of justice. Atticus Finch, in *To Kill a Mockingbird* by Harper Lee, stressed to his daughter Scout the importance of "walking in the moccasins of another." Norman Rockwell (1894–1978), in his iconic painting "The Problem We All Live With," depicted American racism. We see in his provocative work Ruby Bridges, a little girl in a white dress, a lone black student being escorted by government officials to the segregated New Orleans William Frantz School. Rockwell evokes in viewers feelings for the graceful and dignified figure wearing a "mantle of change."

From empathy springs what is natural and good—the desire to assist, to understand, to ease another's way, not out of obligation, not for a college application essay or one's resume, but rather out of knowing, loving, and wanting to do the right thing.

Those members of the butchers union who raised the "problem" of "greenhorn" butchers had somehow lost their way. Like Gyges, they were ready to harm others to benefit themselves—when they thought no one to whom it would be of consequence was listening. Alas, my father was in the room. He grasped the meaning of their words. In unveiling their prejudice, he bent the arc of the moral universe a bit more toward justice.

Where, in the spheres in which you travel, would you like to see greater justice? Identify several local issues that need to be addressed, and choose two or three things you can do to help in particular situations. These need not be monumental acts. Cooking a meal for an overwhelmed family or collecting money for a worthy charity are acts of justice. Creating and sustaining a positive ethos in your place of work is an act of justice.

Where, in the world, would you like to see greater justice? Read the newspaper. Identify a place where human beings are suffering undue harm. Research the problem as thoroughly as you are able. Join an organization that takes responsible action regarding the issue; write a letter to the editor or to your legislator or other leaders who ought to know that people care; raise awareness of the problem among your colleagues and friends.

How can you be sure that you are making progress toward internalizing justice? Self-examination. Reflect, upon realizing any harm you have (however inadvertently) caused, on what you might do to make amends. Is an apology in order? How can you rebuild a burnt bridge or construct a new one? Reflect, too, on the state of your soul, upon whether your choices of action were based on reason or blind ambition or unmediated appetite.

CHAPTER 3

Benevolence

"Kindness is not just for the sake of others." —*Japanese*

∽ ∽ ∽

Benevolence encompasses kindness and generosity, a compassionate heart that feels the empathy of the suffering and strives for others' happiness. As Nobumichi Iwasa points out in the first essay below, kind or generous actions alone do not a benevolent person make, but it is the sustained spirit behind such actions, one's disposition or state of mind, that matter. He further stresses the value of studying great moral figures in history—Jesus, Confucius, and Buddha—whose profound love for humanity and all living things are examples to emulate. While other virtues, such as courage or responsibility, manifest under certain circumstances, he continues, benevolence can manifest in a broad range of situations. It lies "at the very center of the mental functioning of an individual's personality." He explores this centrality of benevolence to character here, evoking Eastern perspectives of appreciation, respect, and recognition of the mutual dependence of people on each other and on the greater world around them. The sphere of benevolence from the Japanese perspective encompasses not just humanity but all that exists, "animate and inanimate, in the universe" and across time from past through the future, recognizing a global network of interdependence. Thus the benevolent attitude expresses itself not just in good actions but also in improved relationships between people and between humanity and the natural world. From such a recognition arises a sense of duty to "strive wholeheartedly to make our selfless contribution to the network."

The next essay recalls a story from World War II when two pastors in France urged their parishioners to protect Jews from the impending Nazi scourge and illustrates the selfless efforts of many nameless individuals to support and hide strangers at great personal risk. Bernice Lerner recalls the biblical story of the Good Samaritan to elaborate on the Western concept of loving one's neighbor as oneself. The history she relates illustrates not simply kindness to strangers, but as with the virtue of justice, also encompasses wise, nonviolent resistance to evil. Empathy arises out of one's own experiences of suffering. Here Lerner connects East with West, citing Buddhist expressions of empathy and compassion, the experience of which leads to more genuinely ethical conduct. She, too, interprets benevolence as incorporating appreciation as well as empathy and compassion, and as leading to improved relations between people.

Benevolence

BY NOBUMICHI IWASA

On March 11, 2011, Japan was hit by the greatest disaster since World War II. Five days after the calamity, Emperor Akihito talked directly to his people. His message of March 16, 2011, gave courage and the spiritual power to continue with their lives to many people in the country:

> I am deeply saddened by the devastating situation in the areas hit by the Tohoku-Pacific Ocean Earthquake, an unprecedented 9.0-magnitude earthquake, which struck Japan on March 11. The number of casualties claimed by the quake and the ensuing tsunami continues to rise by the day, and we do not yet know how many people have lost their lives. I am praying that the safety of as many people as possible will be confirmed.
>
> My other grave concern now is the serious and unpredictable condition of the affected nuclear power plant. I earnestly hope that through the all-out efforts of all those concerned, further deterioration of the situation will be averted. Relief operations are now under way with the government mobilizing all its capabilities. However, in the bitter cold, many people who were forced to evacuate are facing extremely difficult living conditions due to shortages of food, drinking water, and fuel. I can only hope that by making every effort to promptly implement relief for evacuees, their conditions will improve, even if only gradually, and that their hope for eventual reconstruction will be rekindled. I would like to let you know how deeply touched

I am by the courage of those victims who have survived this catastrophe and who, by bracing themselves, are demonstrating
their determination to live on.

I wish to express my appreciation to the members of the self-
defense forces, the police, the fire department, the Japan Coast
Guard, and other central and local governments and related institutions, as well as people who have come from overseas for
relief operations and the members of various domestic relief organizations for engaging in relief activity around the clock, defying the danger of recurring aftershocks. I wish to express my
deepest gratitude to them.

I have been receiving, by cable, messages of sympathy from
the heads of state of countries around the world, and it was
mentioned in many of those messages that the thoughts of the
people of those countries are with the victims of the disaster.
I would like to convey these messages to the people in the afflicted regions.

I have been told that many overseas media are reporting that,
in the midst of deep sorrow, the Japanese people are responding to the situation in a remarkably orderly manner and helping
each other without losing composure. It is my heartfelt hope that
the people will continue to work hand in hand, treating each
other with compassion, in order to overcome these trying times.

I believe it extremely important for us all to share with the
victims as much as possible, in whatever way we can, their hardship in the coming days. It is my sincere hope that those who
have been affected by the disaster will never give up hope and
will take good care of themselves as they live through the days
ahead, and that each and every Japanese will continue to care for
the afflicted areas and the people for years to come and, together
with the afflicted, watch over and support their path to recovery.

Many Japanese people are well aware of how these words express the emperor's benevolent mind, reflected in his wishes for

the welfare of the whole nation, for Emperor Akihito and Empress Michiko had visited the evacuation sites in Kobe after the devastating earthquake there in January 1995. When the couple bent down to talk sympathetically to sufferers and ask about their condition and feelings, the people were deeply moved and gained hope for the future and the will to live.

The benevolent character of Japan's emperors was also well understood by General Douglas MacArthur (1880–1964), commander-in-chief of the Allied Forces in World War II. Emperor Hirohito (1901–1989), father of Emperor Akihito, made a visit to General MacArthur on September 29, 1945. In *Reminiscences*, MacArthur wrote that he was deeply moved by this encounter. Referring to the emperor's sense of responsibility and courage, he spoke warmly of Hirohito as "the First Gentleman of Japan in his own right," while in reviewing his subsequent meetings with him, MacArthur also spoke of the emperor's loyalty. Although MacArthur's account of his experiences did not actually use the term *benevolence*, the theme of this chapter, it is precisely here that we can see the most important aspect of benevolence.

It can be said that what truly motivated Emperor Hirohito in his meeting with the general was a deep concern for the welfare of the Japanese people and for world peace, in just the same way that Emperor Akihito's benevolent mind is clearly expressed in his message cited above. Such benevolent care for the people of Japan and the world found concrete form in various actions. General MacArthur's high regard for them can be seen in his use of terms like *responsibility, courage, loyalty,* and so on. But how do these various qualities combine into an integral personality?

The Different Aspects of Benevolence

Each of us experiences a wide variety of circumstances in our lives, and we behave differently in response to the particular situations in which we find ourselves. Those around us might have some idea about what we might do in a specific situation, either expecting us to act in the most appropriate way or fearing that we would do something less befitting.

If someone's behavior equals or surpasses our expectations, this person might perhaps draw our praise. Somebody might, for example, visit the elderly in the community with a gift of seasonal fruit or some other delicacy. The local community could well applaud such behavior as an example of benevolence, since this is a virtue that people ascribe to an individual who behaves generously and compassionately toward others, especially to those who are suffering or in need.

More considered analysis of such a case, however, reveals that seemingly benevolent deeds in certain situations do not necessarily signify that a benevolent mind is at work prompting such conduct. Acts that appear benevolent can be performed in order to enhance one's own reputation in society or to get something in return from the other party. Moreover, even if individuals do act with a benevolent mind in one particular instance, this does not necessarily mean that they can be relied on to behave benevolently at all times and under all circumstances. Therefore, when discussing benevolence the key consideration is not necessarily whether people act in a seemingly benevolent way on occasion, but rather whether they have a benevolent mind and what role this plays relative to their whole mental functioning. If benevolence really has a permanent presence in the mind and heart, it will in due course find expression in one way or another according to circumstances.

The words of the founder of Reitaku University, Chikuro Hiroike, "Basing each thought, each act, on benevolence," emphasize the importance of a benevolent mind as the constant backdrop to all our thoughts and acts. So does the expression *jojuuzaga*, which literally means "regardless of whether you are sitting or lying." Hiroike used this as a synonym for *always* in such contexts, since he was fully aware of the importance of a constantly benevolent mind whose concern for others informs every act of one's waking lives.

The key feature of true benevolence is the influence that such a mind exercises over the total functioning of a person. Benevolence is not something that appears just occasionally in thought or deed. Rather, it maintains an unceasing and active existence in one's heart, and its desire for the happiness of others manifests in a variety of concrete forms. In summary, we can say that benevolence constitutes the central element in one's personality and way of life.

❧   ❧   ❧

The nature of true benevolence may seem so altruistic that we might be forgiven for thinking that examples of it in daily life would be hard to find. Yet we can at least find qualities that approximate it, such as the love of parents for their children. Such benevolence is both very strong (even, in most cases, instinctive) and certainly not short-lived. However, parents tend to bestow their love only on their own children and not necessarily on others. This may be a limitation of their love as benevolence.

Though if we look back on human history, we can readily find incontrovertible exemplars of benevolence. These include those commonly described as the "teachers of humankind," whose deep love, akin to that of parents for their children, extended to the whole human family and even to the non-human world. For example, Jesus Christ told his followers to love their enemies, and as he was being crucified he asked God, "Father, forgive them, for they know not what they do." Socrates calmly accepted his death sentence from an Athenian court out of respect for its authority and the law of the state. Buddha told his disciples, "If you monks had your joints and limbs severed with a saw by robbers and murderers, I tell you that you would not fulfill my words and heed my counsel if you were aroused to excitement by this." Rather, "a light of loving gentleness should shine forth from you and radiate through the entire world, and a radiance [spread] wide and deep, unlimited and cleared of all anger and malice." Confucius taught that we should "extend benevolence to trees and grass," showing concern for things outside our human sphere.

Thus it can be said that these teachers of humankind displayed a profound love for every person in the world, including even their enemies who would kill them, and indeed for all living beings. This is why they have commanded global respect and have had a tremendous influence on world history. The lives and behavior of these teachers or sages embody the essence of benevolence. We should focus on a study of these models so as to acquire, little by little, their benevolence of mind, which will then begin to find expression in our daily conduct.

When we talk about benevolence from the standpoint of moral education, it is not enough to treat it as one virtue among many. This is the mistake of the popular system of moral education called *the bag of virtues approach*, with the "bag" being a metaphor for a person's thinking as a whole. It is a common enough approach in which moral educators compile lists of a number of different virtues and try to inculcate them one by one, without any clear understanding or discussion of their mutual relationships or their place in the total structure of an individual's character. One problem with this approach is that the list of virtues will vary in number and contents from educator to educator. Even when the same virtue happens to appear on more than one list, its meaning may not necessarily be the same. In addition, it is not clear why certain virtues turn up on the list and others do not.

How do such lists relate to General MacArthur's appraisal of Emperor Hirohito's sense of responsibility and courage? Clearly the general discerned various virtues in the emperor's consistent and unchanging spirit of benevolence. This implies that qualities such as responsibility, courage, loyalty, and benevolence differ widely depending on the situation in which they are displayed. Courage, for example, is a virtue we recognize in a person who behaves dauntlessly in circumstances where many others would be fearful. The virtue of responsibility, by contrast, reveals itself in situations where people obligated to behave in a certain way act in accordance with the understanding that this is their duty.

Most virtues manifest themselves in particular contexts, then; they are clearly situation specific. With benevolence, however, a mental state that involves care for others and behavior that promotes their happiness, the range of situations in which it may manifest is far wider. Hence benevolence is a much more fundamental quality, one that we must recognize as lying at the very center of the mental functioning of an individual's personality. This is why, in an individual's behavior in a variety of situations, benevolence can often appear in tandem with other virtues. If most other virtues are restricted in their situational applicability, our educational efforts should clearly focus more on elements that are central to the structure of moral functioning. So we need to explore in more detail how benevolence is the central concept in human life, or at least in its moral structure.

If we accept benevolence as a mental state that involves caring for others and behavior that promotes their happiness, it clearly cannot be limited to our children, family members, close friends or other important people close to us. It must include all humankind and, beyond even that, all that exists on earth and is connected with our lives, since caring for and respecting all human beings is simply not possible if we exclude the animals and plants that grow alongside us. This is because not only do we co-exist with them, we also depend on their existence to support our own. Beyond that, of course, we are also sustained by our natural, inanimate environment, relying as we do on the sun, air, water, soil, and oceans that provide us with so much of what we need. In respect of human society, too, we receive great benefits in the form of electric power, water and waste facilities, transportation, communication facilities, and so on. Rather than exploiting all these benefits provided by nature and human society selfishly and thoughtlessly, we need to accept all we are given with a sense of gratitude. That will

then form the basis of a caring attitude that should inform our relationships with everything, animate and inanimate, that helps to
sustain our lives.

Thought of in this way, benevolence in its broadest sense means
caring for and respecting all that exists in our surroundings and
thereby enhancing the quality of our relationships with all our surroundings. By taking an active interest in all that surrounds us, by
expanding the sphere of our interactions with it, and by developing a sense of gratitude towards it, we will enhance the quality of
our relationships with our surroundings in the spirit of care and
respect. Of course, we need to be aware that these relationships extend across time as well as space, for we are connected with all that
has existed in the past as well as with all that will exist in the future.
In sum, benevolence of mind can only be acquired by examining
all our relationships in a serious and radical manner.

♣   ♣   ♣

We have seen, then, that the concept of benevolence is a central element in the mental functioning of the human personality, rather
than one virtue among many. It has also become clear that benevolence concerns itself not only with human beings but also with all
that exists on earth. This conception of benevolence as the key element in the structure of all human life is further amplified when
we come to consider it in the light of the concept of the spirit of
"nurturing all that exists."

To understand the full meaning of this, we must appreciate how
all the phenomena of the universe are related to one another. The
fact that the earth on which we live is the only planet in the solar
system on which water exists in liquid form is highly significant.
Only this very rare circumstance makes it possible for all kinds of
living beings to exist and flourish on our planet. Scientific research
has further shown that our universe constitutes a unified system,
and that human beings are only one of many phenomena within it.

Relationships of interdependence exist not only between living things (animals and plants) but also between animate and inanimate things. Therefore, as human beings, we are connected with everything, animate and inanimate, in the universe. However, human beings differ from everything else in that we live in society and enjoy the full benefits of doing so. Society consists in essence of interdependent relationships on a mental level (remembering, of course, that such interdependence extends not only in space but also in time). Since our human lives are therefore linked with everything in the past, present, and future, we must examine our way of life and our thinking about morality in this extended framework.

We may call this comprehensive interrelatedness the *network of interdependence.* In this context, benevolence can be regarded as embodying our fundamental attitude towards the whole world. It encourages us to treat all relationships with great care and it enriches their quality. Cultivating a benevolent mind is therefore the central issue for us as human beings and members of the network of interdependence, and the core concern of moral education as well. But what exactly is this benevolence of mind within the extended framework of the network of interdependence, and how should we go about acquiring it?

The essential characteristics of the network of interdependence (the interrelatedness of everything in the universe) are revealed in the way that nature gives birth to and nurtures all living beings in harmony. The great teachers of humankind actualized these characteristics in the sphere of human society as a deep and impartial love for all beings. This is the spirit of benevolence, and its acquisition is the ultimate objective of moral education.

The first step toward benevolence is to overcome our self-centered mentality. As human beings we are not always free from the impulse towards self-preservation and self-centeredness, and this can deny us a proper understanding of the work of nature in giving birth to and nurturing all living beings in harmony. The self-centered thinking and activity of human beings is the major factor underlying almost all the problems of society. It is very important for us to try to overcome such shortcomings. We cannot cultivate a benevolent mind unless we recognize and acknowledge our tendency towards self-centeredness and make efforts to overcome it.

As we try to overcome our self-centeredness and widen our perspective, we will gradually grasp how the great nurturing powers of nature support our lives and how in human society we also owe much, above all, to those who work very hard to sustain our bodily existence, a safe and orderly social life for us, and a meaningful and satisfactory spiritual life. When we realize the extent of our debt to such people, a sense of gratitude and a willingness to follow in their path and return their favors will grow in us. Acquiring a benevolent mind is greatly assisted by expressing gratitude to our benefactors, and then by repaying them and following their example.

Once we understand the great debt we owe to our important benefactors, we will begin to realize how very little we have done for the network of interdependence to date in the selfish pursuit of our own satisfaction. This recognition, together with a sense of gratitude, will implant in our minds a willingness to act in accordance with the sense of duty we should feel as members of this interdependent network in everything we do. Benevolence of mind will then grow little by little within us as we strive wholeheartedly to make our selfless contribution to that network.

Since the value and meaning of everything depends on our own mental and spiritual condition, it is vital that we ourselves acquire this spirit of benevolence in the manner just outlined. However, it is just as crucial to communicate this benevolence of mind to others and to share an awareness of it with as many people as possible. Through the accumulation of such efforts, the world will become a truly rich network of spiritual interdependence. This is the ultimate goal of moral education.

Benevolence

BY BERNICE LERNER

On June 23, 1940, the day after France and Germany signed the World War II armistice, Pastor André Trocmé (1901–1971) encouraged villagers in Le Chambon-sur-Lignon, France, "to resist the violence that will be brought to bear on their consciences through weapons of the spirit." Invoking Christian duty, he insisted, "We will resist whenever our adversaries will demand of us obedience contrary to the orders of the gospel. We will do so without fear but also without pride and without hate."

Trocmé and Pastor Edouard Théis (administrator of Le Chambon's Cévenol School) had laid the groundwork for benevolent action long before Germany invaded France. While the Nazis gained power in the 1930s, the two pastors urged parishioners to "work and look hard for ways, for opportunities to make little moves against destructiveness." Their sermons focused on the preciousness of each human life and on the importance of attacking evil. The Chambonnais understood that the obligation to love your neighbor as yourself superseded obligations toward any governing authority. They felt concern for victims of unbridled hatred and feared what might and did come to pass—the deportation to concentration and death camps of the Jews in their Haute-Loire region, in the southern zone of France. Believing that "a closed door is an instrument of harm doing," they welcomed refugees.

Surrounded by rugged mountains, the village of Le Chambon-sur-Lignon was difficult to reach. Trocmé and Quaker leader Burns Chalmers (1815–1868), whose followers brought supplies and consolation to concentration camp victims in France's Vichy zone, decided that Le Chambon could be an "ethical space where goodness could overcome evil without hindrance from the outside world." Its conditions were unique—members of most other communities would have been unwilling to share what little they had, to take dangerous risks, and to tolerate such disruption to their lives. In *Lest Innocent Blood Be Shed*, author Philip Hallie (1922–1994) argued that these leaders wished to impart to the children "a strong feeling and a solid knowledge that there were human beings *outside of their own family* who cared for them." Trocmé and Chalmers aimed to "give those children hope and a basis for living moral lives of their own." The two leaders conceived plans during meetings in the nearby town of Nîmes. They sought to alleviate suffering through boarding, nourishing, and educating the offspring of hunted and incarcerated Jews. The "conspiracy of goodness" would be in evidence within a dozen miles in all directions of Le Chambon-sur-Lignon, an area encompassing twelve parishes. The scale of the "conspiracy" would be evident, too, in the area's high school, which would—according to Pierre Sauvage, producer of the 1989 film *Weapons of the Spirit*—grow from eighteen students in 1938 to more than 350 students in 1943.

Though isolated, the Chambonnais had learned of terrible events. Rescue efforts proceeded with urgency after the deportation of the Jews in the summer of 1942. In addition to "weapons of the spirit," the villagers deployed pragmatic tactics such as secrecy, cunning, and discretion. There could be no bureaucratic protocol, no record-keeping, no sharing of information. Only Trocmé knew the whole rescue operation. Each of his leaders operated independently, and these *responsables* could not afford to make a misstep. They thus could not know too much—only one woman from the Resistance kept a list of the children and with whom they were placed.

Though not explicitly stated, the poor farmers of Le Chambon knew that the children they were sheltering were Jewish. They were given very little money—five hundred francs a month—for sharing their daily bread. (Small children were easiest to place, for they did not eat much.) Le Chambon soon gained a reputation for sheltering Jews, and its villagers, who did not think of the danger, were in fact imperiled; if found out, they could have been massacred. They nevertheless resisted evil rule—not for any self-serving or political reason, but rather in obedience to their consciences.

What was preached by the passionate Théis and Trocmé—what Trocmé's *responsables* brought to thirteen different parts of his parish—were messages contained in chosen biblical passages, such as the Good Samaritan story in the New Testament. When Jesus was asked how one could achieve eternal life, he answered, "You shall love ... your neighbor as yourself." And when he was asked, "Who is my Neighbor?" he answered that one's neighbor is anyone who dearly needs help. Biblical injunctions inspired concrete solutions to the problem of sheltering Jews.

Trocmé, a descendant of Huguenots (and on his mother's side, of Germans), and his Italian wife, Magda, modeled unswerving obedience to moral law. In addition to providing for their own four children, they shared what meager goods they had, arranged for counterfeit documents for refugees, and immediately sought to shelter anyone who knocked at their door. Trocmé believed that "help must be given only for the benefit of the people being helped, not the benefit of some church or organization that was doing the helping." He argued that "only a person's conscious obedience to the demands of God could arouse and direct the powers that could make the world better than it is." Talk about the "power of the sciences to transform the world into paradise" was, for Trocmé, empty rhetoric.

The people of Le Chambon could have lived in safety, attending peacefully to their private affairs in the midst of a blood war. They could have adopted an attitude of indifference toward the Resistance and its maneuverings. They could have felt sorry for the persecuted but compelled to do nothing. They chose benevolence, quiet and ubiquitous expressions of compassion and generosity. What factors, we might ask, led to this magnanimous stance?

We may begin by exploring their leader's background. Trocmé's personal history prepared him, in ways, for his role as "the soul of Le Chambon." He was born on Easter Day in 1901 to a wealthy family in Picardy, in northeast France. He became sensitive to the plight of the downtrodden, whose lives contrasted with his own privileged, sheltered existence. His mother was killed just before World War I in a car accident in which his father was driving recklessly. Trocmé learned from that tragedy that both the victim's life and that of one who caused another's death were precious. Another lesson: As a twenty-year-old, Trocmé participated in a map-making expedition of Morocco for the French army. He belonged to a unit of twenty-five men. When his lieutenant learned that Trocmé had refused to bring his gun, he berated the pacifist soldier, whose belief in nonviolence could endanger the entire unit. Trocmé realized that he should have spoken up earlier and not gone on the mission. He learned that, in Philip Hallie's words, "nonviolence could, in fact, increase violence if it was not chosen in the right way at the right time."

As for the Chambonnais, their collective history may explain their receptivity to their leaders' messages, to the idea of non-violent resistance to evil forces. Le Chambon was home to several thousand Protestants—descendants of Huguenots, the first Protestants in Catholic France. These Chambonnais knew discrimination. They had endured three centuries of persecution, from the Saint Bartholomew's Day Massacre of August 24, 1572, to periods of enslavement, starvation, and torture. Their temples had been razed, and for years they could engage only in clandestine worship. It was not until the French Revolution, in the late eighteenth century, that they attained full civil rights. They would retain collective memories of their persecution.

The experience of having suffered, which may sensitize or harden a person, partly explains the Chambonnais villagers. Their benevolence may be traced, too, to their capacity for empathy, the supreme emotion: From this precious human quality springs love, affection, kindness, gentleness, generosity of spirit, and warm-heartedness. Here, West meets East: the kind and generous Chambonnais exemplified Buddhist values such as the inability to bear the sight of another's suffering (Tib. *shen dug ngal wa la mi sö pa*), and great compassion (*nying je*). As *great compassion* belongs to a category of emotions with a cognitive component (empathy plus reason), it is especially effective. According to the Dalai Lama, "The more we develop compassion ... the more genuinely ethical our conduct will be." Put another way, "Ethically wholesome actions arise naturally in the context of compassion."

Benevolence carries transformative power for the actor and recipient alike. Witness the experience of an American girl who volunteered in a Peruvian hospital nursery wherein some babies had no parent. Feeling compassion for one abandoned baby, the fifteen-year-old described her watershed experience in an essay submitted to the Sir John Templeton Laws of Life contest:

> I remember walking towards the nursery one night. I could see, in the hallway, one [lone] crib.... I approached the crib, and inside there lay a baby, crying helplessly, obviously in need of love and comfort. She was slightly bigger than my forearm and her strangely developed face suggested prematurity. "She was born three months early and her mother hasn't come back for her," I was told. I witnessed nurses scurrying around, inside the nursery, feeding and changing the babies of mothers who care, but ignoring the tiny person struggling for attention from inside the crib. "They have to take care of the others first, then, if there is time, she will be fed," someone explained to me. I could not imagine standing by... as this perfect little creature, unable to move her head, struggled to find a comfortable position and at times desperately gasped for a breath due to her underdeveloped respiratory system. I immediately lifted her into my arms and held her close. The improvement within those few seconds seemed... almost unbelievable. The baby stopped crying. Her

hands remained in tightly clenched fists, but I could tell she was relieved. From that moment on, I knew what I had to do. It was my chance to be the person I never thought I could be, the Good Samaritan. Every night ... after midnight, I found my way through the laboring mothers to that baby in the hall-way. I spent hours just rocking her and at times, even singing to her. I began to notice gradual improvements. She seemed to let go of all her worries and anxieties the moment I picked her up each night. By the end of my stay, even her tight, frustrated fists would spread open into wide, reaching hands...

Like Trocmé's parishioners, this girl was inspired by the parable of the Good Samaritan, the man who cared for a stranger who had been robbed, beaten, and ignored by two other passersby. Like the Good Samaritan and the Chambonnais villagers, she stopped to see the humanity of the "other." Any of her own needs became instantly less important than those of the abandoned infant.

Without taking away from her noble actions, let us pause to consider that a helpless baby arouses compassion in ways that others may not. It is difficult to exercise greatness of heart toward someone who is crotchety or nasty. Many of us have encountered school bullies, whiny co-workers, embittered friends. To see beyond the behavior to the deeply hurting individual, to give the best possible interpretation to the actions and attitudes of those sorely in need of understanding, is to demonstrate benevolence. Such cases, of course, test our forbearance. It is particularly hard to check our feelings when we are the object of another's irritability or wrath. Moreover, we must be able to distinguish those who are not in their right minds from individuals with evil intentions who are not deserving of second chances.

It is challenging, as well, to feel kindly toward those we find repellent. In recent times, many have been inspired by the late Mother Theresa (1910–1997), who founded Missionaries of Charity in India and ministered to the poor, sick, orphaned, and dying. At one point, a U.S. television reporter endeavored to film a documentary about the Charity Sisters' work in Calcutta's slums. There he observed a young American nun cleaning sores and infections covering a beggar's maggot-infested body. After capturing her gentle actions on film, the reporter declared, "Sister, I wouldn't do that for a million dollars!" Without taking her eyes off her dying patient, the nun quietly replied, "Neither would I."

The nun displayed *nying je* or great compassion toward a fellow human being, a man whose suffering made at least one foreign observer uncomfortable. Her own welfare was not a consideration. Such purely motivated deeds may be seen when there is no time for deliberation, often in dramatic incidents that capture our imagination.

Newspaper columnists in January 2007 both described and analyzed the behavior of Wesley Autrey, the fifty-year-old man—who at the time had with him his two young daughters—who leapt in front of a New York City subway train to save the life of a stranger who had had a seizure and fallen onto the tracks. Autrey immediately covered the man's body with his own; the train passed over them and they emerged unharmed. Why the fascination with this courageous deed? We need to be shown that spontaneous and noble action on behalf of a stranger is within the realm of human possibility. Thoughtful readings of the incident indicate just why, however, even the most altruistic among us might not act as Autrey did. A navy veteran, he had been trained to move quickly in stressful situations. Not only was Autrey able to immediately empathize with the man he beheld, but he also could draw on his military past, a way of responding that had long become for him automatic, his way of being in the world.

Such anecdotes may serve as touchstones as we confront challenges and opportunities to do some good. Circumstances need not be dramatic in order for our deeds to be of consequence. We need not witness an accident in which someone is about to be killed. We need not be engulfed by war. We need not be exposed to extreme poverty. As we forge and maintain relationships, interacting with family members, colleagues, and friends, there are countless opportunities to display a generosity of spirit called benevolence.

At times, acts of kindness and caring take unexpected forms. A teacher in a large urban high school is known to be incredibly strict with her students. She will not tolerate swearing in her presence. Her students must say "please" and "thank you" or they will be asked to leave. This teacher well knows where her students come from. These teenagers see crime, violence, and drug addiction in their neighborhoods. Some consider school their only safe haven. Some carry knives, which they hide around the school's grounds, to protect themselves. They must be vigilant, understand "the code," never squeal, and know how to steal and manipulate to get what they need or want. They have low expectations of themselves and others and low self-esteem. In order to help these students lead good lives, their teachers must enable them to discern right from wrong, foster in them the desire to do good, and encourage them to take responsibility. In so doing, they may be "cruel to be kind."

One teacher gives these minority students the opportunity to discuss sex, drugs, jobs, and other topics about which they need honest information and guidance. However, she minces no words in telling those who put no effort into their schoolwork that by thinking that academic success means "acting white," they are making a huge mistake. In taking the time to communicate about practical matters, in acting as an authentic role model who can accurately imagine her students' attitudes, this teacher is showing that she cares. The same may be said of the counselor who knows when order is lacking at home, who gives concrete and hard-line instructions to parents, who must provide their teenagers an alarm clock and breakfast and enforce a reasonable curfew. This school's behind-the-scenes lessons in benevolence may be applied to various other settings.

We ought to collect anecdotes that highlight benevolence in its many incarnations. The greater our storehouse of stories, the easier it will be to access examples to illuminate our own choices. Apart from recognizing emblematic episodes as they occur around us, we can find examples of benevolent action in history (e.g., the compassion of President Abraham Lincoln [1809–1865] toward a beaten slave), in literature (e.g., Sidney Carton's heroic sacrifice in Dickens's *A Tale of Two Cities*), in film (e.g., Phil Connor's turn of heart in *Groundhog Day*), and in the news, e.g., one family sheltering another that endured losses in the wake of Hurricane Katrina.

Let us also post eloquent sayings that remind us of our human capacity. How beautiful, for example, are words penned by Emily Dickinson (1830–1886): "If I can stop one heart from breaking, I shall not live in vain." In acting on such precepts, we begin to develop the habit of benevolence. Again, in practical terms, our deeds need not be monumental. It is not difficult to thank unsung heroes, to express appreciation to the person who cleans our office, the friend who listens attentively to our problems, the relative who prepares us a meal. It takes little to act kindly toward the person who cuts our hair, the mechanic who fixes our car, the cashier who rings up our purchase. We might, as a next step, let their supervisors or other clients know of their good work!

Benevolence is displayed whenever we truly see the "other." I observed this lesson in action once on a family trip. A driver picked up our small group at a designated place and proceeded to take us on a tour of Italy's Amalfi coast. It was not long before we realized that we were not going to hear about the sites we were passing; our driver was upset and he went on about negative reviews posted about him on the Internet. While some members of the group grew impatient, my father-in-law noted that the driver was a hurting human being who needed to give vent to his feelings. After we listened to him sympathetically, his anguish subsided and the driver was able to show and describe for his attentive audience a charming, off-the-beaten-track hamlet.

Once we internalize benevolence, we will forever hold the formula for warming our own and others' hearts. Where there are limitless opportunities to lessen another's pain or brighten another's day, there is no room for problems to cloud our world.

CHAPTER 4

Gratitude

"Gratitude is the heart's memory." —*French*

⌁ ⌁ ⌁ ⌁ ⌁

There is no country in the world where people do not return thanks. Gratitude is the universal spirit to recognize and acknowledge one's debt, an act as small as thanking someone who has given us kindness or help and as profound as appreciating the natural world for providing life. The Japanese authors focus on this broad-ranging spirit of appreciation inherent in their culture. They open with a story of poor villagers who rescued Turkish shipwreck victims during the Meiji period and how this gesture by goodhearted citizens nurtured a "chain reaction of goodwill" between Japan and Turkey that has lasted well over a century. We are introduced to the Eastern practice of expressing gratitude toward ancestors and protective gods, reflecting a deeply held value of indebtedness toward individuals, society, and whatever universal powers support the miracle of life. The culture is rich in rituals displaying this deep reverence and appreciation. The authors assert that gratitude is closely tied to kindness and respect, and that cultivating it leads to a sense of humility. They outline several steps one can take to develop this virtue, which range from observation and reflection to learning to appreciate different levels of kindness.

In the second essay, the author relates the story of her father and the poverty he experienced as a young boy, showing how hardship can lead one to develop a grateful heart. Drawing from the words of great Western thinkers, she reaches essentially the same conclusions as the Japanese essay: that an awareness of the vast extent of our indebtedness leads to a humble attitude of appreciation. It fosters the spirit to worship God as well as repay our debts and is thus closely linked to justice, to doing what is right. She points out that while gratitude is often referred to as an emotion, in truth it involves knowledge and thought, that it is an attitude that we can choose, one that requires cultivation and practice. Gratitude allows us to enjoy our lives with greater resilience and inner strength, as has been recognized in contemporary psychology. We need to "refine our lenses of wonder and awe," this essay urges, as well as learn to choose our words wisely, focus on the positive, and reframe the negative in our lives. To both perspectives, it is clear that true happiness cannot exist without this spirit of gratitude.

Gratitude

BY OSAMU NAKAYAMA AND SHUJIRO MIZUNO

There is no country in the world where people do not return thanks. Studying the many different forms in which gratitude is expressed has much to teach those who wish to discover its essential meaning.

The *Ertuğrul* Incident

In 1890, during the Meiji Era in Japan, the *Ertuğrul*, a frigate belonging to the Ottoman Turks, ran aground on a reef in the Genkai Sea off the coast of Kushimoto in Kishu (today's Wakayama Prefecture). Five hundred eighty-seven sailors, including Admiral Ali Osman Pasha, lost their lives in the disaster. Sixty-nine others, though, were saved from drowning thanks to the efforts of local people. The kindness they showed the sailors has turned out to be more than a matter of history, of a dead past. In fact, it set off a chain reaction of goodwill that has had an impact on relations between Turkey and Japan up to the present day.

Immediately after the shipwreck, the residents of the village of Oshima devoted themselves to saving the lives of as many of the drowning men as they could. Their efforts did not cease with the setting of the sun, though. For the next four days until the rescued sailors left their village, they worked steadily to get the wounded to safety, to prepare food for them, and to assist the doctors who came to attend them. Their efforts went far beyond normal volunteering. For one thing, the food situation in the Kushimoto region at the time was extremely difficult: grain and vegetable crops had failed that year, the catch of fish was poor, and on top of all this, the price of rice had skyrocketed. Consequently, well before the accident took place, the number of those suffering from hunger and begging for food in the area had increased greatly. In fishing villages in those days, however, people prepared for an emergency by, for example, keeping potatoes under the floorboards or raising chickens in the back yard. All these supplies they now offered to the injured sailors, immediately and without thought for themselves, even though they knew that they too might be in desperate need of food in the near future.

Their concern for others did not fade even once the year of the accident passed. Every five years since 1890, in fact, the people of Oshima have held a memorial service for the victims of the *Ertuğrul*. Before the war, pupils at the Kashinozaki Elementary School (now the Kushino-Cho Oshima Elementary School) tended to the graves of those of the crew who had lost their lives far from home. Even today, the entire school—pupils, teachers, and the non-teaching staff—spend time every November to tidy the cemetery and sing songs of mourning for the dead sailors.

Nearly a century had passed when the actions of the Oshima villagers suddenly once more found their way into the limelight, this time during the Iran-Iraq war.

On March 17, 1985, the then Iraqi president, Saddam Hussein, designated the sky over Iran as a no-fly zone and decreed that any plane using that airspace for any purpose whatsoever would be liable to attack without warning. This prompted an immediate exodus of foreign nationals from Iran. Japanese citizens living there found themselves stranded at Tehran's international airport. This was partly because no Japanese commercial carriers flew to Iran but also because foreign airlines either cancelled the reservations of Japanese passengers outright or simply refused to allow them to board their flights, giving priority to citizens of their own countries instead. As the conflict with Iraq escalated, the atmosphere of panic surrounding the Japanese trapped at the airport intensified with each passing day.

Under these circumstances, the Republic of Turkey sent two large DC-10 planes to the rescue of the forsaken Japanese citizens, enabling 215 of them to leave Iran for safety. What prompted the Turks to act in this way? A decade later, as reported in the *Sankei* newspaper on November 9, 1995, Necati Utkan, the Turkish Ambassador to Japan, spoke of his feelings about Japan and its people, and made the following interesting comment:

> You are a diligent people, belonging to the only country that has been atom-bombed. This is the impression that I had of the Japanese when I was young. Among the incidents that impressed me about Japan, that of the frigate *Ertuğrul* comes to my mind first … It was a very tragic event, of course, but it was also the beginning of our grass-roots friendship with the Japanese … An account of the incident was published in a textbook in Turkey, and I myself studied the story at school. It is such an important historical event for us that there is no child who is unaware of this story.

Turgut Özal, the Turkish Prime Minister who made the decision to dispatch the airliners to rescue the Japanese stranded in Tehran, explained that he did so because "we have to repay the kindness of the Japanese people." The incident of the frigate *Ertuğrul* must surely have passed through his mind in this connection too.

The chain reaction of goodwill that began in 1890 continues to the present. August 17, 1999, witnessed a severe earthquake in the northwestern region of Turkey. The death toll rose to over seventeen thousand—three times as large as that of the Great Hanshin-Awaji Earthquake of 1995—and the number of those injured reached approximately forty-four thousand. The first people to start fundraising and to lend a helping hand to those living in the afflicted area were precisely those Japanese citizens who had been stranded in Tehran and rescued by Turkish commercial aircraft in 1985. The

Japanese government was also quick to respond to the needs of the victims, offering relief supplies worth one million dollars and giving another million in cash. On September 23, it requested the Marine Self-Defense Force to dispatch the LST (landing ship tank) *Oosumi*, the minesweeper *Bungo*, and the replenishment oiler *Haseya* to Turkey, carrying five hundred preassembled temporary housing units for those who had lost their homes. The instructions that the captain of the *Oosumi* gave his crewmembers on the occasion touch once again on the theme of gratitude:

> At the time of the Iran-Iraq war, the Prime Minister of the Republic of Turkey made the courageous decision to send two jetliners to rescue 250 Japanese citizens from Tehran despite all the dangers involved. As a result, all of their lives were saved. Now Japan must repay the kindness of the government and people of Turkey. Today we must act to return their friendship. We will deliver temporary housing units to Turkey and support people as they struggle to recover from the recent disaster. Our efforts in repaying its past kindness will bind Japan and Turkey in a spirit of fraternity for one hundred years to come. When Japan is in trouble, Turkey will help us, and when Turkey needs our aid, we will not hesitate to give it. Whatever difficulties we may face, it is our responsibility not to break the bond between Japan and Turkey, the bond that our predecessors bequeathed to us ....

Needless to say, the Turkish people were touched by the good-will and support of the Japanese government and people.

It is clear from this that what characterized the people of Japan and Turkey in these matters, what truly motivated them, was a concern for the welfare of others regardless of nationality. Such benevolent care for human beings in general may seem to have been expressed in the form of other virtues like responsibility, courage, benevolence, and friendliness. But it was benevolence that bound all of these together. So how does gratitude manage to combine such various qualities into the single entity that is an integral human being?

In Japan, gratitude is also very frequently expressed to ancestors and the gods who are believed to protect family and country. After paying due respect to their Imperial Ancestors, for example, members of the Japanese Imperial Family are in the habit of communicating items of good and bad news to them. This is the background to the following *tanka* (poem) composed by Emperor Meiji the Great (1852–1912), the great-grandfather of the present emperor:

Today is New Year's Day.
I have asked my attendants how things are going at the Ise Shrine.
The shrine is dedicated to our Imperial Ancestors.
So this is the first thing I must do on New Year's Day.

Members of the Royal family continue this tradition of showing respect to the gods and their ancestors; they express gratitude to them at the New Year, report to them on what has happened in the year just ended, and make promises for the year to come.

This feeling of gratitude is captured in the Japanese word *on*, which strictly speaking, should be translated as "that for which we should feel indebted to somebody" or "that which we owe to others." *On* and *giri* (the responsibility we are required by society to bear) are very important concepts for those trying to understand the Japanese mind, since they underpin much social behavior. For instance, Japanese people often call their teacher *on-shi*, meaning "the teacher to whom we feel indebted," and graduating students hold a "Gratitude Party" to express their thanks to their teachers. Even the "thank-you bargain sales" during which department stores sell goods at special prices as New Year approaches are not entirely commercial in spirit. They are also intended to express gratitude to customers for the favor they have done the stores by shopping there during the year. The all-embracing nature of *on* was demonstrated best by Sontoku Ninomiya (1787–1856), who is famous in Japan for his extraordinary efforts to regenerate poverty-stricken agricultural villages. His view, which was seen as remarkable even in his own time, was that those who just pursued their own advantage or happiness could only expect an empty life. Expressing gratitude to everything under the sun and doing one's best to give something in return would, by contrast, engender good not only for the world but also for oneself.

The *Quotations from Sontoku Ninomiya* include the following insights:

> When they have nothing to eat, people are apt to beg others to give them something. But if they find they are about to starve to death, they don't feel it necessary to wash their tableware.

One of the implications of this is that people should feel thankful to the cooking pans, cups, and plates that have helped them consume food to date, which means they have a responsibility to keep them clean even if they are unlikely to have anything to eat the next day. Sontoku Ninomiya here is urging people not to forget how much they owe to the past.

Buddha, who lived around twenty-five hundred years ago, said people suffer because they cannot free themselves of worldly desires. If they could, they would not experience pain or distress. But people mistakenly desire to live just as they please, only to find this all but impossible. If they want to spare themselves agony, Buddha believed, they should accept everything exactly as it is rather than seeking what they cannot have.

One day a woman carrying a dead baby in her arms came to see Buddha. She had long wished for a child and had been exceedingly happy when at last she gave birth at the age of forty. But the infant died after just three days. In despair she approached Buddha, begging him to bring her baby back to life. Buddha agreed to do as she asked but then said, "There is something I need if I am to accomplish this. Please fetch me some mustard seeds. But they must come from a household in which no member has ever died."

Three days passed, and the woman returned to Buddha. This time she was entirely composed, for she had been unable to find a single household that had never experienced death. Seeing that it visits everybody and should be taken for what it is, the woman had come to accept the death of her own child and ceased to lament it.

The *Hokkukyo*, or *Words of Truth Sutra*, is a Buddhist scripture whose 182nd lesson teaches, "It is difficult to be born a human being. And if you are born a human being, you have to die soon. It is by a fluke that you are in this world at present." It may be significant here that one derivation of the Japanese word *arigato*, meaning thank you, is from *arigatashi* or fluke. In the thinking of Japanese people long ago, saying thank you may have been closely connected with the belief that the miracle of life was a blessing from Buddha or the gods for which we must always be grateful. Certainly, Buddha taught that it is only by a miracle that we are here, and it is on this fundamental conviction that gratitude is based.

Expressing Gratitude on a Daily Basis

Since time immemorial, Japanese people have been accustomed to say *itadaki-masu* before every meal and *gochiso-sama* after it. For example, at lunch, which is provided by the state, students at Japanese elementary schools usually chant these phrases in chorus. Whenever people say *itadaki-masu*, they put their palms together in a fashion similar to *namaste*, the gesture Indians use to pay respect to others. It is said that the Japanese custom derives from Buddhism, but *itadaki-masu* is used by all Japanese people regardless of their religion. The phrase is not just directed towards those who have prepared the meal. Fundamentally it is also uttered to thank all those beings whose lives had been ended in order to provide food for humankind. In this sense, *itadaki-masu* means, "I cannot help sacrificing other animals and plants in order to live."

Also included in the awareness that infuses the phrase are the farmers who provide the indispensible rice and barley. *Itadaki-masu* acknowledges how they spend the entire year preparing the rice paddies or barley fields, planting seeds, nurturing them, and reaping the harvest, as well tending to pigs and cows so that people may have pork and beef. What pains they take! The same is also true of all the other people involved in the transport and selling of food.

When young children first start to say *itadaki-masu*, they are simply copying what their parents do. But as they mature, they gradually come to understand how they depend on their parents and many other people for food. Without all the help they receive, they would not be able to eat every day.

Another common Japanese phrase used to pay respect is *okage-sama-de*, which literally means, "I owe it to you." People say this, for example, in response to an enquiry after their health, and it carries the sense of "I owe it to you that I am in good health." Here, though, *you* refers not simply to the person one is talking to, but rather "everybody and everything around us, *including* you." Gratitude is being expressed not just to the individual present, but also to everyone and everything responsible for one's good health, including Nature, the gods, and the Buddha.

Expressions of gratitude, then, have an extended quality that is also present in schools when students stand up and bow to the teacher at the beginning and end of each class. This gesture of respect is intended not only for the teacher present but also for the many people, alive and dead, who have contributed to the process of learning.

This wide-ranging quality of gratitude is evident, too, in countries where people set aside a place in the house to pay respect to their ancestors. Japanese homes often include a space for a small Buddhist altar, where memorials to the dead are kept. It is here that news of what has happened in the family, good or bad, as well as expressions of gratitude, are communicated to the ancestors.

An awareness of the extent of their obligations to others is also revealed by the fact that Japanese people offer thanks to dead animals and not just in cases where, as we have seen, they provide food for them. A memorial service is sometimes held for animals killed in experiments.

Such rituals have a tendency to lose their original significance over time and degenerate into meaningless formality. However, this does not diminish the importance of gratitude itself in any way. In present-day Japan, where things material are placed above things spiritual, some people mistakenly feel that they need not feel grateful for something for which they have paid money. Thus one may sometimes hear parents say, "Since I have paid for their school lunch, there is no reason why my children should say *ita-daki-masu* before eating it." Others object to students being forced to place their palms together while chanting this phrase, alleging that it is a religious act and that the Constitution of Japan prohibits public (municipal or state) schools from carrying on religious education. But all that such arguments really indicate is a failure to grasp the true ethos of gratitude.

There are a number of steps that can help us to keep the essence of gratitude alive and fresh in our hearts:

1) Reflecting on our lives

   Do we always express gratitude when we should? Perhaps we should call to mind much more often those who prepare our meals every day or support our existence in other ways. University students might remember those who pay their educational and living expenses or others who may have helped them with their studies.

2) Careful observation and a willingness to acknowledge what we owe

   By observing our everyday lives carefully, we will become far more aware of those who care for us, who work to ensure that we feel safe and protected and can live a comfortable life. Without their help we could not be happy, and so we should gauge carefully how much we owe to them. Some, including our parents, are the reason we exist at all. Others support us spiritually. Moreover, we owe much to the state. There is really no end to the list of our benefactors, living or inanimate.

3) Remembering past experiences

Gratitude is due not only for the good we receive in the present. Should we not also remember those who have done us a good turn in the past? We have ties to many people, including parents, friends, teachers, and so on, to whom we owe thanks. Some of them may no longer be alive, but that should not diminish our feelings of appreciation.

4) Expressing gratitude

If we feel grateful, we should give voice to our thanks. Letters or e-mails are one method. Japanese people have a custom of sending greeting cards at the New Year, and others are starting to exchange Christmas greetings as well, and these are good opportunities to let other people know how indebted we feel to them. Of course it is even better to convey heartfelt thanks in person, and we do not have to wait for a special occasion to do so. Nothing can prevent us from saying "thank you" wherever and as often as we like, and being thanked makes very few people feel uncomfortable.

5) Conveying our thanks to all that exists, animate and inanimate

We should feel thankful to all beings, including pets, for example, that show affection toward us. We should also appreciate the things that give us service every day, like items of furniture and kitchen utensils. Grass, flowers, and trees—all these and more enrich our lives immeasurably. Indeed everything in the world, living or not, plays an important part in sustaining our happiness. If we become more conscious of this fact and feel properly thankful for what we are given, our lives will be truly fulfilling.

6) Learning to appreciate the kindnesses done to us on all scales

It is perhaps easiest to appreciate the small acts of kindness done by individuals around us and to thank them. But we find it harder to remember how much we owe to larger entities like the community or the state. Yet we should also thank the social systems that are indispensible to human life. What they provide us are mid-sized kindnesses. And there are few people who appreciate the really large kindnesses we all experience.

The large kindnesses are those which make human life possible, like the gifts we receive from the earth, from various other forms of life, and from the laws of nature. If it were not for the proper ordering of the universe and the solar system, we could not survive. Being thankful for kindnesses on this scale enables us to live truly worthwhile lives.

In addition to the six steps above, introspection, a method of counseling often employed in Japan, can help us refresh our sense of appreciation. In this method, patients are given a theme and devote themselves to solitary meditation. The theme has three elements: "Look back on your past and try to remember 1) the services others have done for you, 2) those you have done for others, and 3) the trouble you have caused to others." It sometimes takes Japanese patients a long time to remember all the incidents they should, but most can recall them after several days, and they often shed tears when they realize how much they have tormented others. Many focus on their mother and realize they have not yet sufficiently repaid her favors; they also become aware of how much they owe to individuals other than her. They begin to feel thankful, which in turn contributes to solving their psychological problems. Perhaps we would all benefit from undertaking the same exercise.

Gratitude is closely related to many other virtues. The most important of these is kindness. Those who are treated with kindness notice the fact, and this kindles a desire in them to pass it on to others. This is why gratitude also has a close connection with one's ability to sympathize with others. If people do us a good turn, we should try to understand their intention, and this can lead to our feeling even more thankful.

Gratitude is also closely allied to respect for others. Parents sacrifice themselves in helping their children grow up. The survival of society is made possible by many sacrifices on the part of a variety of people. Teachers strive to prepare their students to go out into society. Gratitude for all these kinds of help will increase our respect for such people.

Feeling gratitude toward others also encourages a spirit of modesty. The truth that we do not live on our own is a simple one, but grasping it will inspire a feeling of humility in us. Then we will find it easier to refrain from pursuing activities solely for our own advantage and pleasure to the neglect of everything else. We will be better able to control ourselves and share what we have with others. Gratitude, linked so closely with kindness, respect, modesty, and self-control as it is, can thus enrich our human relationships and promote the welfare of individuals and society.

When learning a foreign language, the first expressions we memorize are usually "How do you do?" and "Thank you." Greeting and thanksgiving are universal customs, and expressions of gratitude have traditionally been imbued with deep meaning, as we have seen. However, in today's world, dominated by materialism as it is, such expressions have become superficial, their meaning reduced to a shell, especially in countries with advanced economies.

As a result, people tend to lack sincerity and are unable to depend on one another. True friendship becomes much harder to find, and people are less able to work well together, for they are always pursuing their own happiness to the exclusion of all else. A sense of gratitude can help cure these social diseases. Making greater efforts to thank others will render our society more livable and help to solve our environmental problems.

Why is it that we cannot also express appreciation for the fact that we are alive in this world right now and mean it? Can we imagine sacrificing ourselves out of a feeling of gratitude amounting to love? Looking back over our past, what kindnesses have we received from others that we have already forgotten?

Gratitude

BY KAREN E. BOHLIN

My father was a little boy when the stock market crashed in 1929. By the time he was ten, he knew he needed to make a contribution to the family. He worked for the local grocer pulling weeds from his garden for ten cents an hour. And he weeded his heart out. When he finally sat down and calculated that he had worked nearly three hundred hours, he realized he had earned close to thirty dollars. Instead of requesting full remuneration, he asked the grocer for a quarter to join his friends at the movie theater. He never anticipated the response. "Son, all the money you've earned has gone toward your mother's grocery bill. I do not have a quarter to give you." The refusal stunned him like a blow to the jaw. My father still remembers the store's screen door slamming behind him and his decision never to return. Crestfallen, he recounted the incident to his mother, who dissolved into tears.

He was thirteen years old when my grandfather secured a job that would bring them just enough money to build a bathroom inside the house. For a teenage boy, sharing the outhouse and washbasin with his sister and parents proved increasingly difficult. One day at school the physical education teacher asked all the boys in gym class to sit on the bleachers and take off their shoes and socks for an athlete's foot check. My father's cheeks burned as he slowly removed his socks to reveal his dirty, unwashed feet. The laughter and taunts were immediate—"Hey Blackfoot," one boy jeered. My father hung his head in shame. He was branded for the remainder of his middle school experience. Having an indoor bathroom with hot running water and an opportunity to shower was the hope he desperately held onto. When his father returned from work one evening and announced the loss of his job, the possibility of funding construction at home and my father's hopes were both shattered.

Despite these hardships, some combination of variables conspired to give my father an extraordinarily grateful heart. Perhaps it is a quality of the generation that suffered through the Great Depression. Perhaps my grandparents' resilience, fortitude, and generosity impressed him—for they had welcomed destitute friends and relatives into their home when they had nothing material to share. He never expressed anger or resentment when reflecting on his childhood. The stories he shared with us as we were growing up were tales of his parents' heroism, spirited family gatherings, experiences in World War II, and his courtship of my mother. He always taught us to give people the benefit of the doubt, not to judge a person on appearances, and never to take good things—such as the roof over our heads or the food on our table—for granted. "We have every reason to be grateful," he would remind us often, "and nothing to complain about."

In *Man's Search for Meaning*, Viktor Frankl, concentration camp survivor and psychiatrist, citing Friedrich Nietzsche (1844–1900), writes that we can endure almost any *how* if we have a compelling *why*, in other words, a *reason* to endure. Gratitude is the virtue that helps to keep those reasons before us. My father spent most of his life contributing to his family, work, and community. He was not a complainer, never lamented difficulties, and scolded us roundly if we took to whining. He was also not fond of comparisons and discouraged us from trying to keep up with the Joneses when we worried about the brand of clothing we wore or the kind of car our family drove. He would swiftly remind us to be grateful that we *had* clothes and a means of transportation. It was his deliberate effort to foster gratitude that kept our family happier and more resilient in the face of hardship.

Cicero (106–43 B.C.E.), the Roman senator and orator, wrote, "Gratitude is not only one of the greatest virtues, but it is the parent of all others." It is difficult to think about gratitude without considering the sources of our blessings. Gratitude requires a disposition of humility to realize that we are all indebted to others in some way—for our life, our learning, our livelihood, our health and safety, and so much more. Thomas Aquinas (1225–1274), the great saint and theologian, argued in his *Summa Theologica* that gratitude is part of the virtue of justice, rendering what is due to others—especially to our parents and benefactors. Gratitude, he explains, also inspires us to give God the worship and thanksgiving He deserves. In many faith traditions, gratitude to God or one's spiritual benefactors is fundamental to appreciating blessings we enjoy. The Welsh-born English poet and Anglican priest, George Herbert (1593–1633) captured this sentiment in the following lines of verse:

> Thou that has given so much to me,
> Give one thing more—a grateful heart;
> Not thankful when it pleases me,
> As if Thy blessings had spare days;
> But such a heart, whose pulse may be Thy praise.

Without a grateful heart, without appreciation for the countless pleasures, conveniences, and consolations we experience each day, we cannot truly enjoy them. Gratitude teaches us the difference between feeling entitled to comfort and happiness, which inevitably leads to disappointment, and truly possessing happiness. A grateful heart keeps us grounded in reality, cherishing and acknowledging the people, experiences, and goods that enable us to rise above our circumstances and make the best of them.

Gratitude, as we discover from countless examples in history and literature, strengthens our capacity to live nobly even in the most extreme circumstances. *Left to Tell* is a heart-wrenching autobiographical account of one woman's survival amidst the horrors of the Rwandan genocide. Immaculee Ilibagiza hid with seven other women in a small bathroom for ninety-one days listening to the unspeakable violence just outside the window. She used this time to study English with a dictionary and to drown out evil with intense prayer. It was her focus that enabled her to survive and later secure employment with the United Nations. Her deep faith enabled her to count her survival as a blessing. She began her life anew with a desire not to harbor hatred but to foster peace by forgiving the individuals who massacred her family.

In 1620, the Pilgrims, a group of settlers who left Europe for America in search of religious freedom, arrived to find a wilderness and a winter so harsh that fewer than half survived to see the spring. They dug far more graves than they built homes, and yet they turned to God with thankful hearts for the blessings they did enjoy. After eventually securing a successful harvest, the Pilgrims hosted a three-day feast in thanksgiving, to which they invited the Native Americans who had taught them to farm, hunt, and fish. This feast, proclaimed a national holiday by President Abraham Lincoln in 1863, is commemorated as Thanksgiving Day on the fourth Thursday of November. According to a 2008 Gallup Poll, Thanksgiving is the holiday Americans say brings them the most happiness.

From ancient to contemporary times, and from the perspectives of psychology and social science, gratitude has been linked to happiness. Albert W. Clarke (1916–1944), the professional English football player, put it this way: "In our daily lives, we must see that it is not happiness that makes us grateful, but gratefulness that makes us happy." Positive psychologists Martin Seligman and Jeffrey J. Froh at the University of Pennsylvania, Robert A. Emmons at the University of California Davis, and others explain that we are happier and healthier when we reflect on the specific things we have to be grateful for in our lives and personally thank people. The results of their research suggest that people who are grateful are more resilient, capable of pursuing worthy goals, more likely to help and support others, and more likely to have a positive attitude.

Gratitude is often referred to as a positive *emotion*. According to the *Merriam Webster Dictionary*, however, the word "thanks" comes from the Old English, *thanc*, which means thought, gratitude. Its Latin derivation is *tongere*, which means to know. In other words, gratitude involves knowledge and mindfulness as well as feeling. And while not highlighted as a virtue in his *Nicomachean Ethics*, gratitude meets Aristotle's requirements for moral virtue. It calls for our intelligent choice of action and reaction to the goods we receive. Like courage and self-mastery, gratitude requires a proper response to the right object or person, in the right degree and for the right reasons. In the same way that courage lies on a mean between recklessness and cowardice, gratitude lies on a mean between two vices: one of deficiency, taking all goods for granted and/or feeling entitled to them, and one of excess, seeking to ingratiate oneself with obsequious and excessive thanksgiving.

The virtue of gratitude helps us realize that we stand on the shoulders of giants—our parents and grandparents, our teachers and mentors, our friends and benefactors. Our connectedness to them strengthens and supports us. Additionally, a disposition of gratitude helps us to appreciate all natural, material, and spiritual benefits—including our talents—as gifts to be cherished and shared. As the German Lutheran pastor and theologian, Dietrich Bonhoeffer (1906–1945), argued, "In ordinary life we hardly realize that we receive a great deal more than we give, and that it is only with gratitude that life becomes rich." When we come to appreciate our *inter*dependence as more important than our *in*dependence and that every good we enjoy is a blessing, we are more likely to flourish.

Our happiness is threatened, however, when we focus on what we believe we are entitled to and do not have, such as good health, great wealth, or in my father's case, just remuneration and a hot shower. We can easily fall prey to bitterness, resentment, and envy. Additional threats to happiness include a mistaken understanding of gratitude as an exaggerated sense of indebtedness that incurs onerous obligation (for example, when someone repeatedly reminds us of all the good he has done for us in order to manipulate us or demand favors in return).

American author and lecturer Helen Keller (1880–1968), acclaimed for her valiant struggle with both deafness and blindness, observed, "So much has been given to me; I have no time to ponder that which has been denied." I am reminded of a colleague who while training for the New York marathon suffered a stroke that left her paralyzed on one side and unable to speak. After a year of therapy, she gradually began to regain her speech and movement. The speech therapy was particularly grueling, and for a long time she spoke with a pronounced stutter at a painstakingly slow rate. She came to realize that when she could not speak clearly, people not only assumed that she could not hear and began to shout at her, but they also assumed that she could not think and treated her like a young child. Suffering daily humiliation led her to appreciate the situations of individuals who live with similar impediments and permanent disabilities. She developed both patience and understanding. Appreciation expanded her purview.

For over a decade my colleagues and I have led teachers academies for educators in the most remote and underserved parts of South Carolina. Here you will find the most magnificent human beings and staggering poverty: families living in trailer homes and shacks, families with no running water or electricity, children who breakfast on Kool-Aid and walk to school barefoot. During these academies we work with primary and secondary teachers of every subject area. Together we spend five days studying and discussing what great classical and contemporary narratives reveal to us about the meaning of character and living well. After discussing Tim O'Brien's novel, *The Things They Carried*, and what the soldiers carry—including love letters and dog tags, C-Rations, ammunition, and a dead man's thumb—the teachers examine the significance of what they and their students carry, both externally and internally, and how these attitudes and material items reflect in some way who they are.

At the end of one academy, a teacher related a story about what she had been carrying for years. She recounted a tragic accident she was involved in on a Christmas Eve over ten years earlier. She and her husband were driving along in a snowstorm when a two-year-old boy darted into the street right in front of their car. They braked immediately, but it was too late. The little boy was struck. His mother, who was watching from the kitchen window, rushed outside, scooped up her son, and called an ambulance. Waiting for the ambulance to arrive, she called to the stunned couple outside and invited them into her home. Every Christmas since the tragedy, this mother invites the couple to her son's memorial service. Still deeply troubled and unable to discuss the tragedy, the woman driving the car had never related the circumstances of the event to anyone.

She chose to share this incident because it was something she had been carrying like a lead weight in her haversack. Up until this moment she had been carrying a tremendous burden. She was too consumed with guilt to accept forgiveness. Now she was able to see and relish the enormous debt of gratitude she owed the mother of this little boy.

☘   ☘   ☘

How do we develop gratitude? Gratitude does not come naturally. The British author, Aldous Huxley (1894–1963) once said, "Most human beings have an almost infinite capacity for taking things for granted." Thus, gratitude must be learned and practiced. Gratitude can be developed in many ways. Social scientists advise us to keep gratitude journals and record everyday experiences that constitute blessings in our lives. Leaving the places where we work better than we found them is a way of showing our appreciation for the use of shared spaces. Recycling, taking care of the environment, and conserving energy, natural, and technological resources are among the countless ways we can show gratitude for the goods available to us.

One of the most practical ways we can develop gratitude is by thanking people for the good they do for us. In the famous parable of the ten lepers, Jesus heals ten men of their disease, yet only one returns to thank him for this miraculous cure. Jesus is grateful for his thanksgiving and asks him, "Where are the other nine?" This story reminds us of the need to express our thanks and not to take the good that happens to us for granted. Thanking people in person and writing notes of gratitude are small gestures of thoughtfulness that convey genuine appreciation.

Too often, especially in service industries such as hospitality and education, we fail to pay attention to the thousand and one details professionals get right and only notice when something is missing or has gone wrong. Writing a note of commendation to the manager of someone who has provided an exceptional service and copying the person on the letter is a great practice. Sending our compliments to the chef for a well-prepared meal—whether it is at home or in a four-star restaurant—is another tangible way to show our thanks. We can acknowledge the services we receive each day by thanking the cashier at the local grocery store and the mechanic at the garage. Leaving a note for a colleague who helped us across the finish line of a project, returning a favor, or writing a letter acknowledging a teacher's generous assistance are all powerful ways to communicate gratitude. In the words of G.B. Stern, the English novelist, playwright, and literary critic (1890–1973), "Silent gratitude isn't much use to anyone." We need to put it in words.

Another practical way to develop gratitude is to refine our lenses of wonder and awe. One of my students, Mary Grace, at age twelve wrote the following as part of her short essay on thanksgiving: "I feel that if wonder did not exist, the world would be bland and monotonous." Noticing and appreciating the beauty of the natural world around us provides a compelling reason to be grateful. The great scientist and inventor, Albert Einstein (1879–1955), summed it up this way, "There are only two ways to live your life. One as though nothing is a miracle. The other as though everything is a miracle."

We can also develop the habit of appreciation by learning to choose our words wisely. Proverbs 18:21 reminds us that "the instruments of both life and death are contained in the power of the tongue." Katherine, a sixteen-year-old student, initiated a gratitude project in her school by asking students to track the number of times they complain and to begin replacing complaints—negative words and reactions—with words of appreciation and thanks. She asked students to wear a bracelet on one arm and move it to the other arm whenever they caught themselves whining or complaining. The longer they could keep the bracelet on the original arm, the better. To foster a spirit of gratitude, she challenged the whole school to a complaint-free week.

Gratitude is fundamentally a choice of attitude. The American poet and essayist Walt Whitman (1819–1892) said, "Keep your face always toward the sunshine, and shadows will fall behind you." These are not trite considerations for the foolish optimist; they are dispositions we have the power to cultivate. When a student of mine was diagnosed with a deadly form of cancer at the age of seventeen, she decided that she wanted to dedicate the few hours she had of feeling well each week to enjoying the simple things of ordinary life: relishing the company of family and friends, doing homework, and attending class with her peers. After several rounds of chemotherapy, missed school, chronic weakness, and the loss of all her hair, her mother offered to take her on a special shopping trip so she could buy whatever she wanted. Her response was swift. "Mom, I don't need material things to make me happy… But, thank you anyway."

We can nurture a grateful heart by taking note of the infinite number of selfless things people do for us. On a train ride from Boston to New York, I was talking with a mother whose son is thriving in a new charter school. One of the great challenges for her ten-year-old son, however, is abiding by the strict dress code.

The boys are required to wear a belt every day, as the school is deliberately countering the baggy pants hanging loose and low, a look sported by gang members. If they arrive without a belt, they must return home and get a belt before they can attend class. When this boy set off for school, he walked a few blocks, greeted the crossing guard, and entered the subway. He realized right before his stop that he was not wearing a belt. He panicked momentarily but knew exactly what he had to do. He exited the train, turned right around, and returned by subway to his home neighborhood. As he started across the street back to his house, the crossing guard asked, "What happened? I just saw you leave." Rushing ahead he responded, "I forgot my belt. Can't go into school without my belt." Without giving it a second thought, the crossing guard took off his own belt and gave it to him. "Here, hurry back to school so you're not late." The boy was not only grateful for the belt, his entry ticket to school, but he was also moved by the instinctive response of the crossing guard, whom he hardly knew. At the end of the school day, he returned the belt with effusive thanks.

Finally, we can develop a keener sense of appreciation by deliberately focusing on the positive and reframing the negative in our lives. A friend of mine is a former Olympic athlete and America's Cup sailor. She is also an inspired speaker and author of books on performance excellence. One would never know that she was orphaned as a child, lived in several foster homes, and endured a painful upbringing. She is living testimony of what is possible if we follow the sage advice of the great English novelist Charles Dickens, "Reflect upon your present blessings, of which every man has plenty; not on your past misfortunes, of which all men have some."

CHAPTER 5

Wisdom

"Wisdom and virtue are like the two wheels of a cart."
—Japanese

⁗ ⁗

This chapter will deepen and enrich our understanding of this essential virtue. In the first essay, the authors illustrate that more than simply utilizing knowledge or skill, wisdom entails applying it with the correct spirit of the master. Two aspects of wisdom, it explains, are the one within the realm of daily affairs and that of the great religious and moral teachers. The ability to distinguish between right and wrong is linked to the ethical obligation of education, the wise and moral application of what one learns. We are introduced to the founder of Panasonic, who wrote eloquently on the role of the corporation within society as well as on honesty, fairness, and gratitude, and the story of a courageous visionary in the realm of public works from the Edo period, as illustrations of how wisdom embraces elements of other virtues—justice, benevolence, courage, and self-reflection. The Eastern emphasis on cooperation and concession, of listening and dialogue, of respecting the situation of others, and "tempering justice with compassion" instead of being rigid and opinionated shine through in this piece. To cultivate wisdom, it encourages us to be aware of the intrinsic value of something as well as to learn from those more experienced than ourselves.

The second essay opens with the well-known Old Testament story of King Solomon and two women who laid claim to the same baby. Again, this view recognizes wisdom as something greater than simple intelligence, as the quality that enables one to synthesize knowledge "in order to form good judgments and actions." Wisdom is dubbed "the executive virtue," for through it one can direct the other virtues toward living a happy life. The author also points to the importance of learning from others in the acquisition or development of wisdom: he illustrates a parent's duty to guide children to realize their own worth and acquire wisdom, referencing the Plains Indians' vision quest, a time of reflection and isolation in which the young person can come to understand and embrace his or her unique role in life. Wisdom is not something one has or does not have, but rather something one cultivates through reflection and experience, sifting through the myriad sources of information and knowledge in our lives. It entails rising above a what's-in-it-for-me attitude and thinking of the greater good, and what is true.

Wisdom

BY KAZUNOBU HORIUCHI AND JUN YAMADA

Once upon a time in feudal Japan, there lived a samurai named Shouken, whose life was made miserable by a fierce, old rat that had taken up residence in his house. Finally, he could stand the pest no longer. Asking his friends for the loan of some cats known to be good rat catchers, he let the cats loose in the house. But all to no avail. Next, Shouken tried to dispatch the rat with his wooden practice sword, but he was constantly foiled by the agility and cunning of the beast. Near despair, he sought out the owner of an old cat known for its mastery of the art of rat catching. The man took pity on Shouken and lent him the cat.

Bringing it into the room where the rat lay, he expected to see it bound forward and leap on its prey. The cat did nothing of the kind. Rather, it approached the rat step by slow step. To Shouken's surprise, the rat failed to react as it had done on previous occasions. Instead of scuttling away immediately, it remained utterly motionless in one corner of the room, apparently paralyzed by terror. The old cat sauntered right up to it, effortlessly pinned its neck between its teeth, and took it outside to dispose of it.

Other cats quickly learned of what had happened. Intrigued, they decided to invite the old master cat back to Shouken's house to discuss the matter. A tabby cat and a gray one told of their lack of success with this rat, and then a black cat spoke as follows:

"I come from a family famous for its skill in hunting rats. Ever since I was a kitten, I have dreamed of becoming a virtuoso rat catcher, and I early sought out a master of the craft to learn all that

I could. Under his advice I constantly broadened and improved my skills. I practiced jumping over high obstacles and slipping through tiny holes, hour after hour. I also became adept at strategies like playing dead or surprising a rat while pretending to be asleep. Yet despite all my training and experience, I could not get anywhere near snaring that old rat. I have disgraced myself."

Then the old cat turned to the black cat and said: "It is true that you learned from your master the skills and knowledge we all need for the successful hunting of rats. Your master instructed you well in them, but they were just part of his teaching on the right way to complete your task. In listening to him, you focused only on technique, without seeking to comprehend the selfless spirit of your master. You may perfect your skills all you wish, but you will not enter the way of the cat until you try to learn your master's spirit. Without this, in the worst case, you may even misuse all your skills." (Translated and adapted from "Zen to Kuu-kan," in *A Sequel to Zen and Japanese Culture, Complete Works of Daisetsu Suzuki*.)

This story of the cat and the rat, simple as it appears, had a very important meaning for Daisetsu Suzuki (1870–1966), the eminent scholar of Japanese Buddhism who introduced Zen Buddhism to the English-speaking world. It summed up for him much of the essence of Zen, a branch of Buddhism founded by Bodhidharma in India in the sixth century B.C.E. and introduced to Japan by Buddhist monks such as Eisai and Dogen in the twelfth and thirteenth centuries.

This Zen truth, though, is also a universal one—that seeking for and relying on techniques and knowledge is less important than mastering the fundamental spirit of something. Our greatest need, in fact, is for the wisdom that gives direction and meaning to human powers like skill and knowledge. The black cat in the story concentrated on amassing knowledge and honing his skills, but he should also have tried to grasp something of much greater value, his master's spirit, which is wisdom. So it is with us. We are often successful in our pursuit of knowledge and skills. Having once acquired them, however, we may misuse our gains, to the detriment of society and sometimes even to the point of self-destruction.

So we need a clear understanding of the difference between wisdom and knowledge and how these virtues relate to one another. Attaining this may help us discover secrets that can make our lives happier and more meaningful, as well as lead eventually to the building of a peaceful society.

🍀　🍀　🍀

What is wisdom, as a virtue? In Japanese, it takes two words to define it fully: *chie* and *eichi*. *Chie* refers to wisdom as it appears in the sphere of ordinary life, at home or at work. This is not just the fruit of practical experience, important as this may be. It also has a moral dimension, being defined as "the mental activity that leads us to discern the truth of things and to judge what is right and what is wrong." And since, in the Japanese worldview, there is no clear distinction between the sacred and the profane, it also has a religious flavor to it. *Chie* is the first part of a continuum of wisdom that ascends to *eichi*, which is "the intelligence which enables men to understand profound truth," and which is the essence of the higher ranges of existence, such as the ascetic religious life. *Eichi*, then, is simply superior *chie*.

How does this differ from knowledge and skills? In daily life, we use the words *knowledge* and *wisdom* almost interchangeably. But are they really the same? Kounosuke Matsushita (1894–1989), an eminent Japanese businessmen and the founder of Panasonic (formerly Matsushita) Electric Works Ltd., distinguishes between *knowledge*, meaning the information that someone possesses, and *wisdom*, the ability to distinguish between right and wrong. On this basis, he concludes that the essence of wisdom is revealed in the way in which wise people "use their knowledge." (*Kounosuke Matsushita's Daily Maxims: Wisdom of Working, Wisdom of Living.*)

That wisdom is formed only of knowledge that has a moral dimension has long been understood in the East. In China, for instance, Confucius believed that human sincerity is based on knowledge and that those who behave morally are truly erudite. Confucianism taught that anyone deserving to be called a man of virtue must also be considered a person of great learning. In Buddhism, Gautama Siddhartha was spiritually awakened to a recognition of the law of the universe. But this happened only after he emerged from a state of spiritual darkness in which he could neither see nor hear nor think in the right way. Having gained his profound wisdom, Gautama came to be called Buddha, one who has been enlightened. The oldest extant document of Japanese thought, the *Records of Ancient Matters*, tells how, of the three Imperial Regalia of Japan (the sword, the mirror, and the jewel), the mirror symbolizes knowledge, and the jewel represents moral character.

These examples indicate that true knowledge contains true morality and vice versa; as people gain in knowledge, then, they ideally become more moral and virtuous. If so, we must accept responsibility for using our knowledge ethically and morally. Whenever we employ any of the information or skills we possess, our purpose must be guided by wisdom.

Eichi, the world of the outstanding wisdom of great religious and moral teachers, blends imperceptibly, as we have said, into *chie*, the wisdom of the mundane. So where in our daily lives can we find it, and how does it help us towards the realization of happiness?

The expression *mottainai* has long been in common use in Japan. But recently it has attracted worldwide attention after Wangari Muta Maathai (1940–2011), a Kenyan environmental protection activist, visited Japan the year after she won the 2004 Nobel Peace Prize. She was greatly impressed by the spirit of *mottainai* she found in Japanese culture. Before ending her visit she expressed a wish to introduce the word to the world, and since then she has used it frequently as a key concept in caring for the environment.

Mottainai is a compound of *mottai*, a Buddhist term describing the essence of a thing and *nai*, which negates the noun *mottai*. The meaning thus becomes "what a waste not to use the worth of something to the full." The brief word *mottainai* encapsulates the wisdom revealed in the care with which Japanese people consume food or other objects in their daily lives.

Maathai learned the essence of this term from a number of experiences. Here are just a few that she has talked about. One is the gratitude shown by Japanese people in the way they ensure that they eat every part of a meal that has been served to them. This attitude, according to Maathai, is a clear sign that the spirit of *mottainai* exists in the heart. People explained to her how, in childhood, their parents at home and their teachers in kindergarten instructed them that it was impolite to leave any part of a meal uneaten; they should consume everything set before them, down to the last grain of rice, since it had all been produced with the utmost care by farmers.

Japanese people, Maathai found, display the same feeling of gratitude towards the animals and plants they consume, and even towards inanimate objects that they use. For example, the whole of a fish, including its head, internal organs, bones, and skin, is used in cooking. This practice reflects the perception that human beings, standing at the top of the food chain, exist only at the expense of all other living things; therefore, they should show appreciation towards every single one of them by wasting nothing of what they have to offer. The same is true even of inanimate things, as can be seen in customs such as *hari-kuyou* and *fude-kuyou*, memorial services for broken brushes and rusty needles, respectively. When people find that such tools can no longer be used, they do not throw them away. Rather, they bring them to their local temple or shrine and extend to these objects their appreciation for the hard work they have done, as if they were human.

Maathai was also struck by how the Japanese part with used items (Jap. *osagari*). One example of this is the handing down of clothes that older children have outgrown to their younger siblings or other children in the neighborhood. This tradition, though observed less and less frequently in recent years, was, Maathai thought, an example of the "Japanese custom of reuse."

Today, of course, we live in a highly advanced consumer society. Shops are packed with disposable commodities. An endless stream of relatively inexpensive goods, from computers to electrical appliances and shoes, flows through consumer-driven markets, and industry is so structured that buying a replacement is usually cheaper than repairing an existing model. As a result, our lives as consumers have certainly become much more convenient and comfortable than in the past. But in the process we have also lost the spirit of using things carefully. Given the society in which we live, the wisdom of *mottainai* is one of the key concepts that can keep us attuned to the dignity of life and the importance of inanimate objects.

Our highly developed consumer society devours huge amounts of natural resources; the more advanced it becomes, the more serious is the depletion of those resources. In this context, the wisdom of *mottainai* can add a deeper resonance to our concern to protect the environment that is embodied in, for example, the "three Rs": Recycle, Reuse, and Reduce. Human beings have a duty to safeguard our planet, which nurtures us all, and it is our responsibility to preserve all the other forms of life that share the earth with us. Our well-being, our happiness, is incompatible with a damaged environment. Cherishing and nurturing the spirit of *mottainai*, that is, our sense of love towards all living and inanimate things on earth, can only improve our lives.

In daily life we are not just consumers, though. We are also producers, supplying services or goods for others to consume. So where is wisdom to be found in this sphere? The owner of a private company and an entrepreneur in the public sector provides us with some clues.

♣   ♣   ♣

We have already mentioned Kounosuke Matsushita, the founder of Panasonic. He developed a unique approach to economic activity as the manager of a large company in one of the leading sectors of Japanese industry, that of electrical appliances. In his *Philosophy of Kounosuke Matsushita: How to Live, How to Prosper*, he accepts that "the economy is the basis which supports human life… We humans cannot live without the economy." His wisdom allowed him to see that many surprising conclusions could be drawn from this simple fact.

One very important part of his philosophy was the concept that corporations exist for society and people. Based on his belief that "business belongs to the public," Matsushita referred to the "spirit of patriotism through industrialization" as the first of his company's precepts. This idea also found expression in his 1929 outline of the principles of his company. He wrote, "We are resolutely determined to consider it the duty of businessmen to plan to improve and enhance the quality of our society and life, thus contributing to the development of the culture of the world." If corporations pursue profits to the exclusion of all else, the results can be distressing; they may pollute the environment with industrial waste, for instance, or treat their employees unjustly. Matsushita, by contrast, compared his employees to uncut diamonds and paid great attention to their training and education. When asked, "What does Matsushita Electric Works produce?" he replied, "Matsushita produces fine people, as well as fine electrical appliances." Believing that a fine corporation should create a fine, supportive environment for the whole community, Matsushita took the moral character of his company very seriously. He was also firmly of the opinion that corporations should not seek and depend on financial backing from the government. Just the reverse, in fact: they should act to underpin government and contribute to the advancement of society.

A second element of Matsushita's wisdom was his respect for the spirit of fairness and honesty. He said that for a business to succeed in gaining the trust of its customers, the secret was openness. So, when introducing a new product to the market, for instance, one should not try to cheat customers by charging an exorbitant price. Instead, following the dictates of the conscience, one should let potential customers know the cost price of the product. Resorting to deception with the aim of making a large profit was a sure way to lose the trust of customers and see one's business fail. This was because one was choosing to rely on human knowledge that did not derive from the wisdom of the great religious and moral teachers of mankind.

A third ingredient of Matsushita's wisdom was the spirit of *kansha-houon*. This means the repaying of blessings or benefits received from divine beings, nature, acts of human kindness, and so on, with appreciation and gratitude. Matsushita, contending that this is the most advanced form of moral behavior, thought that its origins could be found in the spirit that actuated a sage Gautama Siddhartha or Confucius. He wrote:

> How happy and how much gratitude he must have felt to be born as a human and how important it was, he must have felt, to repay blessings of this gratitude... The spirit of *kansha-houon* is a source of happiness which gives us human beings the utmost hope and joy, power and progress.

We learn from Matsushita's wisdom as the founder of a private enterprise that managing such a company is not a private but a public undertaking, with the aim of developing fine human beings and building one's nation; that fairness is indispensable in business; and that business transactions based on the spirit of *kansha-houon* will, in times of trial, support us in our sufferings. His belief that a company is not its founder's private possession, and that it should be endowed with a public quality in the conduct of its business, has much in common with the thinking of Eiichi Shibusawa (1840–1931), the "father of Japanese capitalism," who founded and managed some five hundred different companies and institutions, including the Tokyo Stock Exchange and the First National Bank.

It is clear that such practical wisdom differs widely from what passes for knowledge in shortsighted and shallow-minded individuals. It is equally evident that it derives from the wisdom of the great religious and moral teachers of mankind, and contributes not only to the happiness of our social and economic lives as individuals but to the stability and peace of society as a whole.

Both Matsushita and Shibusawa exerted great influence over later generations of Japanese business people. Someone else who did the same lived in earlier, feudal times, during Japan's Edo period. Sontoku Ninomiya (1787–1856) was an eminent agricultural practitioner, as well as a philosopher, moralist, and economist. He devoted his whole life to public works, especially the reconstruction and improvement of villages. As a result, in the course of the twentieth century, statues of him were placed in the corner of every elementary school playground across Japan as a model of diligence. Today he is still considered an outstanding national figure. What can we learn from his wisdom? One episode from his life is particularly worth pondering.

Ninomiya received an order from his lord Tadazane Oukubo (1778–1837), the ruler of Odawara Han (domain), to reconstruct a village in Shimotsuki-no-kuni (the present-day Ninomiya Cho in Tochigi Prefecture, north of Tokyo), and duly crafted a careful plan for the purpose. However, the peasant villagers and even the local administrator did not understand it and refused to cooperate with him. Ninomiya in turn criticized the local administrator and villagers for their lack of understanding and support and tried to push ahead. But he could make no progress. Thwarted, he realized how the stalemate had revealed the limitations of his knowledge and skills and saw the need to seek divine wisdom.

Ninomiya decided to visit Archbishop Shouin at the Shinshou-ji Temple in what is now the city of Narita in Chiba Prefecture.

Shouin advised him that rather than imposing his own plan and methods for implementing it, he should wait patiently until his opponents came around and offered their cooperation willingly. So Ninomiya stayed at the temple for approximately three weeks and underwent hard discipline there. He fasted, read the Buddhist sutras, and washed himself in the open air with cold water, all in the hope of obtaining divine help to resolve this impasse. On the twenty-first night after beginning this ascetic regime, Ninomiya had a dream. In it, he was taught that one cannot move others by justice alone. Benevolence also is needed. On awaking, he interpreted the dream as a message from the Shinto gods and Buddha offering him divine wisdom, and he examined himself searchingly in the light both of the dream and the archbishop's advice.

Returning to the village, he was surprised to find that the local administrator who had resisted him had been recalled to Odawara and replaced, and that the villagers were now ready to cooperate with him. The reconstruction of Sakura-machi proceeded apace and the work was finally finished after ten years.

Three lessons can be learned from this episode. The first is that justice by itself will not touch and move people's hearts. One may feel entirely justified in reprimanding the uneducated, impolite, or lazy, or those who violate the law, but this only arouses their hostility. Benevolence must also be given its place. It is far better to forgive such people and persuade them patiently and benevolently until they change their minds and attitudes voluntarily.

The story is, secondly, a warning against *chuukin no hei* (blind loyalty). The more seriously and assiduously Ninomiya pursued his plan, the wider the psychological distance between him and the local people became, and the more serious the antagonism towards his person and plan grew. The reason for this was his loyalty to his lord. Confident that his efforts were entirely praiseworthy, he became self-righteous and grew more and more critical of the negligence of others. Only later, when he began to examine his own thinking and behavior critically, did Ninomiya realize that he had become a prisoner of *chuukin no hei* and had to work to free himself of its bondage.

While the freedom to express one's opinion to others is very important, especially in the public arena, it is just as vital to understand the situation of those listening. Concessions and compromise may sometimes be the right course. In practical terms, even when one is entirely in the right, sticking rigidly to one's own opinion in the face of the objections of others makes it very difficult to find common ground. From the perspective of higher wisdom, too, a focus on justice or righteousness to the exclusion of all else is an error. One must respect the situation of others and make concessions to them, tempering justice with compassion and benevolence. Contact with someone guided by higher wisdom eventually teaches one the importance of mutual concessions in the search for common ground, to the benefit of everyone involved and society at large.

The last lesson taught by Ninomiya's anecdote is that wisdom is attained through experience, especially of the hardships of life. After undergoing the privations of the temple regimen, he realized that "there were neither foes nor friends when I gazed around me, but only hubris in my own heart." So he recognized that, no matter how mean the opposition to him in the village had been, he had to free himself of anger, hatred, and grudges, to be forgiving and to assume the entire responsibility for what had happened. In overcoming his vexation, Ninomiya attained a state of mind comparable to that of the great religious teachers and confirmed the truth of what Aeschylus (525–456 B.C.E.), the first great tragedian of ancient Greece, wrote in his *Agamemnon*: "πάθει μάθος"—"through suffering, wisdom[or understanding]."

All of us, then, would be well advised not to avoid any of the difficulties that come our way. Rather, we should accept and treat them as clues to a wisdom that can change our lives in a positive way. And even when others obstruct us in our pursuit of what is right, we too can learn, like Sontoku Ninomiya, how forgiveness

and compassion, not hatred, grudges or anger, truly pave the path
of wisdom.

♣   ♣   ♣

The virtue of wisdom exists, as we have seen, in a wide variety of
contexts: in religious traditions, in the work of the great religious
and moral teachers of humankind, and in the daily lives of individuals, among them business entrepreneurs and an agricultural
expert in Japan. Here, finally, we will explore ways to deepen our
understanding of such wisdom in our own daily lives.

One very important quality that can enrich our daily lives is
kizuki, the awareness or realization that something is of interest
and value. Human perception largely depends on how much interest we take in things. Walking along the street, for example, we
may completely fail to notice things that do not interest us. For all
practical purposes, it is as if they did not exist in the world. But it
need not be so. *Kizuki* can be triggered by anything. Say someone's
attention is attracted by a dog barking. That may be enough to
awaken an interest in dogs where there was none before, and once
attuned, the person will rapidly discover how many different types
of dogs are walked by their owners in the neighborhood. Immediately when we become aware of something, our field of vision is
enlarged, influencing the way we look at things. In this way, a sense
of curiosity and a willingness to become interested expand our ho-
rizons, and this growth of awareness leads to wisdom.

In the course of our daily lives, there is much we can learn from
our families, our teachers at school, friends, neighbors, or colleagues at work. A great variety of wisdom is available to us if only
we look for it; above all, it is vital that we seek out those in society
with experience. At work, we can acquire wisdom as well as knowledge and skills from the supervision and guidance of our superiors, from the experience of starting a business, or from negotiating

with clients, to take just a few examples. Students can learn much of value from internships or part-time jobs.

When faced with obstacles in life, advice can be sought from one's family, colleagues, friends, teachers at school, or anyone whom one respects and aspires to emulate. However, when frustration sets in after a disagreement of opinion with somebody, no matter how small and trivial the matter may appear to be, it is advisable to try to practice self-examination as a way of fostering a spirit of forgiveness towards one's opponent, instead of blaming another individual or group.

By way of conclusion, let us return to the insight of Socrates. He believed that consistently asking oneself what is most important for mankind and what is the nature of wisdom is conducive to living a good life and eventually to improving one's own moral character. Might it not be a good idea, then, for everyone to ask themselves, on a daily basis, "What is wisdom?"

Wisdom

BY KEVIN RYAN

One of the most well-known stories in the Bible recounts how King Solomon settled a dispute between two mothers and demonstrated his profound wisdom. Two women, Lena and Mona, lived in the same house and bore infant boys within three days of one another. They were friends and had helped one another in the birthing of their babies.

One morning, a few weeks after the births, Mona woke up early and discovered that in the night she had rolled over on her child and smothered him. Heartbroken and distraught, she conceived a wicked plan. She took her dead infant to the bed where Lena was sleeping with her infant son and quietly exchanged the babies. Shortly after, Lena awoke, discovered the dead baby, and became hysterical with grief. Mona came to comfort her. But then Lena noticed that the dead baby was smaller and had more hair than hers. She accused Mona of the foul deed.

The two women and the baby boy were brought before King Solomon. He asked what brought them to his court, and each told her version of the story. After questioning each of the women, Solomon told them to wait while he retired to consider the case. After a short time, he returned and summoned the two women, asking them again whose child it was. Both strongly proclaimed the baby was theirs. At that, Solomon called for one of his guards to bring him a sword. Then he asked for the baby. Holding the sword and the baby, he said, "The only fair way to settle this is to divide the baby…to cut him in half and give half a child to each of you."

As he handed the sword to his guard, Lena cried out, "No, my King. Give the baby to Mona. Let him live. Please, let him live." Mona, then, turned to Solomon and said, "Go ahead, my King. Yours is a fair decision." At that, Solomon said to his guard, "Put down your sword and give this baby to Lena. She is the true mother. Only a true mother would let me give her child to another in order to save its life. The words of these two women have revealed to me what is true."

While it is doubtful King Solomon would have gone forward with the cold-blooded slaughter of a child, he nevertheless was taking a chance before his court. He had heard the accounts of the two women, knew that one was a liar, and had to come up with a correct decision. He removed himself from the court, carefully reviewed what he had heard, and came up with a way to bring the truth to light.

Throughout history, the method of *splitting the difference* when dealing with counter claims has been used to settle disputes. Solomon knew the law, but he also knew the human mind and, even more, the human heart. He played upon the women's familiarity with this procedure and what he knew of a mother's love for her child. The course of action he chose is emblematic of what has come to be called the *wisdom of Solomon*.

🍀   🍀   🍀

Dictionaries variously define wisdom as "the quality that implies the ability to judge and deal with people" or "the ability to discern inner qualities and relationships." The collective meaning of wisdom is the sum of all the teachings of wise people throughout the ages. While the word implies intelligence, wisdom is much more than that. It is more than the accumulation of great sums of information and knowledge. It is a quality, a singular quality, of being able to marshal facts and impressions and synthesize them in order to form good judgments and actions.

Wisdom is socially recognized. Whether or not we ourselves are wise, we recognize those who are. They are anchored to reality. They are trustworthy. We sense that they are motivated by the right thing. Their judgments and interpretations are not tainted by self-interest or particular prejudices. They are able to sort through paralyzing complexities and point the way.

While we may yearn for wise leaders, they are, in fact, rare. We find more *effective* leaders than truly *wise* leaders. Effective leaders have the skills and qualities to draw people to them and their causes. Part of their capacity as leaders is to elicit from within us an emotional response and a desire to follow them. The effective leader is able to inspire loyalty and move us to action. Sometimes that action is flawed or unsound. While Solomon may have been both an effective leader and a man of wisdom, the combination is uncommon.

As a young man in my late twenties, I was fortunate to have a brush with wisdom. Unmarried and busy as a public school teacher, I was regularly asked on visits home by my much revered father, "Well, son, what are you going to do next?" and, "Son, do you know where you are going?" My father, a businessman, neither fully understood nor quite approved of my chosen occupation as a teacher and my interest in education. After parrying these questions for a few years, surrender seemed the best option, and I grudgingly asked, "Dad, what do you think I should be doing with my life?" He answered, "I don't know, but I know a man who's been an educator all his life, and maybe you should speak to him." With little enthusiasm and rather low expectations, I made an appointment with my father's friend, who turned out to be the retired dean of the Harvard Business School and who was currently an official at the prestigious Ford Foundation.

Going to New York City from the upstate town where I taught and meeting with a "significant man" was an experience in itself. Expecting to be "talked to" by this eightyish-year-old man, I discovered that instead I was being interviewed. He was asking the questions. At one point, he asked, "Do you have a life plan?" As I fumbled to answer his question, we both realized that I had no plan. Grasping for something to say, I asked, "Did you have a plan?" Quietly and modestly, and switching to the present tense, he said, "Yes. I have a thirty year plan." He then told me that his plan for the first thirty years of his life was to prepare himself through education and work experiences for the second thirty years. He saw this as preparation for making what he called "some contribution to society." These second thirty years he referred to as his "career years," in his case lived as a professor of business and in academic administration. "This last third," and here he ruefully remarked that he hoped to reach 90, "I want to do the good I didn't have time to do before I could retire. That was and is my plan, and I'm trying to keep to it." While intrigued by the particulars of this man's life journey, what was new to me was the idea of sitting down and consciously constructing a well thought-out life plan. I had met a wise man.

We tend to associate wisdom with age and maturity. Wisdom seems to be built from many experiences, either firsthand or gained from careful observation of the lives of others. There is a Yiddish term, *menshen kenner*, that describes a person who is able to accurately assess another person's true character. This often takes time and experience, so a popular embodiment of wisdom is the village sage or the wise grandmother or grandfather or anyone who has accumulated and reflected on human events. There are, however, even wise children.

Among a group of elementary or high school students, someone will emerge with the qualities we associate with the wise person. The depth of experience and knowledge of human strengths and foibles may be lacking, but we recognize their good judgment, their ability to be objective and not moved by the opinions of peers. College dormitories are petri dishes for such discoveries. Away from home and family and experiencing new freedoms, college students often find themselves mired in mistakes. Alone and coping desperately with difficulties, they seek guidance from those around them. At such moments, an otherwise unnoticed student emerges as a wise listener and guide. He or she becomes the "go-to person." While we celebrate the existence of wise young people, the hazard of the false guru or easy advice giver is ever present. For some, appearing wise and offering advice is a means to ingratiation or control. It would seem that it requires a touch of wisdom from a young person to recognize wisdom amid peers.

In most advanced nations, the schooling of the young starts early and lasts long. Modern life is nothing if not complex, and its complexity grows daily. There are new facts to digest and new technologies to master. There are new theories to explain the error of older theories. There are new voices that must be listened to, and new skills required of us if we are to keep up. In turn, national leaders across the globe claim, "Education is my first priority," and "Our nation must become a learning society."

This ubiquitous drive for education and self-development is all around us. It is spurred by our natural instinct to learn and also our survival instincts to grow and to prosper. Perhaps this is all well and good. However, it may be the case that the pace of societal change and the drive for more information is, in fact, the enemy of wisdom.

The great majority of people in the modern world are surrounded by sources of information—from books, radio and television, the Internet, and DVDs. Ideas and facts and knowledge pour at us and over us continually. What, then, is the relationship between this barrage of information and wisdom? One can know a great deal of facts but not be wise. The answer would appear to be in what we do with the information, how we *process* it. The accurate processing of what comes to us through our senses takes skill. Human beings early in life develop filters that distort the raw data we take in. Someone once said that it is a natural human tendency to make ourselves the hero of our own stories. We see and hear the world the way we desire to hear it. Also, our egos are continually at work on our memories, frail organs that they are, revising the actual past events of our lives so that we were the right ones in a conflict, or the one who did the actual "good deed," or the one who played the constructive role in a past event. We are the one in the family who came to the aid of a parent in distress. We are the one in the company who warned of what turned out to be a bad decision. We are the heroes in our life's story. The wise person, on the other hand, flees from such self-delusion.

Throughout human history, religious leaders and philosophers have told us that the purpose of our lives should be to seek happiness, and that the path to happiness is to cultivate within ourselves virtues, those excellences of mind and character that enable us to flourish as human beings. Wisdom, however, is unique among the virtues because it is through wisdom that we come to understand the meaning of a good life. The wise person steers his life to that end. His wisdom directs the other virtues of courage, respect, and responsibility to contribute to happiness and a flourishing life. Wisdom, then, can be called the executive virtue. Like my early mentor, the wise executive has a good plan.

Adults should not only guide their lives by having a worthy plan, but they should also aid those following them in the same pursuit. Parents, in particular, should be helping their children develop worthy goals and the means to attain them. While many parents do, many are casual about this. The Plains Indians of North America are instructive in the way they raise their children. They believe that each child has a contribution to make to the tribe, to its overall health and success. Further, they are convinced that each child must discover for himself what his special contribution is. Therefore, at an early age the young person sets out on a "vision quest." He or she engages in a number of practices to prepare to receive an understanding of the purpose of his or her individual life. This is done through prayer, fasting, meditation, and living in isolation, separated for a while from the tribe. The vision quest focus on self-discipline and introspective prayer leads to the individual's understanding and embracing his unique plan for life. This intense process is part of the Plains Indians' commitment to a lifelong pursuit of wisdom, a concept involving mind, body, and soul. Such an individual vision or life goal is embedded in an ancient civilization, which is hardly available to those of us living in the modern world. The question, however, remains: How does a person gain the virtue of wisdom?

The very form of the question, "How does a person *gain* the virtue of wisdom?" is, however, flawed. To say someone *has wisdom* does not mean he or she has the correct, judicious answer to all questions. Wisdom is not a commodity like gold or wheat. It is not a human attribute like intelligence, which lends itself to testing and measurement. To *have wisdom* is rather a way of being, a habit of considering our experiences and making prudent judgments. Wisdom is less an attainment than an approach.

Like all virtues, wisdom is an acquired disposition to act deliberately and thoughtfully. One path to approaching wisdom is cultivating the habit of reflection, a habit that becomes more and more difficult as our worlds become increasingly rife with printed words, media screens of various kinds, and voices insisting on our attention. While this rich flow of information and ideas can be a great benefit, it is leaving modern men and women with little time to process the data of our lives for meaning. Reflection, then, which we will take up in more detail in the following chapter, is nothing more than stepping back from the noise and quietly asking ourselves, "What does this mean? What is this experience revealing to me?"

❦   ❦   ❦

Many years ago when my first daughter was five or six months old, a philosopher friend rested his hand on her head and uttered, "What is the code? What is the code?" When I asked him what he meant, he said, "That is what she is asking herself. You can feel the mental energy. She will never be as engaged in understanding what is going on as she is now. She is desperately trying to figure out what all the noise and sights around her are so she can order it all and then manage it. She is trying to break the code." Reflection is a quieter, less desperate attempt to understand the deeper meanings of what is occurring around us.

From our infancy to our current stage, we have learned much of the code with the aid of languages, both verbal and non-verbal. We also have learned to discern the differences between simple categories of friend-or-foe and hot-and-cold to the more demanding categories of material-or-spiritual and dictatorial-or-democratic. While our processing of the stimuli of our everyday lives into categories is crucial and somewhat automatic, it often leads to pre-judging, to prejudices, and to false interpretations. The habit of reflecting back on events and seeing clearly the "inputs" of our lives is key to moving toward wisdom.

Contemplating the events of our own lives can be disappointing, embarrassing, and painful. Mistakes are in the woof and warp of life. Our actions may humiliate us in our own eyes and in the eyes of others. We want to sweep them off our mental table. We want, as mentioned above, to make ourselves the heroes of our life stories. On the other hand, candid reflections on our failings enlighten our path to wisdom.

Some speak of reflection as taking the "aerial view," of stepping back and looking at situations objectively, trying to see the big picture. One major problem with trying to attain an objective view is our subjectivity. Our self-focus and self-interests are natural human instincts and part of our survival system. The Stoic Greek philosopher, Epictetus (55–135 C.E.), wrote, "On the occasion of every accident that befalls you, remember to turn to yourself and inquire what power you have for turning it to use." Presumably, the use to which Epictetus directs us is to something that advances mankind in general. With that in mind, unless we are able to rise above our "what's-in-it-for-me" impulses, our reflection will lead us down other paths than the path toward wisdom. Above all, it should not be a time for a daily and personal cost/benefit analysis. Socrates famously tells us to "Know thyself." This does not mean making ourselves the center of our concern. Rather, our daily reflection should deepen our understanding of what truly is our nature and what is the nature of the world around us. Reflection should lead us to be more grounded in reality, in truth.

The sages of the Talmud ask the question, "Who is a wise man?" and respond, "He who learns from all men." Another path to wisdom is through encounters specifically with wise individuals. Those who have contact with wise people on a regular basis are particularly fortunate. The constant observation of how they see and process the same realities as we is a powerful teacher. We can learn from their thoughtful objectivity and dispassionate decision-making. But there are other wise individuals whose example is readily available to us. History and biography and even fiction portray sagacious individuals from whom we can learn wise ways. Through the written word, we can "live along" with Nelson Mandela through his unjust imprisonment and his shrewd and judicious steps toward aiding South Africa to free itself from the nightmare of Apartheid. In literature we can follow a developing path toward wisdom in tales such as Jane Austen's heroine, Emma, who eventually comes to see her habitually thoughtless and impulsive behavior when she is reproved by the man she admires most, Mr. Knightley. His scolding helps her to see that she embarrassed and hurt Mrs. Bates in front of her friends. Humiliated by the correction, Emma considers the truth of his words, feels genuine remorse for her unkindness, and consequently makes amends. Indeed, it is the heroes of these stories who can help us escape the blinders of our own stories and gently point us down the path to wisdom.

CHAPTER 6

Reflection

"Know thyself." —Socrates

∽ ∽ ∽ ∽

The essays in this chapter present two notably different perspectives on the virtue of self-reflection. While both cultural approaches understand reflection as an opportunity to gain a clearer perspective on oneself, it is the purpose and focus of such perspectives that reflect unique cultural values and beliefs. In the Eastern point of view we see a focus on self-examination, often while withdrawing from the business of everyday living, in order to perceive one's character flaws and correct them. Emphasis is on developing a "lucid and pure mind" in order to promote one's own moral transformation. The purpose of such transformation is not simply improvement of the individual, but to engender transformation and moral development in the environment as well, based on the belief that a positive change within one life will engender change in the lives of those around that individual. Self-reflection leading to inner development is thus a strategy, in a characteristically indirect manner, for solving problems within the individual's environment and creating a more just and virtuous society.

The Western view, on the other hand, sees as a primary goal of reflection to understand and direct one's own life toward one of greater meaning. This second essay focuses on reflection to fight against living at the mercy of myriad meaningless distractions. It is concerned with how one spends one's time and in directing it toward a purposeful existence. Reflection enables one to reevaluate one's actions, to apply reason and consciousness to them, redirecting one's life along a more meaningful path with an emphasis on moral choice. We see in the Eastern discussion an image of Buddhist-style meditation, while the Western reflection is more intellect-based, pensive, more directed. Both, however, aim toward a state of appreciation, of calmness, empowerment and personal direction, of solution to problems, and ultimately toward a better society through personal moral development—the Eastern individual affecting his or her environment through personal growth while the Western one lives a more fulfilling, meaningful life of tempered passions, transcending the dangers of rationalization and impulsiveness.

Reflection

BY SHUJIRO MIZUNO

The earliest extant Japanese chronicle is the *Kojiki (Records of Ancient Matters)*, which was compiled in the seventh and early eighth centuries. Despite being essentially a work of history, the first of its three volumes opens with a mythical account of the founding of Japan. In the course of this there is a description of an important incident that revolves around self-reflection. This is the story of how the Sun Goddess, Amaterasu Omikami, shut herself away in a celestial rock cave.

Susano-o, the brother of Amaterasu, was very violent by nature. He damaged the rice fields belonging to his sister by breaking down the divisions between them and filling in the ditches. Although such actions were usually regarded as serious crimes, Amaterasu chose to interpret her brother's conduct as an expression of goodwill, saying that he wanted to enlarge her rice fields and improve their condition. She refrained from criticizing his conduct in any way. Next, though, Susano-o urinated and defecated inside the holy shrine. Amaterasu interpreted this incident as a simple mistake, on the grounds that he had been completely drunk. Once again, she made no attempt to criticize her unruly brother but continued to display the same forgiving attitude towards him as before.

Finally, Susano-o skinned a horse alive and dropped it into the shrine where the maidens of Amaterasu were engaged in weaving divine garments, frightening one of them to death. This time Amaterasu, in keeping with her exalted sense of responsibility for everything in the world, became convinced that all these incidents had been caused by the inadequacy of her own moral virtues. She thereupon decided to engage once more in self-reflection so as to enhance her moral virtues, and she shut herself inside the heavenly rock cave.

As soon as the Sun Goddess confined herself in the cave, the country was covered in darkness and all manner of calamities arose. So the eight hundred myriad deities assembled and discussed the best way to persuade Amaterasu to open the door of her cave. Amenouzume, one of these deities, overturned a bucket, stood on it, and started to dance. All the other deities immediately began to laugh at the amusing spectacle.

Hearing them, Amaterasu was curious to know how such happy sounds were possible in such dire circumstances. She opened the door of the heavenly cave a crack to see what was happening and asked the deities why they were laughing. Amenouzume replied, "We are rejoicing because we now have a deity far superior to you." Then Amaterasu noticed her own shining face in a mirror. At that moment, the deity Ameno-Tajikara-o used all his strength to force open the cave door.

Then the eight hundred myriad deities discerned in Amaterasu a grace and nobility that she had never possessed before. Her appearance had changed totally owing to her attainment of higher moral virtue.

Amaterasu, instead of rebuking her brother and fighting him in pursuit of justice, had engaged in serious self-reflection. Having attained a higher moral character in this way, she then exerted a moral influence on others, including her mischievous brother.

The Sun Goddess shut herself in the heavenly cave not because she was frightened by her brother's actions or angry with him, but as a result of being struck with a spirit of profound benevolence. The Japanese word here is *kashikomi*, which means pious, penitent, or respectful. Having completed her self-reflection, she gained a higher moral character and forgave her brother in the spirit of benevolence and tolerance.

Seeing the moral transformation of his sister, Susano-o deeply repented of his violent ways. However, he was still expelled from heaven and had to descend to the land of Izumo. There he slew an eight-headed dragon and brought peace to the land. For this reason he is considered to be the founder of Japan.

♣　　♣　　♣

Self-reflection or self-examination like that of Amaterasu has several characteristics. First of all, it is conducted with a calm attitude, eschewing vehement passions, but with an appreciation of the given circumstances. It does not involve fighting over right or wrong. Instead of seeking justice directly by just means, Amaterasu sought it indirectly by working toward the perfection of her own moral character. Furthermore, it is a process that empowers one in the face of difficulties, humiliation, and loss. And finally, it has a profound moral effect on others, as well as enhancing one's own moral character. Self-reflection or self-examination encompasses six virtuous elements. The first of these is called *shikan*, or concentration and observation.

Shikan is practiced by the Tendai Sect of Buddhism. The first step is to quiet one's mind by stilling one's thoughts and concentrating. Only then can one observe the depths of one's being. If the mind is troubled and full of anxiety, many thoughts, like bubbles rising up through water, will constantly disturb its surface. One can see the truth only after attaining peace of heart and mind. The next element entails the enhancement of one's own moral condition. Two ancient sages in China, the Emperors Yao and Shun, were said to have governed the country solely by perfecting their own moral virtues. It was believed that their attending to their own exalted moral standing was sufficient by itself to bring peace and prosperity to their subjects, without any need for them to intervene actively in government. The explanation given for this was that once rulers paid proper attention to their own characters, heaven and earth were brought into harmony.

It may not be easy at first to see the relevance of this philosophy to the modern world, especially since today's conception of justice is that errors and crimes have to be corrected and punished in the proper way. But we should not dismiss the lessons implicit in the story of Amaterasu too readily. Is it not in fact possible that there are circumstances today where the promotion of high moral virtue will bring peace and happiness to society in the long run? We may not be able to answer this question with complete certitude either way, but the question should at least give us pause before we dismiss such ancient wisdom out of hand. The third aspect of self-reflection, forgiveness, has been defined as a generous gift to a person who does not deserve it. We have seen that Amaterasu did not seek to cast off her brother, nor did she treat his violence as just cause for waging a struggle against him and defeating him. Instead, she forgave him and used the occasion as an opportunity to enhance her own moral virtue.

Amaterasu was a ruler as well as a Shinto priestess. Her purpose in governing was to create harmony between her land and heaven, since there were countless other deities in her world. From her cosmic perspective, she treated even her enemies with benevolence and mercy, which the virtue of self-reflection gives rise to. She tried to avoid focusing on the faults of others or regarding them as evil. Thus she interpreted any evils or vices she saw as indicating deficiencies in her own moral virtue.

To Amaterasu, self-reflection was how one trained to become a better being. In conducting it, she used nature as the reference point from which to view herself and then tried to remove any blemishes she detected. In this way, the virtue promoted her higher moral virtue, which is the fifth element of self-reflection.

Finally, when Amaterasu attained perfect serenity (Jap. *hachimen reirou*) in her heart and mind, her appearance became graceful beyond anything that had been seen before. Like a crystal with many facets, she appeared serene, equable, and affable when viewed from any direction. Such a lucid and pure mind exerts a powerful influence over others. This, too, arises from the practice of self-reflection.

It may seem a long step from the mythical to the world of today. However, the two narratives that follow illustrate how the model of self-reflection described above can be applied to everyday issues in human life.

♣   ♣   ♣

Mr. Ito was struck with tuberculosis at the age of forty-one. Contracting the disease came as a great shock to him, especially as he had always taken very good care of his health. At first he tried to deny that he had TB at all, but unfortunately the disease got progressively worse, and he began losing weight.

In search of the causes of his illness, he decided to engage in self-reflection. Subsequently he came to believe that he must have some deficiency in his character, which he then identified as a lack of sufficient mental resilience to accept that other people were different from him and had deficiencies of their own. He had even been blaming others for what happened to him. After engaging in self-reflection a number of times, Mr. Ito decided that he must take this opportunity to accept what he was at the moment and scrutinize his inner self rigorously. He imagined himself as a stream of running water, which always flows from a higher place to a lower one. Such a stream never decays nor becomes muddy but remains crystal clear at all times. Not having a selfish mind, it simply follows the laws of nature.

With this mental image before him, Mr. Ito regained a calmness of spirit. He no longer held a grudge against anyone, and his mind became as clear and pure as water. He even became grateful for his disease and began to believe that he could live with it. His conclusion was that all human beings are originally healthy, and that if they temporarily lose their balance, they have a natural tendency to regain it and so return to their original healthy state.

As this state of calm took hold of his mind, he began to get better day by day. Although traces of the disease remained in his lungs, he was able to return to his former job after a year of medical treatment.

Mr. Hasegawa was a young executive at a medium-size textile company when, in 1930, Japan was struck by the Great Depression. He became puzzled as to why his company was suffering so badly while the major textile companies seemed relatively unaffected, and in his search for an answer, he consulted a student of Chikuro Hiroike.

He was told that he could solve this problem by conforming his mind and behavior to the model of self-examination taught by Dr. Hiroike. Accepting this, Mr. Hasegawa began to perceive how he could transform his own destiny by following these principles and enhancing his character. His company survived and prospered, even through the dark days of the war.

Then in 1977, one of his factories was completely destroyed by fire. Once again, Mr. Hasegawa seized on such an incident as an opportunity to improve himself still further, even to the point of being thankful for this renewed hardship. His company miraculously recovered from the disaster thanks to the trust of his business associates, which he had worked to build up over many years. Within a month, he had succeeded in importing two large textile machines from the United States to replace those lost in the fire. Importing things like these in such short order was usually very expensive, but Mr. Hasegawa was able to purchase the machines at the regular price.

Mr. Hasegawa had been putting into practice the teaching of Dr. Hiroike that "Deeds should be good from three directions." He expressed his understanding of this as follows:

Your business will prosper when you think three-directionally, that is, in respect of yourself, the party with whom you are dealing, and other people or the public. You can thereby bring certain benefits and happiness to the person with whom you are directly dealing, to the public, to the nation in which you live, as well as to yourself.

Self-reflection is oriented towards the perfection of one's moral character. It is an orientation rather than a goal. Moreover, it is characterized by an acknowledgement of one's responsibility for one's own life. An individual must be prepared to accept who he or she actually is at the present moment. The importance of self-reflection lies in discerning the true meaning of one's experiences, just as the importance of any narrative lies in the meaning of the story being told. The key to self-reflection is to establish security and happiness in oneself as well as in the society in which one lives. This practice is relevant not only to one's own life but also to the creation of a peaceful society.

The Culture of the East and Self-Reflection

Let us now look at self-reflection from the perspective of Confucian and Buddhist philosophy.

The *Analects of Confucius* prescribe three sets of circumstances which should prompt us to engage in self-reflection. The first is if we find ourselves responding in a half-hearted way when asked for help. The second is when we notice that we are responding to our friends without sincerity. The third is if we catch ourselves pretending to know things about which we are in fact unsure.

We often give hasty advice to help friends because we cannot really put ourselves in their shoes. In such cases, though, we should reflect on whether we are responding to our friends' trust in the same spirit. Furthermore, we should ask ourselves whether or not we are talking in an irresponsible manner.

In the East particularly, relationships are considered to be very important, and it is believed that a sincere attitude will produce trust among people. The *Avatamsaka* (*Flower Garland Sutra*), also known as the sutra of penitence, says that we should repent of our greed, anger, and foolishness, and of all the deeds of our body, mouth, and will. In sum, this means repenting of the imperfections of our existence and working toward perfection.

Interestingly, recognizing our imperfections can actually evoke a feeling of hope. Konosuke Matsushita wrote:

If you follow your own destiny, you will gain security of mind and rejoice in spirit. Most important of all you will find meaning in life. You can then say, "This is my life, I am all right with the way I live." Such a feeling is very powerful indeed ....

Matsushita is not saying here that we should give up hope in life, but rather, that we should accept who we are as the reality of life. In doing so, we open up future possibilities for ourselves. If we hesitate or have regrets and fail to accept our destinies, we will have to suffer for a long time, for we will be unable to use what we already possess within. For example, some people may be too small to become sumo wrestlers, but this does not mean that there are not other ways in which they can use their bodies effectively. In order to exploit our potential to the fullest, then, we must begin by accepting who we are. That is why a fundamental aspect of self-reflection is self-acknowledgement.

The Chinese characters for self-reflection, 反省, has two meanings. One is *introspection* or *reflection*; the other is *to eliminate an excess*. We humans are feeble and fallible, so we need to practice self-reflection constantly. If we study our reflections in a mirror, we will see our defects clearly. If we can eliminate our excesses, we will function better. Cleansing our hearts and minds allows us to see ourselves as we really are and so to lead better lives.

Modern conditions certainly make the direct application of the model of self-examination practiced by Amaterasu far from easy. But readers may still reflect upon the following in the light of their own experiences. What makes it difficult for people to see the world in its true aspect? Do you accept the troubles in your life or do you reject them and other people who may be their cause? Should all the wrong actions of others be punished? While it may be difficult to honestly examine ourselves and our faults, the rewards of doing so are plentiful. As Socrates once stated, "The unexamined life is not worth living."

Reflection

BY KAREN E. BOHLIN

When the nationally acclaimed sports journalist Mitch Albom learns that his beloved college mentor, Morrie Schwartz, is dying of ALS (Lou Gehrig's disease), he flies to Boston to visit him. It has been sixteen years since he has seen his favorite professor—his best intentions have been repeatedly challenged by competing demands on his time and attention. As much as he looks forward to seeing his old friend, deadlines and story ideas swirl through his head, and he pulls over several times, franticly checking messages and following up leads. Resisting the temptation to keep working, he resolves to attend fully to Schwartz during his much-anticipated visit.

Albom's first encounter with his seventy-eight-year-old friend—now a wheelchair-bound, shrunken figure with a blanket covering his legs despite the summer heat—stuns him. But Morrie's affectionate welcome and the spirited conversation that ensues transport Albom for hours. Morrie invites him to come again, and Albom returns weekly to learn from his teacher what dying can teach us about living.

Each visit between the two marks a decline in Morrie's physical health. And each visit stirs Albom's soul. Among the many lessons Morrie teaches is why people tend to lead meaningless lives, "half-asleep even when they are busy doing things that they think are important." The problem, he says, is that we are caught up "chasing the wrong things," and this harried running around gets them nowhere. "The way you get meaning into your life," he advises Albom, "is to devote yourself to loving others, devote yourself to the community around you, and devote yourself to creating something that gives you purpose and meaning." Regretfully, Morrie observes, "The culture doesn't encourage you to think about such things until you are about to die." He explains:

> We are so wrapped up with egotistical things, career, family, having enough money, meeting the mortgage, getting a new car, fixing the radiator when it breaks—we're involved in trillions of little acts just to keep going. So we don't get into the habit of standing back and looking at our lives and saying, Is this all? Is this all I want? Is something missing?

Albom's memoir, *Tuesdays With Morrie,* not only chronicles the life lessons gleaned from each visit with Morrie, but also reveals Albom's transformation from a workaholic addicted to his cell phone and email inbox to a person willing to embrace the present and the people before him. His story highlights the need for reflection, "the habit of standing back and looking at our lives."

Human beings are hungry for meaning and purpose. But sometimes we don't feel that hunger because we are falsely satiated. We can be distracted from our quest for meaning by freneticism, workaholism, fragmentation, and information overload, as well as by shallow standards of success. Technology, work, and leisure activities are not the enemies. It is our addiction to these things that cause us to lose our way, our self-possession. But no matter how far we stray, we cannot escape that gnawing sensation: "Is this all? Is this all I want? Is something missing?" A colleague of ours recounts his experience meeting a former student on the train. An Ivy League graduate and successful CEO, this young man had enjoyed enormous good fortune academically and professionally. "But what is it all for?" he asked his former teacher. "At school, I learned to work hard, to be the best and give my best. But we never asked why. What is the point of the long hours, the constant drive to succeed?"

Without studied purpose and direction, we run the risk of chasing the wrong things or pursuing the right things in all the wrong places. When we lose sight of the meaning behind what we do, constant activity no longer fulfills us, and we can become susceptible to sadness or loneliness, even when many people surround us. In order to find and sustain meaning, we need more than learning, competence, and a packed schedule. We need more than success and acclaim. We need to understand *why*. To live a virtuous, happy life requires reflection. Martin Luther King, Jr., once said, "Our lives begin to end the day we become silent about things that matter." Morrie is not silent about things that matter, and his words inspire Albom to take up the task of transcribing their conversations for posterity. Albom is blessed to have had a wonderful teacher to assist him along his journey, someone who cares enough to prompt his ongoing reflection about the point of it all.

The habit of reflection or self-examination is an intellectual virtue acquired over time from example, experience, and self-discipline. When we reflect, we examine the experiences of each day and measure our actions against standards of right and wrong, justice and injustice, truth and falsehood. These moral standards are our compass, and the habit of reflection is the process of checking our compass to chart an accurate course to a purposeful life. Any traveler must periodically check his compass if he hopes to reach his destination. Anyone committed to living a meaningful life must periodically reflect to navigate accurately toward this goal. Reflection prompts us to ask ourselves how we are living virtues such as benevolence, justice, courage, temperance, and gratitude in our daily lives. These virtues are the foundation of lasting relationships with others, and commitment on some level to bettering the world for others is what brings meaning to our lives. Albom was so caught up in his work that he failed to consult his compass. In reconnecting with his mentor, in contemplating life and death, Albom is awakened from his half-slumber to reflect on how he can add meaning to his life and work.

The first step in the right direction is to realize that we have veered off track, that we do in fact need a compass if we are to reach any worthwhile destination. Albom's conversations with Morrie are what prompt him to reflect on his current life track and to strive to correct his course. Thus, mature reflection includes a disposition of humility as its foundation. Humility is rooted in an awareness of our own imperfections and of our need for help from others to guide us along the road to a meaningful life. Our biases and pride, and the endless distractions of a busy life, are quick to cloud our focus. Our ability to reflect is greatly strengthened if we form relationships with people whom we admire and trust for their good judgment and wisdom. They help us to reflect on the right questions and help us to avoid self-analysis and excuses. In T.S. Eliot's *Four Quartets* we read, "The only wisdom we can hope to acquire/Is the wisdom of humility: humility is endless."

Reflection not only helps us realize our missteps and seek the help of mentors to help us get back on track, it also keeps us honest with ourselves and with others. When we reflect, we are striving to learn from mistakes, hold ourselves accountable, acquire perspective, and work towards constructive action. The scientist George Washington Carver (1864–1943) once wisely remarked, "Ninety-nine percent of the failures come from people who have the habit of making excuses." Reflection invites us to check our moral compass and attend more carefully to those internal characteristics that define who we are. Reflection enables us to grow in self-knowledge and to lead a more flourishing life, precisely because it helps us to evaluate the worthiness of our goals and commitments.

When we fail to reflect, we fail to live our lives to the fullest. As Socrates put it, "The unexamined life is not worth living." He challenged individuals to provide an intelligible account of why they believed what they believed. For Socrates, the pursuit of truth is a quintessentially human activity. Only human beings can give reasons. Only human beings can reflect on the morality of their choices. Animals may respond to stimuli and modify their behavior, but they cannot engage in moral deliberation. Thus, we see Socrates exhorting the Athenians to think about the indiscriminate pursuit of money and power and to seek instead "the best possible state" of their soul.

Imagine Socrates wandering the streets of midtown Manhattan or central Tokyo, challenging everyone from tourists and street vendors to stockbrokers and film producers to reflect on what they hope to attain and who they hope to be. In a culture that equates success with happiness, the habit of reflection is often underdeveloped. The fast track to success—getting the highest grades and test scores, earning admittance to prestigious universities, attaining the right degrees, securing the best job and salary—can deceive us into believing that any one of these milestones is a measure of happiness. But external trappings alone cannot help us to attain our "best possible state" of the soul. Reflection helps us to see that money, power, and reputation are not in themselves an obstacle to flourishing. Rather, it is being dominated by them that keeps us from true happiness. In their best-selling book on financial literacy, *Rich Dad, Poor Dad*, Robert Kiyosaki and Sharon Lechter recount why people become enslaved to money:

> Instead of telling the truth about how they feel, they react to their feelings and fail to think. They feel the fear, they go to work, hoping that money will soothe the fear, but it doesn't. That old fear haunts them, and they go back to work hoping again that money will calm their fears, and again it doesn't....

When we "fail to think," we fail to examine the root causes of our feelings, and we can allow ourselves to be dominated by our fear and emotions. Mature self-examination helps us to understand and re-direct our feelings. I am reminded of a friend's exchange with her six-year-old son, who begged and pleaded with her one morning, "But Mommy, I don't feel like going to school today." She wisely responded, "Don't worry, Honey, that feeling will go away."

Passion is an unreliable guide. While it may inspire great energy and enthusiasm, if not tempered by reflection, it can also blind reason. Shakespeare's Macbeth has a consuming desire for the throne. A respected statesman and loyal protector of King Duncan, his lust for power derails him from his once noble purpose. Macbeth repeatedly alludes to his need for time to think, to deliberate, but he never takes the time to do so. In the end, he resists the calls of conscience, dismisses all plans for reflection, and says:

> [F]rom this moment
> The very firstlings of my heart shall be
> The firstlings of my hand ....
> ....
> This deed I'll do before this purpose cool:
> But no more sights!—Where are these Gentlemen?

Lust for power drove Macbeth to kill King Duncan. Failing to consult his compass, he continues along a murderous path. After assuming the throne and conquering every threat to his power, his ambitions are laid waste by guilt and misery. Reflecting on Macbeth's trajectory, Abraham Lincoln, the sixteenth president of the United States and one of the greatest leaders in United States history, read and reread *Macbeth* to engrave in his mind the dangers of unbridled ambition.

What is at risk when we are not reflective? At worst, becoming like Macbeth. Psychologist Erich Seligmann Fromm (1900–1980), reflecting on the Holocaust, wondered how such educated people could do such a thing. Such educated people can commit atrocity when they cut themselves off from the moral purpose of their claims and actions. The perpetrators of gang violence and school shootings, as well as teens who exhibit aggressive behavior, commit crimes of hate or vengeance and sometimes fear. Even when these acts are premeditated, mature reflection is not at work. Rationalization and impulsiveness are. Without clear ethical principles and habits of self-examination, a person has little moral strength and perhaps only a malfunctioning compass to consult.

At best, when we are not reflective we run the risk of floating aimlessly along the surface of life with no real depth perception. This too has its perils. *The Great Gatsby* by F. Scott Fitzgerald (1896–1940) speaks to the need for reflection on numerous levels. Charged with romantic intrigue and boldness, the novel celebrates the allure of a glittering life replete with fancy parties, sparkling personalities, and showpiece cars, but it also points to the evanescence of it all. It illustrates the vagaries and emptiness of some people's lives despite their glamour and fortune. The novel's tragic strain challenges readers to take a closer look at casual recklessness, brutal snobbery, and self-indulgent lust.

At first glance Gatsby seems naïve and perhaps misguided, until we discover that he is dangerously obsessed with Daisy and more of a stalker than a lover. Gatsby is wholly unreflective. There is no Socrates to question him about whether or not he is pursuing the best possible state of his soul. He has no Morrie to ask him to consider the purpose of his pursuits. From his youth Gatsby has been highly imaginative, and his unbridled imagination eventually eclipses reality: "He invented just that sort of Jay Gatsby that a seventeen-year-old boy would like to invent, and to this conception he was faithful to the end." Nick, the novel's narrator, skillfully presents what is reprehensible about Gatsby's choices and commitments and at the same time remains a neutral observer in awe of his "purposeless splendor."

Gatsby could have benefitted from the sage advice of Seneca, the Roman senator and philosopher from the time of Christ. His letters show him warning a correspondent: "You ask me what you should consider it particularly important to avoid," one letter begins. "My answer is this: a mass crowd. It is something to which you cannot entrust yourself without risk .... I never come back home with quite the same moral character I went out with; something or other becomes unsettled where I had achieved internal peace." Seneca called it "the restless energy of the hunted mind." We can be led by the crowd and lose ourselves, or we can reflect on how we spend our time and direct ourselves purposefully. In our culture, the "mass crowd" that can be unsettling to our peace is our unlimited access to mass media. In practical terms, if we do not gain control of electronics, they can gain control over us. Limiting the time we spend checking email, Facebook, Twitter, or surfing the Internet, for example, helps to preserve time and mental space for reflection.

Reflection assists us in developing a discriminating mind, so we can see the difference between material success and deep happiness, between impulse and intelligent choice, between friendship and exploitation, between self-respect and self-aggrandizement, between treating others like equals and treating them as stepping stones. Reflection, then, is a prerequisite to learning. It awakens wonder and awe. The British writer G.K. Chesterton (1874–1936) put it this way, "The world will never starve for want of wonders, only for want of wonder." Whether it is the enjoyment of literature, art, music, natural beauty, or the study of science and engineering, reflection enables us to see, to savor, and to discover the world around us in a new way.

Moreover, practicing reflection in daily life can help us to stave off gossip and shed biases. We are familiar with the sentiment that there are two sides to every story, that we need to give people the benefit of the doubt and to assume the best rather than jump to conclusions. Perhaps one of the most important books on the power of reflection to help a person shed prejudice is *Pride and Prejudice* by Jane Austen (1775–1817). The intelligent and independent protagonist Elizabeth Bennett is blindly taken by Mr. Wickham, the dapper young militiaman, whose amiability both charms and deceives her. She is easily persuaded that Mr. Darcy is haughty and aloof and contemptuously refuses his offer of marriage. When she is in possession of more complete and reliable data, she sees each man for who he is and realizes she has radically misjudged both. Austen reminds us that mature relationships demand generous understanding and openness to the truth—fruits of reflection.

Finally, we need the habit of reflection to help us make sense of the inevitable suffering, adversity, and evil we will encounter in life. In his book, *Man's Search for Meaning*, Viktor Frankl's reflections on his experiences in a concentration camp offer compelling illustrations of how this may be done. He observes those prisoners who, crushed by man's inhumanity to man, lose all will to survive. He also observes those who rise above the obscenity of their situation and choose to share their last crumbs of bread with other prisoners of dire need. Frankl concludes that you can strip a person of everything except the last human freedom, the freedom to "choose one's attitude" regardless of the circumstances. A philosopher who both experienced firsthand and studied the suffering, resilience, and post-traumatic stress of survivors, Frankl concludes there are three fundamental ways we find meaning in life: 1) reflecting on the experiences of work we do well, 2) reflecting on the experiences of genuine love, and 3) reflecting on the experiences of suffering.

CHAPTER 7

Respect

"Respect is mutual." —*African*

◎◎ ◎◎ ◎◎

Respect is defined as a feeling of high regard, honor, or esteem, as well as deference or dutiful regard. In the two essays of this chapter, we find distinctive foci but much that overlaps. Perhaps no virtue captures the Asian spirit as thoroughly as that of respect, which underlies so much of its philosophy and spirituality. Hajime Ide draws from ancient, deeply influential Eastern philosophies, from Confucius to Buddhism to Shinto, as he describes first the elements of respect and then that which makes one worthy of respect. We recognize here the great value the East places on this virtue, which the author defines in part as awe, admiration, and obedience, such as toward nature or one's ancestors, placing self inextricably within the greater universe, bound by relation and duty. Awe toward "something greater than what is human," writes Ide, allows one's life to become more meaningful. He also points to the facet of respect that is admiration, which allows the individual to learn from and emulate others and develop further. Fundamental to the Eastern view, as illustrated by the Lotus Sutra's teaching of the Buddha nature existing within all people, is an understanding of the innate value of every human being, a theme echoed in the second essay.

In agreement with this view, Kevin Ryan asserts that part of re-spect is recognizing the essential worth of people, both in others *and* in oneself, further stipulating that failure to do so lies at the heart of violence in human history. He adds that respect must in-variably include two parts, understanding and action, or recogniz-ing this worth and then enacting that recognition. His essay opens with a tale illustrating the Western (if not universal) value placed on respecting one's parents, which is also indicated in the Japanese piece. While Ide's essay represents the Eastern belief in a oneness between self and environment when it asserts that this virtue is key to forming a peaceful world and avoiding conflict, this is not at odds with Ryan's thoughts on the influence of respect, indicative of maturity, on human relationships. Both authors agree with the importance of cultivating this profound, human virtue toward the goal of building a culture of peace.

Respect

BY HAJIME IDE

Several centuries before Christ, disciples of Confucius collected and discussed their master's words and deeds and committed the results to paper. The work that emerged, known as the *Analects of Confucius*, reveals very clearly that the basis and essence of the relationship between teacher and followers was *uyamau*, or respect. Confucius showed respect to his disciples and they to him.

Yan Hui (Jap. Gankai) is usually judged the most eminent of the disciples of Confucius. The boundless measure of Yan Hui's respect for his teacher's character is evident in his account of their relationship:

> The more familiar I became with him, the better I understood how noble-minded he was. The more I troubled him with questions, the better I knew how firm his faith was. He took great pains to give me a clear idea of everything. He helped me raise the level of my understanding through the pursuit of learning. He taught me how to put courtesy into practice. Thus he made every effort to build up my character. He was too noble in nature, too firm in conviction, and too enthusiastic about education for it to be possible for me to follow in his footsteps.

These words capture very well the feeling of awe that people experience when encountering a character greater than their imaginations could ever conceive.

The following dialogue, taken from the *Analects*, illustrates one of the most striking qualities of Confucius, his gentle and attentive consideration for others.

One of his disciples said to him, "I am very grateful for the chance to hear your teaching on ethics. However, I am a long way indeed from having the capacity I need to put it into practice."

To this Confucius answered: "If you really do not have the capacity and cannot help giving up halfway, you needn't feel at all ashamed. But it seems that you will then regard yourself as good for nothing. That is where you are most to blame."

Confucius shows here how well he understands the kind of trap that earnest people are apt to fall into. Since they are often perfectionists, they are in too much of a hurry to attain excellence, and failure undermines their self-confidence. Faced with a challenge that could open up the way to the future, they therefore have a tendency to doubt themselves and draw back. With his acute insight into human nature, Confucius wanted his disciple to think more highly of himself and respond to any challenge with confidence. In this way, he believed, he would grow into a man of character. His disciple was moved by this advice and understood how sincerely Confucius cared for him, since he did not urge him to do anything against his own will. The disciple made up his mind to act faithfully on his master's advice and in his spirit. This is why he wanted to hand on these words of Confucius to succeeding generations.

The *Analects* offer many examples of the respect that these disciples paid to their teacher. It also gives a detailed insight into what kind of educator Confucius was. He respected his disciples' individuality. To put it another way, he set the proper value on them as they were. This highlights the importance of the mutual respect that permeated the entire relationship between teacher and disciples.

The word *respect* has many synonyms, including awe, admiration, homage, and adoration, each of which reflects a different aspect of this virtue. It adapts itself to circumstances, depending on the nature of the person being respected or the situation the person showing respect is in. Let us explore some of these.

❧   ❧   ❧

Shinto, the earliest religion of Japan, is founded on a feeling of awe of nature. Japanese people love to watch the changing spectacle of the four seasons, as if it were something displayed on a never-ending picture scroll. Many poems have been composed in praise of the ever-varying hues of the seasons that adorn the fabric of the "space-time continuum" of nature. The Japanese divide each season, in turn, into many shorter periods, and this serves to give a rhythm to daily life. Fall, for instance, has three very distinct phases: early, middle, and late. Such subdivisions are just one example of the sensitivity with which Japanese people respond to nature. Festivals, religious services, and even the rituals of everyday life display an intent awareness of the changing seasons and other mysterious forces of nature.

While nature enriches the life of Japanese people in ways like this, it can also threaten them with a variety of disasters. But even when confronted by phenomena whose power far outstrips that of human beings, Japanese people feel the order of the natural world and its power to protect and support everything, living or inanimate. At such moments especially, they are struck with awe.

Another fundamental Shinto teaching is that all things under the sun are inhabited by spirits. Shinto asserts that its followers should feel grateful to these spirits and respect them, which in turn encourages people to pay homage to nature. The Shinto view of existence, in short, is that nature and human beings help one another.

This basic outlook on life explains why Chikuro Hiroike, the Japanese scholar and teacher, began his study of *The Shrines of Ise* with the following words:

Beautiful, dazzling clouds are floating across the sky. Surely, spring is come here in the forest of the shrine. The sacred precincts are far from the secular world, not so much geographically as spiritually. Standing here, we feel purified and vitalized, keen to align ourselves with nature and fortify ourselves. We cannot help being filled with awe, eager to worship and admire the glory of the holy being. What purges us of earthly thoughts is the splendor of our surroundings. We are deeply impressed by the sight of the Isuzu River and Mount Kamiji rising up beyond it. The path to the shrine is lined with tall pine and cedar trees. They have been thick with leaves since time immemorial. The Isuzu River, rising from Mount Kamiji, flows on the same course as it did thousands of years ago. We find something changeless here in the precincts. This is indeed the symbol of the spiritual culture to which our ancestors contributed so much; it is nothing other than Japan's national polity.

As he wrote this essay, Hiroike was picturing the precincts of the Ise Shrine in his mind's eye as they had appeared to him during a visit there. He believed deeply that Japan's spiritual culture derived from this particular place and had been handed down from generation to generation. Respect for the stillness and the sacred atmosphere of the Ise Shrine was, he felt, what made a truly human existence possible for the Japanese people. It was a manifestation of the supreme power of nature that nurtures everything in the world, and human beings owe all that they are to this power. He thought that it was the realization of this that engenders a proper spirit of modesty among the Japanese, who cannot help feeling awe-struck in the presence of nature and its beauties. It allowed them to understand the words of Confucius, "We should have something to look up to." Awe, then, was something Japanese people could experience even in their everyday lives, something that greatly helped them in placing their existence in its true setting.

As the influence of Confucianism swept across China, people began to equate nature with Heaven. They modeled the ethics of human beings (*jindo*, the way of man) on their conception of the order of Heaven (*tendo*, the way of Heaven). The *Analects* report China's greatest philosopher as saying, "Heaven says nothing, but the seasons rotate and everything comes and goes." Since the world of nature moves on incessantly, he believed that people can and should construct their lives on the basis of its transitions. According to ancient Chinese thought, it was obedience to nature that gives people true security and enables them to grow. This was the germ of the feeling of awe in respect of Heaven, and it was of vital importance in helping people determine what to do with their lives. The following paragraph in the *Analects* explains how this is so:

One day, Confucius said with a sigh, "There is no one who understands me." This was natural enough for someone who, like him, preached peace in an age of war. Concerned for his master, one of his disciples asked, "Why can't you make yourself understood?" He answered, "But then, I am happy as long as Heaven understands me." He was confident that he had Heaven's sympathy. If he had not believed that Heaven understood his moral intentions, he could not have gone ahead with his teachings on the importance of morality. Confucius was driven by the conviction that he must fulfill his responsibility, and the foundation of this unshakeable belief was his awe of Heaven. Such a feeling is nothing other than the homage paid to that which is beyond human knowledge. It is the orientation of mind on which life itself is based.

Thus people can stand in awe of something greater than what is human. This, in the view of Confucius, is very helpful in constructing a philosophy to deal with everyday life, for a genuine feeling of awe makes it easy to fill our life with meaning.

Admiration is something that makes its appearance when people respect or stand in awe of a person, but its focus is different. Reading the biographies of heroes or courageous warriors of the past may make people treat such individuals as objects of their awe. But admiration is reserved for an individual's way of life and, as a consequence, involves trying to adopt that way of life oneself. Having come across a person one can admire, one gets some idea as to the kind of life one should live. Confucius is once again an archetype here, for he was someone truly worthy of admiration and emulation.

Confucius was certainly the object of his disciples' admiration. In all that he did, his disciples looked up to him as their role model. Describing his behavior in everyday life, they said, "Whenever he found himself at home, he was free from care, smiling very warmly. When he was talking with us, he looked modest and mild." They added, "He was at the same time both gentle and strict. He was strict but not severe. He was modest and quiet."

Confucius revealed himself to his disciples as someone who was extremely tolerant. He never rejected anyone, and everybody felt at ease in his presence. The following anecdote illustrates this exceptionally broad-minded quality of his.

One day he asked two of his disciples, Yan Hui and Zi-lu (Jap. Shiro), what ambitions they had. Confucius did this both because he wanted to know the purpose for which they were devoting themselves to studying and because he was eager to find out whether his teaching was having the right results.

Zi-lu answered first. "I want to be a man who can share a conveyance and clothes with friends and never feel sorry if they are returned broken or worn out."

Next, Yan Hui said, "I want to be a man who does good and yet who never prides himself on it, someone who would never have others do what he himself would not."

These two had been greatly influenced by their teacher's way of life and tried to make the most of what they learned from him about how to live each day. Their answers showed that they were living up to Confucius's expectations.

Then another disciple asked his master, "Please explain to us your ambition."

Confucius answered: "I should be satisfied if old people felt easy with me, if my friends trusted in me, and if young people loved me."

Compared with the ambition of both his disciples, that of Confucius is natural, simple, and realistic. His disciples had expected something loftier from him, and so they were quite surprised at first. Nonetheless, they learned from this unanticipated answer of Confucius's that "their teacher was a calm and good-natured man. He made much of politeness and decency. He was modest and temperate." Shown the aims of his life, they found themselves respecting their teacher all the more.

Hearing his words and observing his behavior, what surprised the disciples was that there was nothing divine or even superhuman about him. They looked up to him as he was. He was human in every way, living a pragmatic life as a considerate man.

Confucius was admired by his disciples not least because he devoted himself sincerely to teaching, showing them the way to live. More than that, they followed him because he was so obviously a lover of learning who made unremitting efforts to put what he taught into practice.

When he heard the public calling him a sage or a man of character, he denied that he deserved such fame, saying, "I am anything but a great man worthy of such praise," and adding, "I am simply a man who admires the real sages and men of character and one who tries to absorb their teachings. I am always thinking about how to pass on their thoughts to my young disciples. I would like the public to value me as such." What he prided himself on, then, was his respect for traditional culture. Studying the teachings of the ancient sages and educating his disciples through them was enough to satisfy him. He felt he was doing all he could to understand these teachings in their truest sense and to guide young men as they set out on the path of learning. As his disciples said, "This is your most characteristic virtue, the last thing we could acquire." They realized all the more keenly how great their teacher was, and their admiration of him grew accordingly.

Confucius himself said, "When it comes to the pursuit of learning, I always feel I have achieved little. Moreover, I am afraid I will forget what little I've learned." Still, he knew well that he was very fond of learning. The *Analects* contain many references by him to his own enthusiasm for learning as well as detailing his ceaseless endeavors to encourage his followers to pursue knowledge.

To Confucius, studying was a practice through which one paid respect to traditional culture. He believed it was important to follow the beaten path in the world of learning and deeply ponder how to live. Furthermore, he felt it was vital to make the thought of the great men of the past a living reality in our lives. This way of studying he called *sojutsu* (back to the past).

Enthusiasm for learning and *sojutsu* constituted the essence of Confucius's way of living. He invariably acted on these two principles, which shows how high-minded he was. We can see why the more intimately his disciples came to know him, the more they admired him.

Confucius believed that human beings are born good in nature and that education enables them to grow in limitless ways. It was this conviction that encouraged him to devote his life to educating his followers. The *Analects* includes many sayings on this subject, such as, "Education makes men noble or mean. But when they are born, there is no difference between them," and "Men are born alike, but education makes them very different from each other." These well-known axioms attest to the importance Confucius attached to education. As he expected so much from it, he was proud of his enthusiasm for it. The fact that his disciples appreciated his selfless and boundless love of education was another reason why they admired him from the bottom of their hearts.

Confucius believed so strongly in education because he was convinced of the existence of conscience, the magnanimous inner voice that resides in us all. He was sure that humankind is possessed of general goodwill. If everyone were indeed good by nature, then education could bring this into flower. The *Analects* record the following famous sayings of his on this subject:

You should do to others what you would have them do to you.
You shouldn't do to others what you wouldn't have them do to you.

A man of character makes others feel satisfied before he makes himself satisfied.

A man of character lets others reach the goal before he himself arrives there.

Confucius taught that we should be considerate of others, basing this teaching on his firm conviction that everybody is born with goodwill.

Another virtue that Confucius and his followers prized highly was *kodo*, or, taking kindly care of one's parents, which they believed was the layer of goodwill that forms the foundation of the human heart. Confucianism ranked this above all the other virtues.

Confucius often talked with his disciples about how to put *kodo* into practice, and the *Analects* record many of their dialogues. One day, when a disciple named Zi-you asked Confucius about the essence of *kodo*, he answered:

These days, when I hear people say that someone takes good care of his parents, it seems to mean that he provides enough for them. Not that he looks up to them. But if you don't look up to your parents, there is no difference between you and a dog or a horse.

And when Zi-xia asked how *kodo*, which they had so often discussed, should appear in practice, Confucius answered: "Your facial expression in your parents' company should be a mild one." He was implying here that if people did not love their parents from the bottom of their heart, such an expression could not appear on their faces. But if it did, however, their general goodwill would be reflected in their respect for their parents.

Buddhism also has a great deal to teach about respect. Indeed, it makes even more of human goodwill than Confucianism does. According to Buddhist thinking, everybody possesses *bussho*, or the possibility of becoming another Buddha. Thus we can make a peaceful world, one without any conflict, by having respect for everybody, and Buddhism demands that we make every effort to this end. This concept of human goodwill is worthwhile to explore in detail.

The *Hokkekyo* is one of the sacred books of Buddhism, known in English as the *Lotus Sutra*. It includes the following story about a bodhisattva named Jo-fukei:

> Long, long ago, there lived a young novice priest. He didn't practice reading and memorizing the Buddhist Holy Books. He did nothing but pay respect to Buddha every day. To everyone he met, he spoke as follows: "I have profound reverence for you, I would never dare treat you with disparagement or arrogance. Why? Because you will all practice the bodhisattva way and will then be able to attain buddhahood."

This novice priest tried to cleanse the world by awakening people to their own dignity. However, the point of his experiment was lost on the public. Although those who were ready to learn the truth about life understood him, most people were offended by his speech and behavior. Some went so far as to shout at him, "Did we ask you not to disparage us? We certainly wouldn't mind being disparaged by you. You say we can become Buddhas. That's no business of yours. In fact, by saying so, you show that you really do despise us. We won't let you make fools of us."

Some of them even threw stones at him or tried to beat him with sticks. He escaped from them but still continued, though at a distance, to say loudly, "I respect you, I do not disparage you." This is why people called him Jo-fukei-bosatsu, or Bodhisattva Never Disparaging.

What belief was it that enabled Jo-fukei not to despise people but to respect everyone without exception? He believed that everyone possesses *bussho*, the possibility of becoming a Buddha. He respected others not because of their appearance or social status, but because of their *bussho*, which lies buried deep in the heart of every single human being.

All living things have this *bussho* in them. All *bussho* are one and the same and so they should be treated as equals. Jo-fukei accepted that people's outward appearances can differ enormously, varying according to the unique circumstances of their lives. Nonetheless, he believed, all people have this *bussho* in them, and it was therefore unacceptable to refuse to treat it with reverence. This was the conviction that made it possible for Jo-fukei to respect everyone.

The concept of *bussho* is one of the most important in Buddhism. It originally meant the *real nature of Buddha*, or *Buddha nature*. Yet it also came to refer to the *possibility of becoming a Buddha*. Therefore, when people say, "Everyone has *bussho* in them," they mean, "Everyone has the possibility of becoming a Buddha." The belief that people should honor this *bussho* is the basis of respect in Buddhism.

🍀　　🍀　　🍀

The situation of the world today makes us all aware of how many countries have co-existed and continue to co-exist on this earth, each devoting itself to nurturing its own unique history and culture. This situation will continue unchanged far into the future. At the same time, there are many conflicts between the peoples of the world. There are also many examples of different races hating each other within a given country. It seems very difficult for people to hold the same values in common even inside a single nation. Then, too, young people have different views from their elders. The hope that all people will one day be able to share mutual values seems like an empty dream.

But Eastern Asia has developed a culture of peace, which sets a high value on "living at peace with everybody and everything." Such a culture demands that countries should get along with one another, as should humankind with nature, one human being with another, human beings with the gods, and every one of us with our own circumstances or destiny. It is not a culture in which people believe they can be saved by gods or Buddha. Neither do they yearn for the next world to rescue them from the present one. Instead, they try to seek peace in their everyday lives. To achieve this, they believe that people must strive to live a moral life and respect one another, which means they are required to build up their characters and make their lives truly worth living through their own efforts.

The *Analects* record Confucius as saying, "However highly you think of someone in your heart, you may end up being regarded as a rough and impolite man if you cannot observe good manners." In the culture of peace, the most important problem is how to acquire and practice good manners (meaning both politeness and moral behavior) in order to be able to learn respect for others.

It is essential to discover the unique aspects of the cultures of countries other than one's own and to pay respect to the differences one finds. Doing so reveals how all countries should look up to one another. This is a useful recipe for avoiding disputes, even where we find that we cannot agree with the views of others. Exactly the same is true of individual human relationships, for while we may not find it too difficult to respect those who love us, we are seldom capable of adopting the same attitude to those who are hostile to us or do us injury.

We live in an age of distrust. Everywhere we hear of people suffering ill-treatment, bullying, or criminal cruelty. It is in just such an age, however, that we need to heed the essence of the teaching of respect described above; we need to learn to trust in human goodwill and be ready to rely on everyone's potential to do what is right. This will be of real help to us in seeking to respond to the fundamental question posed by the present era: What is the most important principle that we have to stick to as human beings?

The best answers to this question will incorporate the idea that a culture of respect can aid us greatly, both as individuals and in our efforts to create a secure and peaceful world. At the very least, it will illuminate some of the most important steps we need to take to realize this ideal.

Respect

BY KEVIN RYAN

The grandfather had become very old. His legs would not carry him, his eyes could not see, his ears could not hear, and he was toothless. When he ate, bits of food sometimes dropped out of his mouth. His son and his son's wife no longer allowed him to eat with them at the table. He had to eat his meals in the corner near the stove.

One day they gave him his food in a bowl. He tried to move the bowl closer; it fell to the floor and broke. His daughter-in-law scolded him. She told him that he spoiled everything in the house and broke their dishes, and she said that from now on he would get his food in a wooden dish. The old man sighed and said nothing.

A few days later, the old man's son and his wife were sitting in their hut, resting and watching their little boy playing on the floor. They saw him putting together something out of small pieces of wood. His father asked him, "What are you making, Misha?"

The little grandson said, "I'm making a wooden bucket. When you and Mama get old, I'll feed you out of this wooden dish."

The young peasant and his wife looked at each other and tears filled their eyes. They were ashamed because they had treated the old grandfather so meanly, and from that day on they let the old man eat with them at the table and took better care of him.

♣   ♣   ♣

This story, "The Old Grandfather and His Little Grandson," was written by the great Russian novelist Leo Tolstoy (1828–1910). It is, however, a tale that has appeared in the literature of many cultures. In the Chinese version, the grandfather breaks a valued porcelain bowl, and the family decides to remove him from the dining table. In another Asian version, the grandfather becomes a financial burden to his family, and in his frustration the son decides to throw him in the river. He begins weaving a carrying basket, but stops when one of his own young sons asks him to bring back the basket so that it can be used when he gets old and becomes a burden.

Like all universal stories, this one captures enduring truths. One truth is that we humans learn primarily from example. We are an imitative species. The eighteenth century British parliamentarian Edmund Burke (1729–1797) stated, "Example is the school of mankind," acknowledging the powerful learning we derive from those around us. This truth could not be more evident than in the actions of the young grandson. Children are like sponges, absorbing the attitudes and behaviors of people around them. The mother, burdened with her own narrow concerns, gave into her annoyance with her father-in-law. And the father had grown too indifferent to care. Young eyes were watching. Young ears were listening.

A second truth, and our focus here, concerns the virtue of respect. The frustrated daughter-in-law lost sight of the old man's humanity and treated him like an annoying object or a troublesome pet. It was not until she and her husband were shamed by their son's actions that they realized the profound disrespect with which they had treated the grandfather. The story, then, is one of loss and recovery of respect.

A root meaning of the word "respect" is to give something or someone particular attention or consideration. To respect another human being is to acknowledge and give consideration to the fact of his or her personhood. Respect transcends our feelings of liking or disliking a person and helps us to acknowledge his or her essential dignity and worth. It is not an overstatement to say that the virtue of respect is the habit of recognizing the intrinsic value of the other, which is at the very core of civilized life. Without respect, families, communities, and nations cannot hold together.

Without respect, international relations crumble.

Many doubt that respecting the other is part of human nature. A second century B.C.E. Roman playwright wrote, "Man is a wolf to man" (*Homo homini lupus*). This same dark view was developed by the British philosopher Thomas Hobbes (1588–1679), who described men as "poor, nasty, brutish and short." This failure to respect others—evidenced in the extreme by savagery and warfare—is at the heart of much of world history. In the modern world such breakdowns of respect can be catastrophic, too. Like all virtues, respect has an opposing vice, a deficiency of care and consideration for others.

Lack of respect is the disregard or failure to acknowledge the fundamental worth of the other. It can range from self-absorption and indifference to outright contempt for another person. Disrespect is not confined, however, to how we treat others. The person with low self-esteem who habitually neglects his own welfare lacks self-respect. And those who have no regard for knowledge or who pollute our environment can be faulted for their disrespect.

The virtue of respect, on the other hand, requires two things of us: understanding and action. We must come to the realization that the "other" is like us in that he or she has feelings, desires, and needs. He or she also has fundamental human dignity and worth. It is hardly a settled matter that humans are born with an instinctive respect for others. Many believe that a child comes into the world with a primitive drive to survive at all costs. Babies may fascinate their parents and others, but their world is one of self-absorption. They are the center of their own universes. They are, in this view, selfish—concerned with satisfying their own needs and desires. Growth and maturity entail overcoming innate selfishness and learning to appreciate the needs and desires of those around us. Full development as a person is characterized by a deep understanding of our shared humanity.

While understanding is essential, respect needs to be operational. Respect needs action. In the above story, the boy's parents not only had to recognize again the humanity of the old man, they needed to act. Without deeds, their respect would be empty. Essential to every virtue is a ready disposition to choose and act well.

We first learn about respect in family and in school. This tale is so poignant because a powerful lesson in respect and disrespect is being learned at home. These parents had an epiphany and changed their ways, drawing the grandfather back into the affectionate care of the family. He ultimately was treated with the dignity he deserved. Some children do not learn the fundamentals of respect at home. They go to school prepared to fight, reflecting the attitudes and behaviors they absorb at home.

Civic life is another arena where positive or negative lessons of respect are learned. Political regimes, whether democratic or totalitarian, are defined by their view of the individual. Is the dignity of the individual citizen respected or is it sacrificed to the power of the state? But civic life also involves the everyday street life of a community, the way people treat one another in stores and on the roads. The presence or absence of respect in our ordinary interactions with neighbors and strangers can profoundly affect the quality of our civic life.

The laws that govern a nation or a community are the encoded moral vision of its people. Laws are made to reflect and enforce decisions about how people can treat one another and, in turn, be treated. Good laws have at their heart a deep respect for the individual, and they require us, whatever our feeling toward the other, to acknowledge and respect his or her personhood. Still, we cannot respect the criminal activity, the offense, or wrongdoing of another, but we respect them as citizens entitled to a fair hearing or trial. Law-enforced respect is, therefore, a limited form of respect.

A deeper and richer form of respect is found in the great religions of the world. Religious-based respect is not based on family socialization, civic traditions, or legal mandates. It rests on the view of the person as transcendent, as a "child of God," and therefore commanding our respectful attention. If God loves and respects our neighbor, then who are we to deny him the same?

♣   ♣   ♣

In his seminal book, *Man's Search for Meaning*, Viktor Frankl, concentration camp survivor and existential philosopher, captures the resilience of the human spirit even amidst the most desperate circumstances. Drawing on his years of brutal imprisonment in a Nazi camp, he argues that regardless of what has been stripped of a person—materially or physically—no one can strip away "the last human freedom," that is, "to choose one's attitude."

To lead a fully flourishing human life, we need to appreciate and practice virtue, those cultivated dispositions of mind, heart, and action that enable us to use our freedom *well*—in family, school, professional, and civic life. Only human beings have the capacity for intelligent self-direction, to orient and lead their lives in pursuit of worthy and noble goals. Because we are rational and free, we need not become enslaved by impulse, addiction, or blind ambition. We have the capacity for reflection and self-correction. We have the ability to break those bad habits that undermine our health, our relationships, or our moral and spiritual wellbeing, our flourishing.

Respect helps us to flourish individually and collectively. It helps us to overcome biases and prejudices. It calls our selfishness into check. It helps us to attend to others, to listen and to learn from them. Respect teaches us to recognize their intrinsic value, not simply their utility. Respects calls forth the best in us and challenges us to regard others as we would like them to regard us.

The son and daughter-in-law in Tolstoy's tale are initially unaware of their disrespect, wholly unreflective about how they are treating the grandfather. When they discover their son is building a wooden bowl for them to eat from when they grow old, their own disrespect is illustrated in bold relief, and they are horrified. They needed to be prodded or jarred into the realization of their glaring disrespect.

From childhood, we come to learn the fundamentals of respect. Respect for elders, respect for the law, respect for the truth, respect for others, especially those who are different from us. Respect is the virtue we invoke when we teach children to take turns and to play fair. It is what motivates them not to taunt, ridicule, swear at, or bully another child. Respect is the reason for teaching manners and common courtesy, even though the specific manifestations of these manners may vary from culture to culture. We flourish. We live more excellent and happier lives when adults and children treat others with the respect they deserve.

Respect is the virtue that enables us to create and sustain a harmonious family life, to build healthy relationships, to be better friends, colleagues, mentors, and citizens. Without respect, relationships disintegrate to mere contractual agreements; employees are instrumentalized in the workplace; friends descend to objects of utility or pleasure. Respect needs to be an animating principle in our lives if we are to be happy and contribute to a culture of peace based on respectful dialogue, mutual support, care for those in need, and a responsible stewardship of our natural resources.

We all fail to greater or lesser degrees in the virtue of respect. For instance, when we don't agree with someone's religious or political views, we mentally lower them in our esteem. We find it difficult to have regard for people with annoying habits, such as talking too much or being sarcastic. We too often enjoy laughter at the expense of others. Many American schools are riddled with what is called a "putdown culture," where students vie with one another over who can be the more insulting. On the other hand, we all possess some form of respect. We respect the abilities of a skilled athlete or the talents of a singer. We find a friend's constant references to himself annoying, but we admire his skill as a conversationalist. Thus most of us do have respect, but its depth and reach in our everyday life is often wanting.

There are several ways to deepen the virtue of respect. One important way is to have people with highly developed respect as our mentors and models. In Tolstoy's story, the parents, as they always are, were the models for their son, and their son became the inadvertent mirror for his parents, forcing on them the realization of their failure to respect the grandfather. Our daily lives are filled with conscious examples of respect. In the car, a driver lets us go ahead of him. A younger woman holds a door for an older woman. A television commentator ignores the opportunity to interpret a public figure's particular embarrassing action in a negative way, but instead comments sympathetically on the situation. While being aware of these moments of public respect, they are no substitute for having one's own model of respect.

Some fortunate few have a model of respect nearby, in their own family, in their neighborhood, or at work. That person's presence and behavior is a continual reminder of how we should honor the intrinsic value of others. We witness daily how a respectful person behaves. In a manner of speaking, their good behavior rubs off on us. Or, at least, it can. One of the reasons committed parents monitor with whom their children associate is because the opposite is also true. Certain friends' disrespectful behavior can seep into children's thoughts and actions.

In our quest to deepen the virtue of respect, we are not limited to flesh and blood models. Stories, true and fictional, present us with models of respect in action. One of the strongest justifications for the reading of literature and history is that it ignites our moral imagination. We encounter people like ourselves, struggling to behave with respect often at times of great stress. We get an inside perspective that is typically veiled from us by the living models in our lives.

🍀 🍀 🍀

One of the realities of modern life is that we are inundated with stories. As opposed to earlier periods when people told stories to one another or read stories if they were available, now we have television and movie theatres, books on tape, films on discs—seemingly endless access to illustrations of the human condition. The great benefit coming from our exposure to all these historical and fictional lives is that they offer us the opportunity to empathize with those who struggle. In a way, we are allowed to walk in others' footsteps, and in our minds face their dilemmas and decisions. This modern exposure to so many lives provides us with a vast storehouse of data. And therein lays a problem.

When Tolstoy wrote his story in nineteenth century Russia, his audience had a much smaller storehouse of stories. The person hearing or reading about the grandfather and grandson probably reflected quietly on the story's events and meaning as he went about his farm chores or she tended to her family's needs, or on long walks to school or the village. They had opportunities to reflect on the mean-spirited disrespect of the son and daughter-in-law and think about its meaning for their own lives.

In contrast, the very volume of stories to which we are exposed can keep us from noticing and thinking about their moral message. We can, however, counter this tendency through acquiring the habit of reflection. To reflect means to mentally go over our experiences, actual or illusionary, trying consciously to extract personal meaning. (See Chapter 6.) "What happened that caused the daughter-in-law to lose sight of the grandfather's humanity? Are there people in my own life that I have stopped "seeing?" Are there people whom I have put in a mental box, which I have labeled in such a way that I have stopped recognizing their qualities and need for recognition?"

People with the habit of reflection are continually probing the meaning of their experiences, seeking to extract ways of perfecting their lives. And as we have stressed throughout this volume, habits can be learned, unlearned, and strengthened. A professor friend of ours teaches the virtue of respect by showing his students the film, *Groundhog Day*, a light romantic comedy. The plot involves a man who is completely selfish, with little or no respect for those around him. However, he is trapped in a particular day, Groundhog Day, and keeps having to relive it, meeting over and over the same people, encountering the same events, and unsuccessfully pursuing the same woman. Through many, many repetitions of Groundhog Day, he gradually confronts his lack of respect for others and begins his path toward virtue and true happiness. Many students who have seen the film previously realize that they had simply skimmed its surface and missed its deeper meaning. The professor shows the film not only to teach his students about the virtue of respect, but also to illustrate the habit of reflecting on the significance of our everyday choices and actions.

🍀　　🍀　　🍀

Finally, as with all virtues we wish to establish or strengthen, we need to consciously practice them. In the case of our deficiency of respect, we can take actions to bolster up this virtue—for instance, by giving attention to those we previously may have ignored; listening carefully to understand and appreciate those we normally don't take seriously; asking for clarification and seeking all sides of a story before drawing conclusions; fighting our preoccupation with self by being attentive to the needs of others and practicing courtesy in our words, tone of voice, and gestures; being punctual and respectful of people's time; being positive in the way we speak about people, mindful that our words can build up or tear down a person's reputation or esteem; being thorough in our work out of respect for those we serve and those we work with and for. While such actions may at first feel artificial, practice will change that. We learn that the other has more to offer than we thought and that there are human satisfactions to being respectful to others. The American psychologist Scott Peck (1936–2005) recommends that "we fake it until we make it." That is to say, practice the virtue even though doing so seems awkward and inauthentic, for it will one day become a natural habit and simply the way we respond to those around us.

CHAPTER 8

Responsibility

"Be the change you want to see in the world."
—Mahatma Gandhi

ⓒⓒⓒⓒ

Responsibility is an attitude in which we perceive our role and the duties tied to that role. Accepting roles and duties positively develops our character and protects as well as builds better relationships and communities. Devotion to one's duty is deeply rooted in Eastern culture, where fulfilling one's duty is both crucial to the successful functioning of the community and determines whether one will be admired or criticized by others. Masahide Ohno illustrates two types of responsibility with moving stories of individuals involved in tragic accidents. We see here again the Eastern focus on the interrelationship between individual and world, the network of human relationships, and on debt and gratitude; interestingly the same elements show up in the Western discussion. A description of the two-way flow of responsibility echoes the Buddhist view of the non-duality of self and environment. Another Buddhist concept evoked is cause and effect, in which one's circumstances reflect past actions, just as one's future will be determined through correct moral action in the present. This leads to a willingness to accept blame, where even seemingly arbitrary mishaps may be attributed to one's lack of virtue. We see responsibility as a voluntary weight, not something imposed by others, unless it is tied to fortune bestowed by heaven. This ancient view turns modern in a discussion of large corporations as being in service to the public.

The Western perspective comes through as a willingness to admit one's errors, regardless of the potential repercussions of doing so. We see the negative effects of not assuming responsibility through reference to a 1960s psychology experiment that showed people can ignore the effects of their actions on others by relinquishing personal responsibility. Here is a belief in the innateness of this virtuous attitude, which will emerge or not when situations calling for it arise. At such times, argues Bernice Lerner, responsibility is a choice and therefore within our power to bring forth. Like Ohno, she stresses recognizing one's role as key to being responsible. To both East and West, accepting and fulfilling one's various levels of responsibilities are seen as personally empowering, as a means for living constructively and directing one's own destiny. Both authors stress the power of a positive attitude for breaking through life's obstacles, quickly solving one's problems, and advancing.

Responsibility

BY MASAHIDE OHNO

In August 1985, a Japan Airlines Boeing 747 on a domestic flight from Tokyo to Osaka suffered catastrophic structural failure. The resulting explosive decompression blew apart the plane's tail fin and completely destroyed its hydraulic systems. With its flight controls disabled, the jet slalomed around the sky for thirty-two minutes before crashing into a mountain in Gunma Prefecture. Five hundred twenty of those on board were killed; only four survived. It remains the worst single-aircraft accident in history.

Several final notes written by doomed passengers during that dizzying, terrifying ride to death were recovered from the crash site. Keiichi Matsumoto told his wife and son, "A bang and we're starting to fall. Be brave and live." Hirotsugu Kawaguchi, fifty-two, left a message saying, "To think that our meal together yesterday was my last… I have had a happy life until now, and I am thankful for it." Ryohei Murakami, forty-three, listed the names of his wife, son, and daughter, telling them, "Farewell and live well …." Mariko Shirai, twenty-four, wrote "Scared, scared, scared, help, not feeling well, don't want to die …." She too listed the names of all her family members. Masaharu Taniguchi's message to his wife said, "Michiko, I leave the children to your care …" Michiko still has that paper and told newspaper reporters fifteen years after the accident, "My husband died thinking of us to the last minute, so we must not give up easily." All their children have grown into fine young men.

Completely out of the blue, with scarcely any time to prepare themselves, those on board were confronted with death. Amid the complete turmoil on board, some were able to pen their notes of farewell. All their messages indicated deep and strong love for their families, as well as fear and regret at having to end their lives in such a manner. Of the 520 victims, 254 were the main bread-winners for their families. Seventy-five were under fifteen years old.

The accident was a tragedy for all those whose lives it took or touched. Nonetheless, it serves to teach us something about the responsibility we have for our own lives and those of our families and others. We all accept the fact that death will part us from those we love someday. But none of us knows how long, nor under what conditions, we will continue to live. The 520 victims of the crash had no inkling of their end, or how to prepare for it, until shortly before their plane crashed into the mountain ridge. Many people who read their story, though, report coming away with the feeling that they themselves should behave more responsibly in safeguarding their family ties and their interactions with others, lest they too are caught unawares.

The same reaction is found among those who have read the story of another disaster, one that occurred just off the coast of Japan on April 15, 1910. Submarine Number Six of the Imperial Navy was practicing a dive in the bay of Hiroshima when it began to fill with water and sank to the sea floor. Over a period of about four hours, the remaining air on board gradually became noxious, and Tsutomu Sakuma, the captain in command, died together with all his crew. The submarine was salvaged the next day, and a thorough investigation was immediately ordered. The officer in charge of examining the vessel had been Sakuma's superior. Before opening the hatch he was overwhelmed with anxiety about what he would find. He knew of a similar accident in Europe where fear and desperation had led to panic and a chaotic fight for attempted survival among the crew. Their bodies had been found piled on top of each other just below the hatch. Such shameful behavior would do no honor to Sakuma or the Imperial Navy, the officer feared. But on opening the hatch of Submarine Number Six and seeing how things had gone inside the vessel, he cried, "Very good!" and burst into tears. Twelve of the fourteen crewmen, including the captain, had died at their posts. The other two seemed to have been trying to repair the gasoline pipe, which had ruptured and was leaking poisonous fumes. It was clear that none of the crew had abandoned their allotted duties even in their death agonies.

When Sakuma's body was examined, a note he had left was found in his breast pocket. It was written on thirty-nine different scraps of paper. In the opening sentences he apologized for losing the submarine and causing the crew's death. He reported that all his men had continued to perform their duties until the moment of death without any loss of self-control. He then analyzed the causes of the accident, explaining exactly how and why the catastrophe had occurred. In this, he was anxious above all to let those concerned know exactly what had happened for fear that the loss of his vessel might hold back Japan's development of its submarine fleet. In concluding his letter, he asked the Emperor to ensure that the bereaved families of the crew were not reduced to poverty.

In the case of a submarine crew, their superiors demand that they obey orders and carry out their duties to the letter. In times of peace, if they fall short of such expectations, they are blamed and, in some instances, punished. But in an emergency like the accident described above, there was no punishment to fear. Yet in this case all the crew members still performed their duties to the point of death. Only a genuine sense of responsibility could have made this possible, and it was doing their duty of their own free will that brought honor to their lives. A willingness to accept our responsibilities and work sincerely to fulfill them is one of the highest virtues.

We feel responsibility as something that flows in two directions between ourselves and others. The first current is deeply personal and proceeds outwards; from within the heart, a feeling akin to care and love prompts us to do all we can for the welfare of those close to us. The second is more impersonal, a matter of duty; here the flow is towards us, requiring that we faithfully live up to what others expect of us, even when we do not know them at all well.

The final moments of those on board Japan Airlines Flight 123 illustrate both these kinds of responsibility. The last words of those who were regarded as the heads of their families speak of their sorrow at being unable to carry out the responsibility they felt they owed to those who depended on them. On the other hand, just like Captain Sakuma and his fellow submariners, the members of the crew of Japan Airlines Flight 123 had a second kind of responsibility. One final letter reported how the flight attendants did their best to maintain calm on board even amid such a dire emergency. The flight recorder also revealed how the crew at the plane's controls did everything possible to save the lives of the passengers right up to the last moment. The captain did not abandon his responsibility, even in the final seconds. He died struggling to lift the plane clear of the looming mountainside: "Raise the nose, flaps up, pull up!"

In the case of Captain Sakuma, trapped aboard his naval vessel, it might be presumed that his concern for his public duties did not leave him time for any final words to his family. However, this was not the case; he fulfilled the second part of his responsibility in a heartwarming final message to his family that was found together with his last official report. In this private note he wrote, "Nothing remains the same; everything is in transition in this world. I leave these last words in case something serious happens to me; otherwise my family will be left helpless, or a conflict may arise over my estate. So I give the following directions about how to distribute my estate." He then added one more sentence, and one only, referring to himself: "If I die, my body is to be buried alongside my deceased wife in my hometown."

Captain Sakuma had married his wife, Kasuya Tsugiko, in 1888. The following year she died after giving birth to her daughter, Teruko. Even though their marriage had lasted less than a year, the love between them was richer and deeper than the ocean that took Captain Sakuma's life, and his body was buried in the same tomb as his wife in accordance with his final request.

In the last hours and minutes of their lives, under the most difficult circumstances imaginable, the concern for others shown by so many aboard Submarine Number Six and Flight 123 stands out as a beacon, and a definition, of true responsibility. It is the reason why many of those who read these stories feel they should become more responsible in their daily lives. How, then, is this to be done?

♣   ♣   ♣

As members of a variety of communities, from family to urban or rural neighborhood to country to humankind as a whole, we all exist in a network of human relationships, supporting others and being supported by them. Each of the many communities we belong to requires us to play a particular part. Once we realize what it is, we want to live up to the community's expectations, and this forms the basis of our sense of responsibility. Advocates of individualism, though, believe that human beings should be independent of others as isolated entities. Their starting point is the dignity of the individual human being, which is why they hold that society came into being in order to enable such beings to live together in cooperation. In Asia, including Japan, on the other hand, it has traditionally been taken for granted that every individual is bonded to society by nature. The belief here is that people are born and brought up in a society, so that as they grow, they are supported by many others. It is not too much to say that individuals can only exist in a network where they can depend on and be depended upon by others.

Communities vary greatly in size from the smallest, the family, to the largest, human society in general, but they form a stratified whole. Each functions and develops properly only if all their members perform the duties allotted to them. Every member, then, is required to make a contribution to the community, and so people must understand what is imposed upon them by each community and act on that recognition. Carrying out our duties willingly means that we can be said to be acting as responsible people. At the same time, we can strengthen our sense of responsibility by being considerate of others who belong to our community.

Every individual belongs to many communities, and since these differ so much in character, the responsibilities imposed on an individual vary from community to community, meaning that a person may be required to shoulder many kinds of responsibility. With the family, for instance, all its members need to help one another in order to sustain their life together. Above all, if there are young children, or an elderly, sick, or handicapped family member, it is practically ordained that all the others assist and provide for them. Of course, parents cannot escape the responsibility of giving their children an education that enables them to live a proper social life. The sense of responsibility in this instance is based on love.

Then again, with a neighborhood, people have the responsibility to help maintain and develop its social life and to take care of weaker residents. This is usually not a legal, but rather a moral responsibility, so every member has to choose to participate in the activities there if local society is to develop properly. In the world of business, on the other hand, it is the responsibility of both parties concerned to carry out the terms of a contract to the letter. Failing this, some penalty is supposed to be imposed. In corporations, all employees are required to perform the duties given to them. Especially in Japanese corporations, where teams are often organized to carry out a task, employees are required to help each other so that the team can perform what is expected of it.

What about the country as a whole? People are legally required to contribute to the state's finances by paying tax. But when it comes to human society as a whole, there is no obvious form of community. Nonetheless, as will be discussed later, people have begun to insist that we should feel a responsibility towards future generations, at least as regards global environmental problems.

Some of the above-mentioned responsibilities are legal requirements, but most of them are moral responsibilities. If people carry

them out, they may be admired; if they don't, they may be criticized. However, they will not be punished by law, which means that
all members of the community must recognize their responsibilities
and try voluntarily and dynamically to contribute to it. Only then
will the community become able to function entirely as it should.

In Japan, people base their sense of responsibility on the idea
that all individuals should recognize their *honbun* (the responsibility allotted to them) and accept that it is one of the highest virtues to carry this out faithfully. *Honbun* refers to the sphere within
which a person is supposed to play an active part jointly with others, and it conveys something of the essence of the English words
"share" or "portion." It also implies, though, that people should accomplish not only what is expected of them by the community but
also the duties allotted to them by Buddha and the Shinto gods.

This belief originated within the Samurai elite but was adopted
by other classes from the middle of the Edo period (1603–1868)
on, when philosophers like Suzuki Shozan (1579–1655) and Baigan
Ishida (1685–1744) conveyed its essence to the common people.
As this fitted well with the contemporary ethics of work and social structure, the public in general was receptive to it. Ishida said,
"If you devote yourself to your job, it will help you build up your
character." His many disciples helped to spread this idea throughout the country, and it became known as "Ishida's heart learning"
(Jap. *sekimon shingaku*). At its core was the belief that while everyone had to labor partly in order to earn a living, work was also a
matter of living up to the expectations of society. It was not that
people were simply forced to work hard against their will by those
above them; now they were also encouraged to decide of their own
free will to come to grips with their calling. They were encouraged
to carry out their responsibilities voluntarily and settle down to labor willingly. This became the culture of work in the Edo period.

If people decide to forge their own characters by devoting themselves to their jobs, sooner or later they are bound to acquire a
self-motivated sense of responsibility and a belief that they should

nurture their lives by their own efforts. Buddhism teaches the law of cause and effect: doing good will lead to people reaping a good harvest; doing wrong will bring them misfortune. Although this belief is not as strongly held as before, it is still the basis of the moral consciousness of the Japanese. Put another way, whatever our lives are like, they are the result of what we did in the past. This idea does much to enhance a sense of self-responsibility, encouraging us to deal actively with our own lives and not just passively await change. With this perspective, we can develop a spirit of self-help. Japanese people believed that their future was not decided by external factors, but that people could change their futures by their own efforts. This concept made people hopeful and encouraged them to do their best in every phase of their lives, rousing within them virtues such as diligence, honesty, and frugality, which have played an important role in developing the country's modern economy.

There are many instances in life where we cannot be sure who is to blame for a problem. It may, for instance, be the result of a coincidence or some unexpected event. In such cases, though, people are apt to avoid shouldering the responsibility themselves and blame it on others instead. As a result, conflicts arise that prevent them from finding a speedy solution to the problem.

Occasionally, however, even when it is not clear who is to blame, someone involved assumes responsibility for the unfavorable turn of events and is willing to take the blame. As the *Analects of Confucius* says, "A respectable man blames things on himself, whereas a mean fellow finds fault with others." Willingly bearing the blame is regarded as one of the highest virtues in the East.

A Japanese person who suffers a misfortune may say, "This was caused by my lack of virtue." Even if the misfortune may well appear to be the result of external factors, such people believe their lack of virtue has offended Buddha or the Shinto gods and so they are experiencing misfortune as a punishment. The law of cause and effect accepted in the East allows people to acknowledge that everyone can encounter some unexpected misfortune. But this is not to be used as an excuse to feel pessimistic. Instead, people should recognize misfortune as a problem for which they are responsible. This way of responding to adversity is intended to encourage people to adopt a positive attitude, to face up to their problems squarely, and so be able to solve them more quickly.

It is often said that the higher one's social status, the more responsible one will be held for things in general. For people with influence, then, responsibility is not something imposed on them by others, but a weight that they should shoulder voluntarily. This has a lot in common with the European concept of *noblesse oblige*, which holds that as people become more and more "public" as they rise in the world, so more and more is rightly expected of them.

Monarchs and other figures of influence are expected not to confine their interests to the small community of their relatives and friends but to assume responsibility for the care of the larger community and to ensure that the people have comfortable lives and are physically and psychologically happy. Such a considerate attitude on the part of those with power, called *jin* in Japanese, is prized in East Asia. To live up to *jin*, people in authority must cultivate their character. They are required to become wise enough to decide how things are going in the world, thoughtful enough to feel sympathy with the public, and have judgment enough to make impartial decisions without prejudice. All this constitutes *jin*, the highest morality to which every statesman should aspire.

Uesugi Yozan (1751–1822), a famous feudal lord in the Edo period, is one of the most respected statesmen in Japanese history. When he retired from ruling his lands, he wrote a letter to his adopted son and heir explaining how he should govern the fief (territory). This famous document is headed, "On Occasion of Entrusting the Fief to the Heir," and reads as follows:

1) The fief is what you have taken over from your ancestors and you will hand down to your descendants. You must not regard it as your private property.

2) The people belong to the country. You must not regard them as your private property.

3) The lord exists for the good of the country and the people. It is not the case that the country or the people exist for the benefit of the lord.

His letter says, in short, that the lord must devote himself to enabling his people to live in comfort and peace.

Much the same point was made by the thinker Sato Issai (1772–1859), who also lived in the Edo period. In a philosophical work entitled *Genshiroku* (*What I Want to Say*), he wrote:

> Both territory and people were given by heaven. It is the lord's duty to provide for the people and give decent status and a proper job to each of them. If he makes the mistake of regarding them as his own property and treating them as he wishes, this amounts to stealing what belongs to heaven.

If we give too much attention to the interests of a small community, we may well satisfy those who belong to it, but at the same time, we run the risk of neglecting the demands of the larger communities to which we also belong. We may, for instance, be guilty of misusing our power for the advantage of those close to us. Instead, we should give priority to carrying out the duties given us by heaven, and men of high rank should not hesitate to forgo private interests in favor of the public. This was certainly the belief of Japanese people in former times.

Modern Japan has been blessed with many excellent entrepreneurs possessed of a strong sense of their responsibility as public figures. The late founder of Panasonic, Matsushita Konosuke, is perhaps the most famous of these. He strongly believed that "A corporation is a public organ" and thought that its mission is to contribute to the prosperity of society and the happiness of the people by providing them with a variety of products and services.

Profit is simply the reward given by society in return for such activities. Today, more and more corporations in Japan are trying to base their management philosophy on a sense of responsibility that requires them to benefit society.

This awareness reflects the fact that we exist in both space and time, extending from the past to the future. No community exists in the present alone. Every community passes itself on to the next generation, perpetuating and renewing itself. Japanese people have traditionally accepted this fact as a matter of course, which is why religious services for one's ancestors have been regarded as of great importance. Whether it is family, neighborhood, corporation, or country, Japanese people see the value of a community in the fact that it has existed in the past and will form part of the future. Since they wish such entities to be eternal, every generation has thought of itself as under an obligation to develop the communities it receives from the preceding generation and to hand them on in good condition to the next.

Historically speaking, the basis of Japan's modernization since the Meiji Restoration (1868) has been a strong sense of responsibility. In the Meiji Era (1868–1912), many youngsters studied hard in order to rise in the world. Some went on to start enterprises. They were sustained in this by the strength of their will and the hope of opening up a path through life by their own efforts. Many of them were confirmed in this hope by reading the book, *Self-Help*, by Samuel Smiles (1812–1904), which had just been translated into Japanese and had become a best seller, with total sales of more than a million copies.

Such young people did not seek after success for themselves alone. They were also desperate to help make Japan as strong a power as any European country. What animated them most was a sense of their responsibility to play some part in building up their nation's strength.

Robert Neelly Bellah, a U.S. sociologist of religion, has drawn attention to the influence of Baigan Ishida and other Japanese teachers on these developments. He argues that Ishida's moral asceticism is the Japanese version of the Protestant work ethic and that it was the key factor in the development of capitalism in Japan. It is true that, later, there was some criticism of Ishida's view for helping to entrench the class system. Nonetheless, even after the Meiji Restoration, Japanese people never discarded the belief that everybody should devote themselves to performing their duty. This was the basis on which Japan grew to be a modern country.

A genuine self-motivated sense of responsibility gives us the feeling that we are not controlled by others, that we are determining our own direction in life, and that we can enjoy good fortune in the future by relying on our own abilities and character. Such conviction will encourage us to strive toward that end. At the same time, rousing ourselves to an awareness that we are responsible to others and to the community means we can regard ourselves as people of worth. We will also feel confident that we are important members of the community, needed and wanted by others. Thus encouraged to take on a larger role in the running of the community, we will find ever greater enjoyment in life.

Such is not the case in an extremely divided society, though, where making an effort doesn't always pay off. In such a society, people lose a sense of responsibility even for their own lives. In addition, the very poor are sometimes excluded from the community. Then people do not feel they have real relationships with anyone, which prevents them from developing a sense of responsibility toward others. So while it is of course necessary to encourage people to feel responsible, it is also vital to make the community congenial enough for them to want to do their best to contribute to it. Only then will people living in the same community feel a duty to improve conditions there.

♣　　♣　　♣

How can we strengthen our sense of responsibility? A variety of practices can help us here.

We should begin by paying attention to the fact that we already owe a lot to many individuals. Various people have helped us in every conceivable way since we were born. People in the Eastern world refer to such support received from others as *on* (goodwill or benevolence). We should feel grateful for such *on* and try to repay what we owe. This responsibility falls on every individual.

Buddhism teaches that we must not forget the four important *on* from which we all benefit: these are the *on* we receive from our parents, from the monarch, from our teachers, and from the public, or society. If we are to be properly human, we must acknowledge our debt to every kind of *on*. However, expressing our obligation openly is meaningless if we do so only because others force us. We must believe in our heart of hearts that we do owe these debts of gratitude and then act accordingly. In some cases, though, we don't have to repay a kindness to the person from whom we receive it. If we do good to others or to the community, we can be said to have fulfilled our responsibility to do something in return for an act of kindness. Human interactions like these are what enable us to grow, and we must never forget that we can best fashion our character by feeling gratitude and trying to devote ourselves to others and to the community.

It is up to each of us to decide the proper way to show appreciation for and repay the *on* we receive. If we try to list all the people who show concern for our daily welfare, we may find there are various individuals whose help has largely escaped our notice. Developing an awareness of their concern for our well-being gives us the comfort of knowing that we are not alone in this world, and a feeling of gratitude for their care then awakens in us. Such thankfulness, though, should also be extended to the kindnesses we have received from those who are already dead. Since we cannot return the favor in these cases, we must instead do good to those who are still alive, as if we owed this debt to them.

Secondly, we should review what parts those around us expect us to play. We all belong to a wide variety of communities at any one time. We should ask ourselves about our role in each of these communities and what we contribute to them. Of course, it is beyond any of us to satisfy all the demands placed on us on a daily basis. So we need to decide for ourselves which are more important and which are less so.

Lastly, when contemplating a course of action, we should make a list of the people who would be made happy or unhappy by our doing or not doing it. Then we should consider our choice in this light. Today, as people become more aware of the social responsibilities of corporations, ever greater consideration is given to how stakeholders are affected by a business's activities. How many and which of them will be made happy or unhappy by a particular decision? How will they suffer or benefit from what is done? Corporations should try to answer these questions precisely and definitively before they embark on a course of action. This approach can also be adopted by individuals. We should press ourselves to do all we can to ensure that our actions have positive rather than negative outcomes. As we become more accustomed to making this effort, we will find it easier to develop a true sense of responsibility.

As we have seen, responsibilities are of two kinds. One involves living up to the expectations of those around us. We must faithfully perform all the duties required of us. The other is to make sure that all our actions result in good done to others. We must discard vague ideas and use our imagination to the fullest so that we can predict the outcome of our actions more accurately.

Responsibility

BY BERNICE LERNER

In 1962, Grumman Aerospace Corporation received a contract to build lander portions for Apollo spacecraft. Its engineers set about designing thirteen structurally and aerodynamically sound lunar modules, enabling six spacecraft to successfully land on the moon between 1969 and 1975. How did these engineers create what was arguably the most reliable component of the Apollo system? Through trial and error over several years. None of the modules' parts could be ordered; all had to be handmade. Landing gear had to be tried out on different surfaces, at different angles, under various conditions. Other considerations included weight, safety, and the avoidance of potential problems.

In one test, a leg of the landing gear snapped. Working late into the night, an engineer involved in the module's design pored over figures. When he realized that he had made an error, he was crestfallen. This was no simple mistake—months of work had been based on his miscalculation. A NASA launch might be delayed on his account. What to do?

The very next day, the young engineer went into the office of Tom Kelly, head of the lunar module design team. He showed his calculations to his boss, who quickly realized the error and its ramifications. Taking full responsibility, the dejected engineer expected to be fired. Kelly, though upset, famously responded: "As long as people speak up about their mistakes, we've got a shot, okay? They try to sweep [them] under the rug, and we're not going to New Jersey, let alone the moon."

Imagine the sleepless night this young man endured. Imagine

what it took for him to bring to his boss's attention such a conse-
quential error. Others in like positions might not have come forward. Most employees care about their reputations; they feel
embarrassed when their work is discovered to be sub par. They fear
disappointing their colleagues and bosses. And then there is the
matter of conflicting responsibilities, such as having bills to pay and
possibly a family to support. When one's livelihood is at stake, one
might wish for one's mistakes or missteps—of which even the most
conscientious are capable—to go unnoticed. And, of course, it is human to avoid what is painful. In the words of former presidential
advisor Bernard Baruch (1870–1965), "Even when we know what
is right, too often we fail to act. More often we grab greedily for
the day, letting tomorrow bring what it will, putting off the unpleasant and unpopular."

To lead a good life, it is imperative to own one's deeds and, if
necessary, face the unpleasant. In so doing one realizes one's strength
and gains self-respect. The lunar module engineer did not blame
anyone else for the error or resulting design flaws. By accepting responsibility he might have paid a severe penalty, but he preserved
his ability to move forward with integrity.

To further appreciate this young engineer's moral decision, let
us consider that he was but an intermediary, a link in a chain of action. In such a position it is, according to psychologist Stanley Milgram (1933–1984), "easy to ignore responsibility." After all, "the
buck stops" with the boss. One in an intermediary position has an
excuse at the ready.

The most extreme examples of this are cases wherein interme-
diaries knowingly harm or murder innocents. Milgram was particularly concerned with cogs (such as World War II concentration
camp guards) who carried out others' orders. While teaching at
Yale University in the 1960s, he conducted several social psychology experiments involving the administering of (ostensible) electric shocks for wrong answers given on a word pair test. Seeking
to determine how much pain one person would inflict on another

before stopping to mete out increasingly intense punishment, Milgram observed most subjects' discomfort. As voltage was turned up, an actor would scream and then bang on a wall separating himself and the subject. After specific verbal prods to continue on, most, even hesitant, subjects obeyed the experimenter, whom they saw as an authority figure. One theory explaining this behavior: the obedient person views himself as the instrument for carrying out another person's wishes and therefore does not see himself as responsible for his actions. Another theory suggests that the subjects suffer learned helplessness: powerless to control the outcome, they abdicate personal responsibility.

Of course, failure to take responsibility for one's actions is seen not only in those who defer to authority figures but also in those who lead. One need only follow the news to learn about morally bankrupt politicians—or certain captains of investment banks who cared not whether they could injure their clients or could trigger, by means of excessive leveraging and investment risk, a worldwide financial crisis!

Examples of irresponsibility abound, too, in the arts. One protagonist who epitomizes this vice is the U.S. Navy lieutenant, Pinkerton, in Puccini's opera *Madame Butterfly* (story by John Luther Long (1861–1927)). During a stopover in Nagasaki, Japan, the dashing figure becomes enchanted by a geisha, fifteen-year-old Cio-Cio-San. Aspiring to "make his treasures on every shore," Pinkerton pursues the beautiful girl, a "butterfly" whose wings he will damage. Cio-Cio-San marries him, embraces his Christian faith, and, while Pinkerton is away, bears his son. Eagerly awaiting his promised return, Madame Butterfly gazes out to sea. Three years pass. Finally, Pinkerton returns—with his new American wife! The woman approaches Madame Butterfly and claims the little boy. Devastated, Cio-Cio-San commits suicide by means of hara-kiri—a tragic outcome of Pinkerton's egoism.

Judging actions so evidently reprehensible helps us to hone our understanding of human decency. We see that we are responsible, above all, for how we treat others. And that no matter one's station in life, right action under duress reveals strength of character. It is important to note that the person who rises to the occasion during crises is likely one who displays responsible behavior as a matter of course. In the words of the first female African bush pilot Beryl Markham (1902–1986), "If a man has any greatness in him, it comes to light, not in one flamboyant hour, but in the ledger of his daily work."

What are those everyday ways and contexts in which we display responsibility?

As members of families, schools, religious organizations, and neighborhoods, we may execute chores, support local businesses or charities, participate on a conservation commission or library board, vote, or assist the disadvantaged or disabled. Young people may likewise volunteer for community service in their schools and local communities and consciously shape positive lifestyle habits, such as handing in neat assignments, putting things back where they belong, recycling and using recycled products, and helping to maintain congenial classrooms. In all such instances people act responsibly by not waiting for someone else to do what they themselves are capable of doing. They abide by the sentiment, "I must do something," rather than "Something must be done."

The responsible "something to be done" will vary according to one's role. Responsible doctors treat the patients before them as though they were the most important individuals in the world. Responsible teachers model diligence and caring. Responsible store clerks show up on time and provide good service to customers. And responsible journalists tell stories that are accurate and serve the public interest.

At the time of this writing, November 30, 2010, *The New York Times* began publishing articles based on a sampling of 250,000 cables—a body of secret or confidential correspondence between the U.S. State Department and more than 270 American diplomatic outposts around the world. These field reports, intended only for senior policy makers in Washington D.C., were obtained by WikiLeaks, an organization bent on exposing official secrets.

With its publication of the first such diplomatic documents, the *Times* issued "A Note to Readers." Explaining its decision to thus illuminate aspects of American foreign policy, the newspaper made clear that it had excluded any "information that would endanger confidential informants or compromise national security" and that it shared its careful redactions with other news organizations, hoping that they would similarly edit documents before posting them. The *Times* also invited Obama administration officials to challenge any of the cables they planned to publish; they would consider additional suggested redactions.

The documents would be made public regardless of the *Times* decision. WikiLeaks provided the material to several news organizations and intended to publish the full archive on its own website. The *Times* could not ignore the material. Nor could it deny its readers thoughtful analyses of selected cables that tell "the unvarnished story of how the government makes its biggest decisions." Weighing the dangerous effects of disclosing private, diplomatic conversations, the *Times* editors strove to exercise responsible journalism.

Unanticipated leaks aside, consider that the responsible person is one to whom we would entrust a secret or our dearest possessions for safekeeping. And we will be thought responsible if we are for others that trustworthy person. Consider, too, that the responsible person acts not only in the moment, but also with a view to the future. He or she may prepare for a career that enables self-sufficiency and engagement in worthwhile work, cultivate enduring relationships, and save for a "rainy day." Consider that the responsible person will have reverence for both man-made and God-given treasures, acting as an appreciative trustee of the younger generation and of art, architecture, and the environment. Theodore Roosevelt (1858–1919), the twenty-sixth president of the United States, exemplified such responsibility. "Do what you can, with what you have, where you are," said Roosevelt. Another of his mottos: "When you are asked if you can do a job, tell 'em 'Certainly I can!' Then get busy and find out how to do it." In what ways did this man born to a wealthy family, who at age forty-two became the youngest person to assume the U.S. presidency, proceed to discover and fulfill his duties?

In 1906 Roosevelt responded to American author Upton Sinclair's *The Jungle*—depicting horrific conditions in meat packing plants—by passing the Meat Inspection and Pure Food and Drug acts. He built the Panama Canal as a contribution to civilization. He saw to federal insurance that would provide for the elderly, sick, and jobless. He also passed the Antiquities Act, which led to the creation of eighteen national monuments. Among his greatest legacies was conservation. During his presidency, from 1901 to 1909, he created fifty-one wildlife refuges and the National Park Service. He established five national parks and protected 150 national forests and 230 million acres of national land. For Roosevelt, natural resources, in danger of being squandered for private, improper uses, were precious. Motivated by the belief that "Forests are the lungs of our land, purifying the air and giving fresh strength to our people," he ensured that his nation would preserve its "soul." Future generations would be the beneficiaries of Roosevelt's profound sense of responsibility.

Theodore Roosevelt actively shaped his destiny. Abraham Lincoln, Albert Einstein, and Eleanor Roosevelt are also among American leaders who left significant and positive marks on their country and our world. The life stories of such leaders can inspire us to forge noble paths. What do we look for in these stories? Evidence of responsibility as a *disposition of choice*.

The psychiatrist and philosopher Viktor Frankl has deepened our understanding of human flourishing. He identified three forms of destiny. The first of these, one's biological endowment, involves inheritance and concerns matters about which one has no say. Individuals possess—to greater or lesser degrees—innate temperaments and talents. One person may have athletic skills, another may have an ear for music or perfect pitch. One person may have inborn enthusiasm or spiritedness, another may be temperamentally subdued. One's biological endowment can limit or expand one's possibilities for achievement in numerous areas.

The second form of destiny, one's external environment, is—especially in the early years of one's life— also not chosen. Our destinies *are* partly shaped by the milieus we are born into and those situations that we navigate throughout the course of our lives. Young people may flourish or suffer on account of their home environments, their neighborhoods, and the schools they attend. (Some schools are academically rigorous; some have strong traditions; some lack a sense of decorum and order.) Adults may grow or stagnate at their places of work; the climate therein makes all the difference.

But it is the third form of destiny, one's attitude, that is determinative. Given our capacities, given the situations in which we find ourselves, what should we think, say, or do? What approach should we adopt? Our choices, from among a range of possible responses, will determine how we fare. Our attitude is our destiny.

People who choose a responsible course shape their destiny in powerful ways. A counselor who works with hundreds of homeless children in western Massachusetts explains that many of them do not have notebooks, let alone computers. Despite their disadvantages, some of these children work extremely hard. "They will," she predicts, "break out of their circumstances and improve their lives." Are these ambitious kids academically gifted? Not necessarily. According to the counselor, "*It's all about attitude.*"

An inner city high school teacher works with students recently arrived from foreign countries. She is concerned that they will pick up certain American teenage habits, such as rude and rowdy behavior in the hallways. At the risk of stereotyping, she shares an observation: "Immigrants who know that they cannot return to the countries from which they came have a strong work ethic—they appreciate opportunities given them and try to achieve goals." After a moment's reflection, she adds, "They have such a positive attitude."

Most every teacher can relay a story about a student whose fortitude and sense of responsibility have helped him or her to overcome difficulties. And all of the adults in a school—administrators, teachers, secretaries, and librarians—can encourage students, no matter their temperaments and abilities, no matter the circumstances of their lives, to practice responsibility. Rights, freedoms, and privileges do not alone ensure human flourishing. Frankl argued that the Statue of Liberty on America's East Coast should have a corollary Statue of Responsibility near California's shore.

❧   ❧   ❧

Responsibility is realized in positive action. It is what we do and not what we think or feel that ultimately matters. Even those who find pleasure in fulfilling their duties may at times wish for respite, freedom from burdensome tasks. They nevertheless care for a sick relative, plug away at grueling work, and ably balance communal and family obligations. Such individuals carry responsibility gracefully, without complaint. But they ought not to take over others' jobs or manage more than they should.

Helping the young to embrace responsibility entails providing for them opportunities to make age appropriate, right-sized contributions. According to advice columnist Abigail Van Buren, "If you want children to keep their feet on the ground, put some responsibility on their shoulders." Purposeful activities include setting or clearing the table, babysitting younger children, preparing a meal, or running errands. To the extent children are counted on to assist at home, they realize their capacities. Author Booker T. Washington (1856–1915) noted: "Few things help an individual more than to place responsibility upon him and to let him know that you trust him."

While responsibility begins at home, with proper education, it spreads. It is the moral obligation of adults to help young people not only exercise responsibility locally, but also to embrace causes larger than themselves, in all spheres of life. In his "An Essay on Man," Alexander Pope (1688–1744) wrote:

God loves from Whole to Parts: but human soul
Must rise from Individual to Whole.
Self-love but serves the virtuous mind to wake,
As the small pebble stirs the peaceful lake;
The centre mov'd, a circle strait succeeds,
Another still, and still another spreads,
Friend, parent, neighbour, first it will embrace
His country next, and next all human race ....

The little prince, in Antoine de Saint-Exupéry's book by the same name, saw responsibility as "a question of discipline." "When you've finished washing and dressing each morning, you must tend your planet," he said.

A dimension of tending one's planet is standing up to injustice. The Babylonian Talmud offers a striking perspective on this matter:

> One who could prevent a family member from doing wrong and does not protest is held responsible for the wrongdoing.
> One who could prevent a fellow community member from doing wrong and does not protest is held responsible for the wrong-doing.
> One who could prevent wrongdoing anywhere in the world and does not protest is held responsible for the wrongdoing.

Bystanders are morally culpable. How can we help young people to become "up-standers," to speak out against bullying, hatred, and that which is harmful or destructive? Lest we feel overwhelmed, let us consider that the question is not "What can we do that will actually make a difference on a global scale?" but rather, "What modest action on my part can improve the lives of others?" The following poem, by songwriter and former teacher Bob Blue, illustrates a boy's journey to responsibility.

COURAGE

A small thing once happened at school that brought up a question for me
And somehow it forced me to see the price that I pay to be cool.
Diane is a girl that I know. She's strange and she doesn't belong.
I don't mean to say that that's wrong. We don't like to be with her, though.

And so when we all made a plan to have this big party at Sue's
Most kids in our school got the news, but no one invited Diane.

The thing about Taft Junior High is, secrets don't last very long.
I acted like nothing was wrong when I saw Diane start to cry.
I know that you think that I'm cruel, it doesn't make me very proud
I just went along with the crowd. It's sad but you have to at school.

You can't pick the friends you prefer. You fit in as well as you can.
I couldn't be friends with Diane, 'cause then they would treat me like her.

In one class at Taft Junior High, we study what people have done
With gas chamber, bomber and gun, in Auschwitz, Japan and My Lai.
I don't understand all I learn. Sometimes I just sit there and cry.
The whole world stood idly by to watch as the innocent burned.

Like robots obeying some rule. Atrocities done by the mob.
All innocent—doing their job. And what was it for, was it cool?

The world was aware of this hell, but nobody cried out in shame.
No heroes and no one to blame. A story that no one dared tell.
I promise to do what I can to not let it happen again,
To care for all women and men. I'll start by inviting Diane.

CHAPTER 9

Temperance

"Moderation is medicine, excess is peril." —*Burmese*

ᘓᘐ ᘓᘐ ᘓᘐ

At last we come to the final chapter of our exploration of virtues and happiness in the East and West. Temperance can be broadly understood as restraint or self-control, and these essays reveal the subtleties, risks, and benefits of this virtue. The first opens with a profile of a baseball player, tying his habits of self-discipline to his Major League successes. We will see again in the second essay another baseball player, this one exemplifying a different facet of temperance, one who controlled his desire for success in order to honor his faith and do what he felt was right. Temperance collaborates with wisdom to enable us to avoid two main obstacles to this virtue—self-indulgence and laziness. Moreover we need it to cultivate in our hearts such character strengths as kindness, generosity, patience, and diligence.

Temperance in the East refers not just to partaking of activities in moderation but also encompasses control of one's strong emotions; it is considered good manners to conceal them. Manners arise in the discussions from both East and West, implying within this virtue the influence of others, such as respect and appreciation. Haruo Kitagawa and Shujiro Mizuno caution that while the benefits of temperance include accomplishments and transcending differences between people to achieve greater goals, it is not without its risks; an over-concern with self-control can lead to repression or a self-centered existence.

The self-mastery that arises from practicing this virtue can benefit us, writes Karen Bohlin, in developing competence and self-possession; the ability to respond well under pressure, to control our emotions, to deal with the vicissitudes and injustices of life; the ability to live a life of greater value, accomplishment, and contribution to our world. In fulfilling our potential, in living true to our hearts, to our true values, unswayed by destructive or tempting influences, we can open up ways to true happiness and a more just and harmonious world.

Temperance

BY HARUO KITAGAWA AND SHUJIRO MIZUNO

In 2010, Ichiro Suzuki, who plays right field for the Seattle Mariners, recorded his tenth consecutive 200-hit season, the longest streak by any Major League baseball player. According to *Baseball America's Best Tools*, since 2001 Ichiro has been selected as one of the top three American League players in at least one of the following categories every year: Best Base-runner, Best Bunter, Best Defensive Outfielder, Best Hitter, Best Outfield Arm, Fastest Base-runner, or Most Exciting Player.

Ichiro's success is built not only on his outstanding natural abilities and the support he receives from his family, but also on the outstanding self-restraint apparent in the way he conducts his daily life. In his book *Ichiro's Way of Life*, Keizou Konishi offers these insights into this important quality:

To Ichiro, training, eating, and other daily habits are all part of the preparation involved in being a baseball player. He prepares for what he does deliberately but also in a way that allows for spontaneity. His attitude may sometimes seem too stoic, since not even by an inch does he make concessions to various temptations. But the method works. Let us take a look at his routine as he walks to the batter's box.

First, he starts to stretch his side and upper body muscles by swinging a heavy warm-up bat. Next he stretches both his thighs and, legs apart, twists his body twice to the left and then to the right. Then he changes to the slender regular bat and stretches his legs once more. On reaching the batter's box, he first takes the bat in his right hand and points it at the pitcher, and then pinches the uniform around his right shoulder with his left hand. Every time he walks to the batter's box, he goes through this same series of rhythmical movements.

Repeating this unvarying sequence is an important part of Ichiro's preparation, because it allows him to create the conditions in which he can concentrate exclusively on batting. Further in his regular routine, he then checks certain points around the field, including the positions of the pitcher and the fielders and other important features. In this way he gains a variety of relevant pieces of information about his surroundings.

Until 1994 Ichiro found himself unable to focus properly on his batting. Up to that point he was easily distracted by fears and a variety of other concerns when occupying the batter's box. Once he became a professional player, though, he had to achieve a state of complete concentration in which nothing could distract him from batting.

A batter swings his bat as a reaction to the ball that is pitched, so he is always in a passive situation. While it is natural for batters to want to learn as much as possible about the pitcher they are facing, too much information will make them less spontaneous. This is why Ichiro created a series of simple movements that sets him free from the various distractions in his surroundings. By repeating his routine, he gains a psychological calm, and by checking various points around him, he rids himself of fears and distractions.

During the season, Ichiro almost always eats the same meals, since if he became adventurous and tried something new, it might upset him. Regular eating habits therefore give him a certain security of mind, and he is particularly loath to change them if he is away from his home field. He seems to be trying to conserve his energy so that he can concentrate exclusively on the game.

Kazuhiro Sasaki, a fellow Japanese pitcher, is the opposite of Ichiro. Sasaki drinks and is fond of parties. But Ichiro once told us that if Sasaki imitated his lifestyle, his pitching would be affected. Ichiro tries not to over-regulate his life, but he has clearly created the method outlined above in the belief that it will help him become a good batter.

The virtue of temperance is well exemplified by the lifestyle of Ichiro Suzuki described in this account. Temperance means moderation or self-restraint in action, and Ichiro certainly controls his appetite, emotions, habits, and behavioral impulses in order to achieve his goal, that of batting to the best of his ability. Authorities, however, have disagreed about who benefits most from this approach to life.

Plato, for example, held that temperance was a virtue of particular importance to manual laborers who could be easily distracted from pursuing what is good by various temptations. Followers of Confucius, on the other hand, recommended the virtue of temperance to the leaders of society: "The way of great learning involves manifesting virtue, reforming the people, and abiding by the highest good."

What is meant here by "manifesting virtue"? The idea is that if less virtuous people live alone, they have no need to manifest virtues to others, and so they will often betray their own conscience. However, when even such people as these meet someone virtuous, being struck with guilt and reverence, they try to conceal their immoral traits and attempt to act ethically. Yet such vicious tendencies cannot be hidden entirely, and what lies deep in one's thoughts will reveal itself unbidden. A virtuous man, on the other hand, is able to practice temperance both in solitude and when living among people. As Confucius said elsewhere:

Things being investigated, knowledge became complete.
Their knowledge being complete, their thoughts were sincere.
Their thoughts being sincere, their hearts were then rectified.
Their hearts being rectified, their personalities were cultivated.
Their personalities being cultivated, their families were regulated.

Their families being regulated, their states were rightly governed. Their states being rightly governed, the whole kingdom was made tranquil and happy.

In his study *Bushido*, the art of self-control, which was universally required of the samurai, Inazo Nitobe wrote:

It was considered unmanly for a samurai to betray his emotions on his face. "He shows no sign of joy or anger," was a phrase used in describing a person of strong character. The most natural affections were kept under control. A father could embrace his son only at the expense of his dignity; a husband would not kiss his wife—no, not in the presence of other people, whatever he might do in private!

According to Nitobe, people of integrity did not allow their facial expressions to reveal their emotions because this disturbed the feelings of those around them and so was seen as a violation of the virtue of consideration for others. Therefore in public it was felt that people should not, as a matter of courtesy, express even the most natural emotions, such as affection towards their own children, at the expense of their dignity. Equally, young people, who were often moved by passionate feelings toward those of the opposite sex, should try to control their passions. It was believed that what was hidden deep in one's heart should not be expressed openly because only superficial and insincere people reveal their innermost thoughts.

Even nowadays Japanese people try not to show their real emotions. For example, if someone sharply points out their faults, they smile calmly as if nothing were disturbing them. They intuitively control their emotions and try to maintain their usual composure. Japanese smiles often serve to conceal a perturbed mind, and it gives them the time to restore their inner balance. In this way, both anger and sorrow can lie concealed behind a smile.

If people take this tendency towards self-control to extremes, however, they cannot express warm and caring love even when it is appropriate to do so. As a result, they may be thought of as prejudiced, hypocritical, or even insensitive. Therefore even though self-control is an eminent virtue, one must be aware of its negative aspects. The essence of self-control consists, in fact, in maintaining a calm and poised mental attitude, neither expressing nor repressing one's feelings in an extreme way.

If self-control shades into self-repression, it may reveal a destructive aspect. For example, exercising patience and self-control to the extreme can make a person appear self-centered, conceited, stubborn, and unwilling to admit defeat. Temperance and self-restraint are only virtues when they are practiced in the proper way, as *The Doctrine of the Mean* makes clear.

> The state before the feelings of pleasure, anger, sorrow, and joy are aroused is called equilibrium (*chung*, centrality, mean). When these feelings are aroused and each and all attain their due measure and degree, this is called harmony. Equilibrium is the great foundation of the world, and harmony its universal path. When equilibrium and harmony are realized to the highest degree, heaven and earth will attain their proper order and all things will flourish.

There is a further negative aspect to temperance. If self-control becomes the goal and is seen as the most important virtue, it poses dangers for people. Attaining the desired goal by controlling one's other desires can bring one great joy. However, if self-control itself becomes the goal of life, one may reach the point of self-obsession. It is therefore vital to ask oneself for what purpose one is denying one's desires and sacrificing oneself. If the goal of life is selfish, self-control may lead to only self-satisfaction. One can even sacrifice oneself in the course of a successful bank raid, but no praise accrues for such a virtue. Self-restraint, though, does have extremely valuable aspects, and some of these are revealed in the following tale by the Japanese novelist Kan Kikuchi (1888–1948), who based his *Onshu no Kanata ni* (*Beyond Vengeance*) on a true story. The central character is a monk of the Tokugawa period who spent more than twenty-one years digging a tunnel through rock using only a hammer and chisel. Kikuchi tells how, about three hundred years ago, the priest Zenkai, on his journeys through the country, witnessed some travelers and their horses falling from a narrow mountain path down a steep rock face. Zenkai decided to dig a long tunnel through the mountain so that this would not happen again.

At first glance this may appear to be a heartwarming story of self-sacrifice. However, the fact was that Zenkai had once been a thief and murderer. He had killed his master and run away with Oyumi, his concubine. Thereafter he committed as many crimes as Oyumi desired, until one day she asked him to kill an old man who saw her face while they were committing a crime. Zenkai found that he could not carry out her wishes and decided to escape from her. Having done so, he came to repent of his crimes and decided to become a monk. After many years of training, he began travelling throughout Japan with the aim of making amends for all his wrongdoings. He prayed to God to allow him to carry out his intention of atoning completely for his past crimes.

Twenty years after he began work on his tunnel, there came to the village nearby one Jitsunosuke, the son of one of the men who Zenkai had murdered. This Jitsunosuke was also traveling throughout Japan, but in his case he was questing for vengeance. However, since Zenkai had by now progressed a long way with his tunnel, the local villagers prevented Jitsunosuke from killing him. So Jitsunosuke decided to stick as close as possible to Zenkai until the time finally arrived when he could avenge his father. Eighteen months passed with Jitsunosuke sitting alongside Zenkai as he continued to cut at the rock. Then Jitsunosuke decided to lend a hand himself, at first with the intention of helping to complete the task more quickly and bringing the day of vengeance closer. However, as time gradually passed, he forgot about this and devoted all his energies to the task for its own sake. One year in mid-autumn, Zenkai and Jitsunosuke were sitting together late at night hammering at the rock, when all of sudden moonlight shone upon them through a small hole. Through it, they looked out upon the river on the other side of the mountain. Deeply moved, they joined hands and shouted with joy. Jitsunosuke looked at Zenkai and saw not the object of his vengeance, but an old man, nearly blind, who was filled with the joy of accomplishment. Jitsunosuke himself was also struck with awe at what they had succeeded in doing together. Both men could only weep with joy.

This is a story of how a desire for vengeance was transformed into a great achievement. Everyone had considered the digging of such a tunnel to be an impossibility, so it really was a magnificent deed. It is easy enough to condemn Zenkai for his various crimes, but we cannot deny that he displayed the supreme virtue of self-restraint for the sake of accomplishing his goal. It vanquished even Jitsunosuke's lust for vengeance.

Self-restraint or temperance is therefore a virtue only when our goal is worthy of attainment. The tragedy of the story is that Zenkai had to devote twenty-one years of his life to a task as atonement for his past crimes. If he had accomplished such a great deed from other motives, such as the wish to save other lives at the expense of his own, he could indeed have become one of the sages.

His story does, however, have something to teach us about the connection between temperance and failure. No matter how hard people work for a goal, employing all their self-restraint, some-times they do not achieve it. An illness, an unfortunate accident, some unexpected occurrence, or even their own shortcomings may serve to discourage them. They may in fact become so disheart-ened or so disgusted with themselves that they fall prey to despair and come to hold a grudge against the world. But this did not hap-pen with Zenkai. Self-restraint came to his aid here, and this en-ables us to understand why failures can be called creative illnesses, provided we respond to them in the right way, with self-control. Failure can teach us to become aware of the many people around us who give us their support. When things are going well, we tend to ignore such help and come to believe that things are achieved solely through our own efforts. Failure can give us the chance to set out once more in pursuit of our goal but in a different way, provided that we react to it in the spirit of temperance.

As the story of Zenkai and Jitsunosuke shows, self-control can bring about entirely unexpected results. Not only friends but also enemies may find out how to work together side by side, fulfilling a task that was originally conceived out of a concern for humanity and a desire to save the weak. Self-restraint that opens up the path to such a goal is indeed praiseworthy, enabling us to help one another in seeking to create something good in the universe. Then things will be in accordance with the words of Mencius (372–289 B.C.E.) in the *Way of Great Learning*, "The way of Heaven reveals the truth; the way of Humankind makes that truth a reality."

Temperance

BY KAREN E. BOHLIN

Several years ago I led a group of students on a literary and theatre tour of London. One of my tenth graders, a TV junkie, confided her fear that our schedule might not accommodate her appetite for television and shopping. Sarah was a capable student but completely disengaged from academics. She slid by, meeting minimum requirements. She spoke articulately about two of her favorite soap operas, *All My Children* and *As the World Turns*, and faithfully recorded these programs, sacrificing sleep to watch taped episodes.

At the end of our tour, Sarah had an epiphany on our late-night visit to the Tower of London. Just inside the Traitor's Gate, we gathered to witness the centuries-old Ceremony of the Keys. Sarah had completed a research project on the Tower of London prior to the trip, and I couldn't help but notice her wide, animated eyes piercing through the fog that enveloped our intimate group. After the formal exchange of keys and a cry of "All's well," the ceremony drew to a close, and Sarah confronted me. "That was awesome— and I can't believe how much I've enjoyed this trip." She paused for a moment. "I wanted to let you know that when I go home, I am never going to watch soap operas again."

My shock soon gave way to admiration. This was not a fleeting resolution. Upon returning to school, Sarah spearheaded the school's first literary magazine. Later, she served as editor-in-chief of the yearbook, dedicated herself to volunteer work, became a youth leader in her church, and secured a part-time job to finance an educational trip to Italy. Her experience in England—from the British Museum to the Tower of London—brought history and literature to life and sparked new possibilities for her. The melo-drama of her soap operas had now lost its appeal. Sarah's experi-ence in England signaled a pivotal moment, but her transformation did not take place overnight. Her new interests required commit-ment, training, and the relinquishing of old, familiar habits. Sarah retained her new focus into adulthood, founding an elementary school at the age of twenty-two, becoming a lead human resources recruiter, and later a university administrator. What she prized most, however, was her marriage and family.

If on our trip to London, fifteen-year-old Sarah had pursued only what she felt like doing, she would have spent her leisure time shopping and watching television in her hotel room. If I had ex-cluded Sarah from the trip altogether because her aspirations were not up to par, she may have taken a much longer time to venture beyond her comfort zone. If she had not developed an apprecia-tion for literature and culture, she would not have sustained the sacrifices necessary to develop a literary magazine. If she had not reflected on the way she had been using her time, talents, and ener-gies prior to the London trip, she may have never committed her-self to the discipline required to launch new initiatives.

It is a mystery how an event can be a transforming experience. It is difficult to know all of the factors—internal and external—that prepared Sarah for this change. Sarah had a full-fledged addiction to her favorite television programs. She had no desire to part from them until she discovered other activities worthy of her time. It took focus, time, practice, and effort for Sarah to replace old habits with new ones. Nevertheless, the rewards of her self-mastery were great. She experienced the satisfaction and enjoyment that accom-panies hard-earned competence and productive service.

A colleague of mine was absolutely astonished to learn that his eighteen-year-old daughter, who reluctantly dragged herself from bed each morning throughout her high school career, was now, of her own volition, rowing on her university's crew team at 5:30 every morning. What prompts such change and disciplined commitment? How do we come to relinquish comfort-seeking habits and replace them with discipline and diligence? What enables a person to gain command of conflicting desires? In short, how do we develop self-mastery? Despite popular opinion, temperance is not a boring and dull virtue. It is not simply about restraint or the repression of desire. Self-mastery or temperance is the settled disposition to enjoy and take pleasure in what is good, true, and beautiful and to feel aversion toward what is evil, false, and ugly. Temperance leads to our enjoyment of all activities that contribute to human excellence and improve the quality of our lives.

Wisdom or good judgment collaborates with temperance. Wisdom helps us to avoid the two chief challenges to self-mastery: excessive desires for self-indulgence on the one hand and insensitivity or lack of interest in channeling one's desires productively on the other. Temperance allied with wisdom keeps us from confusing sex with love, a good high with a good time, body image with self-esteem. Self-mastery helps us to assess our cravings for what they are and say no to our baser inclinations. Sarah ultimately learned to substitute her cravings for television with more satisfying and productive activities.

According to Aristotle, the temperate person does not desire pleasurable goods more than he or she ought. Nor does he crave the wrong sorts of pleasures—those which are base, mean, or cruel, like those of the bully eager to seek his own fun at someone else's expense. The gluttonous person is self-indulgent because he eats more food than he needs. The person addicted to pornography lacks self-mastery because he seeks what is base—turning people into objects of pleasure.

Temperance includes the ability to say no ourselves and delay gratification. Eating three desserts is not healthy. "I will not go on a shopping spree because my family needs this money for food." "I need to stop playing video games so I can spend time with my children." "I need to moderate my drinking so I can drive safely." Self-mastery includes, then, the practice of good manners, listening before speaking, and being a good host who notices and anticipates the needs of others. One of the most important lessons Annie Sullivan instills in her undisciplined blind and deaf pupil, Helen Keller, is how to sit at the table respectfully and eat with a fork and a knife from her own plate.

Self-mastery is a cardinal or hinge virtue. Several other virtues depend on it. Patience requires temperance to help us to hold our tongue and control our anger. Kindness needs temperance to help us listen and understand before imposing our own ideas, tastes, and opinions on others. Generosity is born of tempering our selfishness and noticing the needs of others. Diligence demands temperance to help us overcome laziness and work well.

Self-mastery brings freedom, self-possession, and maturity, whereas there are no solid rewards or salutary effects to living intemperately. American culture in particular is ravaged by a lack of temperance. Medical professionals, parents, and educators are currently striving to respond to the dangers of childhood obesity, drug and alcohol abuse, wanton sex, and various internet addictions.

What are the primary threats to self-mastery? And how have they enslaved us rather than fulfilled their promise of liberation?

The media lures us with powerful stimuli, trying to capture our interest on a daily basis. Young people are a prime target. Experts in psychology, media producers know how to motivate us to imitate fashion and trends. They know how to activate our desire and make us want to buy that which we do not need. Unfortunately, they have little concern for what is good for us as human beings.

Our media diet is high in "saturated fat." It is up to us to control what we consume. According to the findings of the January 2010 Kaiser Family Foundation study on the media consumption habits of eight- to eighteen-year-olds, the average American child spends more than fifty-two hours a week using some form of media and has an increasingly "multimedia bedroom." Twenty-eight percent of children watch television without any parental supervision or input on what they are permitted to view.

In 1997 the Bronx mourned the loss of an outstanding and beloved high school teacher. Jonathan Levin was knifed to death in his apartment, apparently for his ATM card. The assailant was a former student, a young man Levin had tried to mentor years earlier by offering personal advice and academic support. However, another more penetrating education dominated this student's life: the influence of drugs and Gangsta rap music, a genre of music riddled with violent, angry lyrics and antiauthoritarian themes.

Young people are being exploited around the world in sweatshops and for sex trade. In these environments they are systematically habituated to evil, and the virtue of self-mastery is methodically destroyed. The movie *Blood Diamonds* depicts the devastating indoctrinating and ruin of countless African boys. They are kidnapped from their families, taught to hate their parents, and trained to murder and steal. Part of their training includes a steady diet of pornography, drugs, and senseless violence.

There are less dramatic yet more pervasive and insidious threats to self-mastery in our culture: the frantic keeping up with the Joneses competitiveness that drives people to spend beyond their means on clothing, cars, and real estate; the desire for success that drives parents to over-program their children and micromanage their lives both within and outside of school; the desire for immediate gratification that rises up to make our whims and pleasures our god at the expense of our family and work. We also witness a lack of self-mastery in disproportionate responses to perceived problems that put state legislation above common sense and the cultivation of virtue. Carelessness in speech and in basic courtesy in writing and social interactions are all signs of a decline in self-mastery. Learning to practice manners is a basic step in impulse control. When we give people the courtesy of our full attention, when we remove our earphones and put our phone away in meetings, we show respect and self-mastery.

To cultivate the virtue of temperance in our lives and battle omnipresent threats to self-mastery, we need to tackle fundamental misconceptions about happiness and appreciate the various ways that self-mastery enables us to truly flourish.

A contemporary myth is that happiness is the freedom to do whatever you want, whenever you please. In the 1993 Columbia Pictures film, *Groundhog Day*, Bill Murray plays Phil Connors, a self-centered, cynical television weatherman who finds himself caught in a time warp: every day is Groundhog Day in Punxsutawney, Pennsylvania. At the end of several consecutive February seconds, a jubilant Phil declares, "I'm not going to live by the rules anymore." He gorges himself on cream puffs, doughnuts, plates of eggs and bacon; he chain-smokes and guzzles coffee; he seduces multiple women. After days of wanton self-indulgence, he finds himself feeling empty. He turns his attention to Rita, his intelligent and beautiful colleague. If only he can "win" Rita, then he will be satisfied. Then, he will be happy. He spends days studying her preferences, trying to capture her interest. When she finally exclaims, "I could never love someone like you, Phil, because you'll never love anyone but yourself," he learns why he has failed to win her heart. This motivates Phil to change his ways, to become the kind of person who can earn the respect of someone as virtuous as Rita. He uses each day to learn—he reads great literature, takes piano lessons, and even learns to ice sculpt. He spends his time overcoming his own desires and develops inclinations for helping those in need, assisting two elderly women with their flat tire, saving a boy who falls from a tree, and trying to rescue a homeless man from malnutrition and death. The more Phil grows in self mastery, the more attractive he becomes to Rita. This movie humorously concludes that happiness is not achieved by the freedom to do as we please. Rather, happiness is the result of tempering our selfish desires and investing ourselves in the pursuit of noble ones.

With self-mastery also comes competence and self-possession. But these rewards are hard earned. A brilliant lawyer and a self-described "disappointed drudge," Sydney Carton, the protagonist from Dicken's *Tale of Two Cities,* is a memorable and sympathetic portrait of the struggle for self-mastery. Known for his late-night drinking binges and restless wanderings, Carton believes that his "low, base habits" prevent him from attaining the ideal of self-mastery and a virtuous life. What motivates Carton to begin to take action and change his habits is his friendship with Lucie Mannette and her family. Spending time in their company, he comes to see the importance of self-sacrificing love. Lucie's affection for her father, a former prisoner of the Bastille, and her loving family challenge him to reflect on his "wasted, drunken" ways. He is grateful to her for raising these noble ambitions, but ashamed and discouraged by his inability to turn them into practical commitments. He lacks the self-mastery to escape his "low companions and low habits."

When, however, the need arises to help Lucie and her husband, Charles Darnay, during the French Revolution's bloody grip on Paris, he refocuses his desires. He takes no drink. He deliberates, plans, and dedicates all of his strength and intellectual energies to securing a safe rescue for the Mannette family. A disciplined sense of purpose and precise action characterize Carton's unnoticed work in Paris as he stealthily makes his way into the prison, exchanges places with Lucie's husband, and heroically goes in his stead to the guillotine.

Carton's self-mastery is won even though he has indulged his wanton desires for years. He was able to master them because he had enough self-knowledge to realize they were keeping him from leading a happy life. This realization alone was not sufficient motivation, but it was an essential starting point. He was able to distinguish a flourishing life from a dissipated and miserable one. He experienced friendship, and this enkindled his desire to master himself and serve others. All of these factors conspired to help him shed his self-indulgent habits and put his talents to good use.

Self-mastery also helps us to respond gracefully to stress and pressure. We cannot control our circumstances, but we can control our choices and reactions. Anger is an emotion that increases the more we reflect on what provoked our anger. Self-mastery helps us to deal with feelings of anger and resist the temptation to nurse resentments. Resentment comes from the Latin *re-sentire*, meaning to feel again. When we are not in command of our emotions and we brood over resentments, we can give in to grudges and even rage. Self-mastery prevents us from indulging our anger, helping us instead to hold our tongue and practice restraint when we are provoked, fatigued, or on edge.

Finally, self-mastery helps us to deal with mistreatment—intentional or unintentional. Throughout the course of our lives, we will encounter some form of injustice, even if it is only minor. Our response to this pain can either alleviate it or exacerbate it. Learning to respond with self-mastery and principled action are powerful antidotes to injustice.

Hank Greenberg (1911–1986), the great Jewish-American sports hero, is not impressive simply for his incredible batting average and legacy in the Baseball Hall of Fame. What stands out about Hank Greenberg is his extraordinary self-mastery. Despite his outstanding skill as a ball player, he was consistently met with cruel jeers and taunts from the stands, "Kike" and "Go back to Palestine." He endured bitter anti-Semitism throughout his career but never lost his dignity or his focus on the game. When a major game of the World Series was scheduled on Yom Kippur, the holiest high holiday of the year, every rabbi and every Jewish child waited to see what he would do. He went to temple and was met with a standing ovation from the congregation. In his absence his teammates lost to the Yankees five to two, and they lost the World Series as well. But Greenberg remained a hero for resisting the temptation to put fame and personal glory above his faith convictions. Later he resisted the temptation to go after the highest batting average in history and dedicated several years of his career to military service during World War II.

Certain individuals by fortune or fate are cast into the limelight and inevitably become role models. Their example of virtue carries that much more weight because so many people are watching with admiration and desire to emulate them. Literature, film, current events, family, and friends are replete with inspirational stories of heroic individuals whose greatness stems from hard earned discipline and temperance. They also abound with portraits of degradation wrought by self-indulgence and misery born of insensitivity. Identifying individuals who love what is true, good, and beautiful helps us to retain images of what self-mastery looks like and why it is attractive.

Temperance is a tough virtue because its fruits are known only after committing oneself to real personal struggle. It takes dedication to play a sport, learn a skill, or master a musical instrument. It takes commitment, energy, and discipline to grow in self-mastery. And it all starts with knowing oneself and naming one's demons. Armed with this self-knowledge, we can set limits for ourselves in areas of weakness and channel our desires to more worthwhile activity. The brain is highly malleable, and we can develop fresh neural pathways by changing our habits and reactions. For example, if we drink too much when we are nervous, we can substitute a healthier response such as going for a walk or meditating. If we eat when we are sad, we can replace food with reading, playing an instrument, or going to the gym with a friend. To create the new habit, however, we must commit ourselves to repeating the alternative response over and over again. Some researchers say it takes twenty-one consecutive days to build a habit; others say it can take up to sixty-six. Either way, replacing self-indulgent habits with activities that are healthy and rewarding is worth the determined effort.

Conclusion

Two Kinds of Reading

The collaborative enterprise that resulted in this book was a dance of understanding, with the individual authors in two lines facing one another across the meridian. Partnerships then formed, American and Japanese writers pairing off to address one particular virtue. The resulting volume may therefore be approached in two ways. Readers can focus on each chapter as an entity in its own right. Here they have a chance to compare and contrast the perspectives of the two individual writers and try to clarify for themselves the nature and importance of the virtue being discussed. Or readers may proceed virtue by virtue, and in this way, they may well become increasingly aware of generic differences between the two perspectives, those of the East and the West. Neither set of authors, of course, would claim to be totally representative: there is much more to the West than the United States, and much more to the East than Japan. Setting even that aside, there is still vastly more both to the United States and to Japan than the two universities with which the writers are associated. Nonetheless, it remains the case that these individuals cannot escape a degree of identification with their greater national and cultural wholes, that they do possess much of what is characteristic of each of those wholes. The essays can serve as a point of departure on a quest to transcend East and West in search of the essence of these nine virtues.

The first task, then, must be to delineate the broad differences that distinguish the two perspectives. The root of the matter here lies in how they conceive of the human self in its relationship to the world.

The Autonomous Self and the Related Self

One of the most striking features of the essays by the Western authors is how often they enjoin the practice of the virtues as an aid to self-development, to self-improvement. Thus, as one exhortation among many reads, "Courage, like the other virtues, needs exercise. It needs performance. It needs practice." This is indeed very American—practical, energetic, engaged with the world. It is also quintessentially Aristotelian, as we read in *The Nicomachean Ethics*, "A man becomes brave by doing brave acts." But perhaps inevitably with such an emphasis, our picture of that world is of one where the individual self seems to occupy much of the foreground—he or she is the primary agent of his or her own character formation. This perspective is only tempered by the Judeo-Christian ethic, which also imbues these chapters. We find Bernice Lerner's father, a normally reticent Holocaust survivor, speaking out on behalf of many in a post-war situation where justice is violated. We see that dispositions of character—virtue—are formed in the context of relationships through the good example of parents, friends, and mentors. The Western account does acknowledge, as Karen Bohlin writes in her chapter on gratitude, "When we come to appreciate our *inter*dependence as more important than our *in*dependence… we are more likely to flourish."

Still, we cannot help but notice that in the Western view the focus tends to be on how virtues are to be cultivated within the self and practiced on rather than for others. Thus it is natural that we read, "One of the most practical ways we can develop gratitude is by thanking people for the good they do for us." This does, of course, involve a relationship with others, but there is also a distance, something of the world of subject and object, of the self that seeks its own development by the practice of thanking. Others are inevitably placed at something of a remove, serving as a backdrop to the individual self, which is therefore, to a degree, isolated in the spotlight. It is a conception that lends itself readily to an alliance with psychology, both ancient and modern. The teaching of Plato is invoked, as in, "The person who acts justly has a well-ordered, harmonious soul." What does this mean? His "reason," assisted by his "spirit," governs his "appetite." Moderation spreads through the whole of his soul, assuring that all three of its parts are appropriately tuned. Much too is made of the logotherapy of Viktor Frankl, with its search for meaning and purpose that renders the self wholly responsible. Meaning in Frankl's view is pursued in work and loving relationships and the ability to make sense of suffering.

Though the predominant direction in all of this is the development of the self, it is not pure individualism by any means; it is far from being the pursuit of self-interest at every turn. It indeed calls for reflection and some degree of self-giving. Though the objective is primarily internal, the greater good tends to loom large at many points. So we are to practice the virtues not least because of the benefits they bring us, because they constitute our path to happiness, to personal flourishing.

With the essays by the Japanese authors, by contrast, there is much less of this emphasis on the good of the self. We encounter instead the self in context, set amidst its relationships with all that is not the self. There is more to this than the familiar story of the Japanese group ethos, though it is certainly true that we find the individual self firmly anchored in the family, in the local community, and in the nation at large. We note too that these are established relationships, often given at birth, and still permanent in cases where there are established later. But beyond that, the self is placed in the widest possible setting, in its relationship to all that the universe contains, as in the broad formulation of the "network of interdependence." The relationships that serve to define the individual self are not just human, those involving one's parents, one's ancestors, classmates, fellow workers, or the Japanese people united symbolically in the person of the Emperor. They also extend to all else that lives, as in the expressions of gratitude to the animals and plants that one eats, and beyond that to the inanimate world, such as to the needles that one uses and must comfort when their usefulness is at an end.

This will perhaps appear somewhat odd to those in the West, with its traditional dichotomy between the animate and inanimate realms. But that dichotomy is not perceived as existing in Japan, where the animate is held to merge seamlessly into the inanimate realm. Today it may even have begun to disappear in the West, where people are becoming much more ecologically conscious, as can be seen in contemporary movements such as "deep ecology," which stress biocentrism as a useful antidote to the poison of human domination over and exploitation of nature.

Even so, Japanese Shintoist, Buddhist, and Taoist philosophies seem to extend to realms into which biocentrism does not penetrate, and inherent in such an outlook is the concept of an individual self that does not push forward to occupy the foreground of the picture of the world, nor concern itself primarily with its own development. On the contrary, it is self-effacing, almost self-forgetful. Relationships matter far more, and especially the spirit created by the common endeavors that bind people together, even when they are enemies of one another, as in the story of Zenkai and Jitsunosuke. The preoccupation of the self here is with the health of all its relationships, and consequently it acts unbidden to preserve and enhance the good of others. This is evident in the delicacy of concern that characterizes the answer of Confucius to his disciple who was lacking in confidence, or in the tact and attentiveness to the welfare of all parties with which Mr. Isobe handles the unmasking of Chibi's talent. There is much that is very Japanese in Mr. Isobe's conduct—quiet, understated, modest, even in his role as teacher, where he might be expected to be the focus of attention. The focus in fact remains resolutely outwards and on one's relationship with others; the self retreats into the background so that if we notice it at all, we see it in perspective, surrounded by all that it touches and is touched by. The virtues from this view do not primarily concern the self; they characterize relationships.

The truth about anything is never to be fathomed in its entirety, so there are, of course, insights of value in both of these different conceptions of the self, autonomous and related. How, each in their different way, do they bring us closer to an understanding of the virtues?

The Autonomous Self and the Responsibility of Choice

One of the great advantages of a focus on the autonomous self is that in isolating it to some degree from others, proper stress is placed on the self as the locus for virtuous action. It is the individual and the individual alone who occupies the ground of responsibility—no one can hand off that burden to other beings, either individuals or groups. Moreover, this focus highlights the distinctively human capacity we have for intelligent choice. Education in virtue is about helping young people subject impulsive, primarily self-centered responses to thoughtful and just behavior. Hence we perceive the importance of the experimental work of Stanley Milgram about the abdication of responsibility discussed by Bernice Lerner, work that has also been cited by Christopher Browning in his study of the "ordinary men" who formed the advance guard of the Holocaust in Eastern Europe. It is clear that following orders, whether those of party, nation, or race, did not excuse them, nor will it excuse any of us. It is we ourselves, each of us in the isolation of our own self, who are answerable individually and in full for the decision to act virtuously or not.

For, and this is the second great benefit of attending to the autonomous self, the virtues always and only manifest themselves in acts of choice. As the essays in this volume clearly show, each virtue is in fact defined best by its opposite, which together form the dark matter of the moral universe that has traditionally been called vice. So wisdom is illuminated most clearly by folly; justice by injustice; gratitude by ingratitude; benevolence by selfishness;

responsibility by irresponsibility; courage by cowardice; respect by contempt; temperance by self-indulgence; self-reflection by self-ignorance. The essence of each virtue is present in life even when it is disregarded; indeed, its vital significance, its centrality, is grasped most clearly perhaps when it is ignored, as Chibi's classmates came eventually to understand.

To behave virtuously always involves making a choice. How are we to act *now*, at this instant, in this particular situation? To be—unjust, or just? Responsible, or irresponsible? Those are indeed the questions, and they are insistent ones. They block our path at every turn, but our answer to each of them is good only for this time and this place. We are never done with the virtues, with the need to choose; the questions will be put to us many more times in the future, and perhaps in circumstances that are utterly inconceivable to us now, accompanied by pressures that we may find unendurable.

They are, in essence, the same questions for all of us, for we experience aspects of a single world, never exactly the same but never utterly different either, and this is the common element that allows us to comprehend one another when we talk of the virtues and of character, and which also makes stories so attractive and important to us. Still, it is in the privacy, the sanctum, of the autonomous self that, whether we wish it or not, we are all asked to make our choices, and there is no escape, East or West, from this, the ground of our being.

The Related Self and Our Responsibility to the World

But what are our choices in respect of the virtues actually about? Their essence is that they affect not just our autonomous self but other selves as well. It is here that a sense of perspective, of the relative significance of our place amid all that has been, is now, and is to be, gives us an avenue of escape from the insistent claims of self-interest. A focus on the relationships for which the self is responsible brings with it a degree of self-forgetfulness, of modesty, that enables us to see and accept that there are more important things than what we take to be our own well-being. Such a perspective is not something that fades and reappears repeatedly over time. It is a constant, part of the fabric of our being, that makes itself felt with the onset of every situation where a choice between the virtues and their opposites presents itself to us. It helps to clear the path to virtue.

Even so, that path is never straight or well paved, and here the related self has a second gift to offer. An awareness of the delicate intricacy of our connections with all that is not our self illuminates the scale on which the consequences of our choices will play out. This is why Chikuro Hiroike placed such great emphasis on the concept of moral causality, the often mysterious connection between our actions and their consequences. At the moment of moral decision, of choosing between a virtue and its opposite, we can never be aware of the entire chain of consequences, for either good or ill, that will flow from our choice. Hiroike taught, however, that good actions (where our choice is one of the virtues) will lead only to good results, while failure to choose the virtuous course can only have bad consequences. This is not just a matter of self-interest, because the jurisdiction of the law of moral causality operates far beyond the span of our individual lives.

Here once again the self is placed in its full context, in this case in its relationship with what it can never be fully aware of. Our choice between the virtues and their opposites will have effects on others that we will never know in times that we will never see. This serves as both encouragement and warning. It tells us that any good we may do will continue its work long after we are gone. Thus those whose lives were saved by the villagers of Le Chambon-sur-Lignon during World War II were given the possibility of creating families of their own, and these new lives, and all the countless others that will flow from them over time, stand as testimony to the courage of Les Chambonnais. It is equally the case that the failure to choose the virtuous course will also have unknown consequences of its own across time, but as a legacy that can only be damaging and will be resented (an argument heard very often today in connection with our despoiling of the environment). The related self is aware of its place within the scheme of the generations, of its own fleeting nature, and so of its status as trustee, not owner, of all that lies within its seeming power.

The Western account invokes classical biblical narratives from the Old and New Testaments—the Wisdom of Solomon, The Good Samaritan, The Cure of the Ten Lepers, all of which are steeped in the moral imagination of Americans and help to reveal the transcendence of virtue. These narratives elevate virtue from the American tendency toward self-interest and self-reliance to those dispositions that invite us to contemplate and stand humbly before the benevolence of a wise, merciful, and just God. These narratives teach us that virtue properly and more fully understood is motivated by love, not self-improvement; by gratitude, not the pursuit of our personal well-being. This broader understanding of virtue enables us to steward creation and bring peace and joy to others.

Beyond East and West: A Crisis of the Virtues?

Readers of the essays in this volume will also come away with a sense at various points that our world today, East and West, is one where the virtues seem to be under particular pressure. Kevin Ryan, in discussing respect, describes how "[M]any American schools are riddled with what is called a 'putdown culture,' where students vie with one another over who can be the more insulting." Karen Bohlin, in her essay on temperance, expands on this, pointing to the fact that "[m]edical professionals, parents, and educators are currently striving to respond to the dangers of childhood obesity, drug and alcohol abuse, wanton sex, and various internet addictions." But, she goes on to say, adults seem just as vulnerable as the young, owing to:

> ...the frantic keeping up with the Joneses competitiveness that drives people to spend beyond their means on clothing, cars,

and real estate; the desire for success that drives parents to over-program their children and micromanage their lives both within and outside school; the desire for immediate gratification that rises up to make our whims and pleasures our god at the expense of our family and work.

This sense of the virtues in crisis is not so obvious among the contributors from Japan, but it is there. Hajime Ide, for example, is clear that "We live in an age of distrust. Everywhere we hear of people suffering ill-treatment, bullying, or criminal cruelty." All ages no doubt have their unique problems and challenges, but a sense that the virtues are no longer prized today as they once were is common to both East and West, and it is both worrying and frustrating.

One way out of this impasse may be to draw upon the strengths of both Eastern and Western understanding of the self as these pertain to the virtues. Stressing the autonomy of the self reminds us of not only our individual responsibility for enacting the virtues, but also draws attention to the value of the self, which derives ultimately from its uniqueness. Each self is indeed but a very small part of a network of relationships that extends far beyond the vision of a single individual. But infinitesimal as each self may be, it is a unique entity endowed with a responsibility that cannot be shouldered by any other self. Its uniqueness of being is complemented by the unique set of needs of the world in which it is situated. Here emphasis on the connectedness of the self and the need for the utmost attentiveness in seeking to grasp the particular, unique requirements of the time and the setting in which the self is placed is indispensible. The match between what we each alone are equipped to do and what the world asks of us has to be brought into the full light of consciousness. It is call and answer—or rather, an ever-changing sequence of calls and answers extending through an individual's life. Once the purposes that the self is called upon to achieve begin to emerge, the virtues will appear unbidden as they are needed.

Finding an exit from our current impasse, then, involves looking at ourselves and at the world surrounding us from a different angle. The importance of this new perspective extends well beyond our immediate personal circumstances, for it also reveals the first and fundamental requirement for solving the multiple problems we face in common. Economic globalization has produced and continues to produce the universalization of human greed, exploiting remorselessly our weakness in seeking to pursue our own interests and satisfaction so that we pay less and less attention to the world outside the self. Unless individually and collectively we address and seek to overcome our egotism, our self-centered mind, every single one of the world's problems, whether global or local, will not just remain unsolved but continue to fester and spawn others.

Adopting a new perspective on our being will show us that beyond self, family, community, or nation, beyond even East and West, the world lays on each of us a duty to act as co-responsible members of the global network of interdependence, a duty that is the modern incarnation of the virtue of benevolence. Shouldering this duty involves no diminution of self, but rather the achieving of the fullness of its being. Our egotism must dissolve and yield to the demands of the common good, and this can only come about through a change of perspective. Then and only then will we arrive at a full understanding of our true place in the world, learning to embrace in a spirit of humility, and as our individual and global responsibility, moral principles of a higher order that know no national or regional boundaries.

Here, then, is the sketchy outline of a path that will lead us beyond East and West. With time, thought, and effort, we may be able to achieve a new balance between a self that is the all-in-all and a self that is nothing. We may eventually come close to reaching a point of equilibrium, so poised that we are able to acknowledge the importance of our individual self without any loss of perspective, to contemplate a self that neither dominates the picture nor is lost from view in the mass. Along this path we may each stumble finally upon our own individual self in its proper setting, its unique place in the world, and move on from there to a realization of our duty to the world in its entirety, most of which lies beyond our immediate vision. And perhaps, just perhaps, in this never-ending process of deepening our self-understanding, we may find that we are becoming happy without even noticing it.

Osamu Nakayama

Further Reading

Arthur, James. *Education with Character*. London: Routledge, 2003.

Bohlin, Karen. *Teaching Character Education Through Literature*. New York: Routledge-Falmer, 2005.

Chamberlain, Basil Hall, trans. *The Kojiki: Records of Ancient Matters*. Hong Kong: Tuttle Publications, 2005.

Chazan, Barry. *Contemporary Approaches to Moral Education: An Analysis of Alternative Theories*. New York: Teachers College Press, 1985.

Coles, Robert. *The Moral Intelligence of Children: How to Raise a Moral Child*. New York: Plume, 1997.

Confucius. *The Analects*. Translated by D. C. Lau. London: Penguin Classics, 1998.

Durkheim, Emile. *Moral Education: A Study in the Theory and Application of the Sociology of Education*. Edited and translated by Everett K. Wilson; translated by Herman Schnurer. New York: The Free Press, 1961.

Frankl, Victor E. *Man's Search for Meaning: An Introduction to Logotherapy*, (third edition). New York: Simon & Schuster, 1984.

Gruber, Howard E. and Jacques J. Voneche, eds. *The Essential Piaget: An Interpretive Reference and Guide*. New York: Basic Books, 1982.

Hiroike, Chikuro. *Characteristics of Moralogy and Supreme Morality*. Kashiwa, Japan: The Institute of Moralogy, 1930. English trans. 1966.

———. *Towards Supreme Morality: An Attempt to Establish the New Science of Moralogy*. Kashiwa, Japan: The Institute of Moralogy, 1928; English trans. 2002.

Kreeft, Peter. *Back to Virtue*. Fort Collins, Ind.: Ignatius Press, 1992.

Lewis, C. S. *The Abolition of Man*. New York: Macmillian, 1947.

Lickona, Thomas and Matthew Davidson. *Smart & Good High Schools: Integrating excellence and ethics for success in school, work, and beyond*. Cortland, NY: Center for the 4th and 5th Rs and Washington, D.C.: The Character Education Partnership, 2005. (Available at www.cortland.edu/character/highschool.)

Matsushita, Konosuke. *The Path: Find Fulfillment Through Prosperity from Japan's Father of Management*. New York: McGraw-Hill, 2010.

Nitobe, Inazo. *Bushido: The Soul of Japan*. Radford, VA: Wilder Publications, 2008.

Suzuki, Daisetsu Teitaro. *Zen and Japanese Culture*. Princeton: Princeton University Press, 2010.

Tomita, Kokei and Tadasu Yoshimoto. *A Peasant Sage of Japan: The Life and Work of Sontoku Ninomiya*. Charleston, SC: BiblioBazaar, 2009.

Contributor Profiles

Special Contributor:

Thomas Lickona, Ph.D., serves on the board of directors of the Character Education Partnership and the advisory councils of the Character Counts Coalition and the Medical Institute for Sexual Health. He has been named a State University of New York Faculty Exchange Scholar and is the recipient of the Distinguished Alumni Award from the State University of New York at Albany. Recent books include *Character Matters: How to Help Our Children Develop Good Judgment, Integrity, and Other Essential Virtues* (2004) and *Character Quotations* (2004, with Matthew Davidson). His recent work includes directing a two-year study of high school character education and co-authoring with Matthew Davidson *Smart and Good High Schools: Developing Excellence and Ethics for Success in School, Work, and Beyond* (2005).

Editors:

Kevin Ryan, Ph.D., is the founder and director emeritus of the Center for Character and Social Responsibility (formerly the Center for the Advancement of Ethics and Character Education [CAEC]) at the Boston University School of Education, where he currently is also professor emeritus. He is the author and editor of many volumes, including *Moral Education: It Comes with the Territory* (1976); *Reclaiming Our Schools: A Handbook for Teaching Character, Academics, and Discipline* (1992, with Edward Wynne); *Those Who Can, Teach* (2007, with James M. Cooper); and *Building Character in Schools* (1999, with Karen E. Bohlin).

Bernice Lerner, Ed.D., is a senior scholar at the Center for Character and Social Responsibility (formerly the CAEC) at the Boston University School of Education and director of Adult Learning at Hebrew College. She has published several articles pertaining to character and ethics education, and her book, *The Triumph of Wounded Souls: Seven Holocaust Survivors' Lives*, was published in 2004.

Karen E. Bohlin, Ed.D., is a senior scholar at the Center for Character and Social Responsibility (formerly the CAEC) at the Boston University School of Education. She is also the head of the Montrose School in Medfield, Massachusetts, which has been recognized for its character education program. She is co-author with Kevin Ryan of the widely acclaimed study, *Building Character in Schools* and its companion professional development hand book, *The Building Character in Schools Resource Guide*. Another of her recent publications is *Teaching Character Education Through Literature: Awakening the Moral Imagination in Secondary Classrooms* (2005).

Osamu Nakayama, Ph.D., became the president of Reitaku University in April 2007 and is the director of its Center for Moral Science and Education. He is a well-known Milton scholar and the former president of the Milton Association of Japan. One of his major publications in English is *Images of Their Glorious Maker: Iconology in Milton's Poetry* (2002). He is also author of *The Philanthropic Spirit of the Japanese People* (2011), and he is known as a translator of more than thirty books as well as for his many original works.

Shujiro Mizuno, Ed.D., is a professor at Reitaku University and vice president of the Japanese Association of Certified Professional Counselors. His specialized area of study is counseling and human development. He edited *Searching for a Common Morality in the Global Age: The Proceedings of the International Conference on Moral Science in 2002* (with Haruo Kitagawa and Peter Luff, 2004) and wrote "The Self-examination of Dr. Chikuro Hiroike and Its Application to Counseling" (*Studies in Moralogy, no. 61*, 2008).

Kazunobu Horiuchi, M.A., is a professor at Reitaku University, where he teaches sociology, American society (in Japanese), and Japanese religious history (in English), as well as English. He also serves as the director of the Center for International Exchange. His research interests include American society, religion, and politics, and he has published many articles and books in Japanese, including *America and Religion* (2010).

Contributors:

Toshitaka Adachi, Ph.D., is a research fellow at the Research Center of Moral Science, the Institute of Moralogy. His specialized fields are bioethics and medical humanities. His publications include "Theories and Practice of Bioethics Education" in *Bioethics & Biomedical Ethics* (ed. Masami Maruyama, 2004) and many articles in learned journals on the ethics of medical professionals.

Hajime Ide, M.A., teaches at Reitaku University, where he currently serves as assistant to the university president. His specialties include Chinese philosophy, with a focus on Xunzi and the life and thought of Chikuro Hiroike. He is the author of *Turning Points in the Life of Chikuro Hiroike* (1995).

Nobumichi Iwasa, Ed.D., The focus of Dr. Iwasa's research is on the distinction between conventional morality and supreme morality from the perspective of life-long moral development. His publications include "Postconventional Reasoning and Moral Education in Japan," (*Journal of Moral Education,* vol. 21, no. 1), *Japanese Frames of Mind: Cultural Perspectives on Human Development* (ed. Hidetada Shimizu and Robert A. LeVine, 2002).

Haruo Kitagawa, M.Ed. Professor Kitagawa's research interests center on the philosophy of education and personality development throughout life. He is the author of "The Ethical Domain" in *Areas of Learning Basic to Lifelong Education* (ed. Paul Lengrand, 1986); "Social Education in Moralogy" (*Moral Education Forum,* vol. 13, no. 2, 1988); and "Aging and Facing Death as Tasks of Lifelong Learning" (*Reitaku Journal of Interdisciplinary Studies,* vol. 5, no. 1, 1997).

Masahide Ohno, M.A., is an associate professor at Reitaku University and vice director of the Research Center of Moral Science, the Institute of Moralogy. His major concern is the relationship between economics and ethics, with a particular focus on voluntary activity and altruism. He has published many articles on these subjects, including "Altruism in Economics" (*The Annual of the Society of Economic Sociology,* no. 22, 2000).

Jun Yamada, M.A., is vice executive director of the Lifelong Education Section at the Institute of Moralogy, where he is also one of the teachers of moral education at Reitaku University. He has published extensively on human rights education in Japan, including *Democracy and Dowa Education in Japan* (1985) and *Notebook for Human Rights* (1988).

Editorial Consultant:

Elisabeth Carter, Ed.M., M.F.A., has taught college, business, and remedial writing at several universities across the United States as well as conducted private creative writing workshops in the Boston area. She currently serves on the Dean's Advisory Board at the Boston University School of Education and on the Advisory Board for the Center for Character and Social Responsibility and works at McLean Hospital in Massachusetts. Ms. Carter also wrote the introductions to the nine chapters in this volume.